To Carolyn -

Happy _year's sleated_
the new Institute -
Going to visit you!

Jean Saoiuille

Jean Sanville

The Social Work
Psychoanalyst's Casebook

∞

The Social Work Psychoanalyst's Casebook

∞

Editorial Board

The Social Work Psychoanalyst's Casebook

∞

Clinical Voices in Honor of Jean Sanville

edited by

Joyce Edward
Elaine Rose

THE ANALYTIC PRESS

1999   Hillsdale, NJ   London

HV
689
.S69
1999

Published by The Analytic Press, Inc.
101 West Street, Hillsdale, NJ 07642
www.analyticpress.com

Typeset in Baskerville by Laserset, New York City

Library of Congress Cataloging-in-Publication Data

The social work psychoanalyst's casebook : clinical voices in
honor of Jean Sanville / edited by Joyce Edward, Elaine Rose.
        p.   cm.
    Includes bibliographic references and index.
    ISBN 0-88163-256-2
    1. Psychiatric social work. 2. Psychoanalysis.
    I. Sanville, Jean. II. Edward, Joyce. III. Rose, Elaine.
HV689.S69   1999
616.89'14—dc21   99-32594
                                                         CIP

Printed in the United State of America
10 9 8 7 6 5 4 3 2 1

∞

Acknowledgments

We would like to thank all those who helped with the development of this book. First, we extend our gratitude to the National Membership Committee on Psychoanalysis, Inc. (NMCOP), which is affiliated with the National Federation of Societies for Clinical Social Work, Inc. Its establishment of the National Study Group on Social Work and Psychoanalysis made this project possible. It is this Study Group that has constituted the Editorial Board for the book and has in various ways supported this endeavor. We especially wish to thank Dr. David Phillips, President of the NMCOP, and Dr. Marga Speicher, Chair of the Study Group, who offered their wise counsel at many points in this journey.

We are very grateful to Dr. Paul Stepansky, who was willing to publish this collection out of his admiration for our honoree, Jean Sanville, whose book *The Playground of Psychoanalytic Psychotherapy* The Analytic Press published in 1991. We also wish to express our appreciation to Joan Riegel and to Nancy J. Liguori for their fine efforts on behalf of this volume. To our editor, Eleanor Starke (Lenni) Kobrin, we offer our very warmest thanks. She gave abundantly of her time, expertise, and patience. This book could not have reached completion without her generous spirit.

We would also like to acknowledge our debt to our colleagues Gertrude Blanck, Victoria Hamilton, Susan Mendenhall, Diana Siskind, and Helen Ziskind, who provided us with their invaluable time and information, and to our secretary, Rita Testa, whose efforts turned unreadable notes into computerized pages.

We could not have continued our editing without our husbands: Jess Edward, who proofread, assembled pages, cooked meals, mailed manuscripts, and in all ways encouraged and supported this endeavor; and Elaine's husband, Nathan Kaproff, who discussed musical terms, cooked, shopped, picked up litter, and gave emotional strength. And our love and thanks to the numerous Rose children, who edited, proofread, and kept their heads when Elaine was losing hers. We offer them all our resounding appreciation.

We also extend our gratitude to our authors who made this book possible. It is their dedication to psychoanalysis and their effort, creativity, skill, and persistence that has brought this book to fruition. Finally, these acknowledgments would not be complete without an expression of thanks to those analysands who inspired and informed the writings of our contributors.

Contents

❦

Contributors

Samoan Barish, PhD, BCD[*] is Dean, California Institute for Clinical Social Work; and Training and Supervising Analyst, Institute for Contemporary Psychoanalysis and Southern California Psychoanalytic Institute.

Karla R. Clark, PhD, BCD is Consulting Clinical Faculty, California Institute for Clinical Social Work; and is in private practice in San Rafael.

Joyce Edward, MSW, BCD (Editor) is Training and Supervising Analyst, Society for Psychoanalytic Study and Research; and Training and Supervising Analyst and Honorary Board Member, New York School for Psychoanalytic Psychotherapy in Psychoanalysis.

Laurie S. M. Hollman, PhD, BCD is President and Training and Supervising Analyst, Society for Psychoanalytic Study and Research, Long Island, New York; and Adjunct Assistant Professor, Shirley M. Ehrenkranz School of Social Work, New York University.

Kerry Leddy Malawista, MSW, BCD is Teaching and Supervising Faculty, The Center for Professional Psychology, The George Washington University; and Member, The New York Freudian Society.

Peter L. Malawista, PhD is Teaching and Supervising Faculty, The Center for Professional Psychology, The George Washington University; and is in private practice in Tyson's Corner, Vienna, Virginia.

Monica J. Rawn, CSW, BCD is Training and Supervising Analyst, New York Freudian Society; and Faculty, Training and Supervising Analyst, National Psychological Association for Psychoanalysis.

---

[*] Board Certified Diplomate by the American Board of Examiners in Clinical Social Work (ABE)

Elaine Rose, MSW, BCD (Editor) is Training and Supervising Analyst, Los Angeles Institute and Society for Psychoanalytic Studies; and Teaching and Supervising Faculty, Wright Institute, Los Angeles, a center for the pre- and postdoctoral education of psychology trainees.

Ellen G. Ruderman, PhD, PsyD, BCD is Training and Supervising Analyst, Institute of Contemporary Psychoanalysis, Los Angeles, California; and is in private practice in Encino and Westwood.

Jean B. Sanville, PhD, BCD is Training and Supervising Analyst, Los Angeles Institute and Society for Psychoanalytic Studies; is a member of the International Psychoanalytic Association; and is on the continuing education faculty of Smith College School for Social Work.

Cathy Siebold, DSW, BCD is an advanced candidate at the Massachusetts Institute for Psychoanalysis; and is Associate Professor of Social Work, University of Southern Maine.

Gail Sisson Steger, PhD, BCD is Faculty, Training and Supervising Analyst, Los Angeles Institute and Society for Psychoanalytic Studies; supervisor and field advisor in several programs, including Cedar Sinai Medical Center and Smith College Certificate Program.

Toni C. Thompson, CSW, BCD is Faculty and Supervisor, New York School for Psychoanalytic Psychotherapy and Psychoanalysis; and Supervising and Training Analyst, New York Freudian Society.

From the President of the NMCOP

David G. Phillips

The National Membership Committee on Psychoanalysis in Clinical Social Work (NMCOP), established in 1980 by Crayton Rowe, is affiliated with the Clinical Social Work Federation. The founding of the NMCOP resulted from the awareness that it was of vital importance to provide a base for clinical social workers who were seeking psychoanalytic training, becoming involved in the organizational life of analytic institutes, and practicing in a psychoanalytically informed manner.

As the NMCOP developed, its leadership became increasingly aware of both the excellent work done by analytically informed clinical social workers, and the extent to which analytic concepts have profoundly influenced social work theory. The observation of this interface, and the wish to explore it further, led to the formation of the National Study Group on Social Work and Psychoanalysis. The current chair of the Study Group is Marga Speicher, Ph.D. This is the second book to be produced by the Study Group, under the aegis of the NMCOP.

Jean Sanville was a founding member of the National Study Group and coedited its first publication, *Fostering Healing and Growth*. Well known as a psychoanalyst who has made significant contributions to analytic theory, Dr. Sanville has maintained her identity as a social worker, retaining her roots in social work values and principles. This volume, showing the way in which clinical social workers practice psychoanalysis, is a fitting and very deserved tribute to her. The NMCOP is proud to be associated with it and to have participated in its preparation.

David G. Phillips, D.S.W., B.C.D.
President, NMCOP

Publications of Jean Sanville

1947
(as Livermore, J. with Futterman, S.) On putative fathers. *Journal of Social Casework,* 28:174–178.

1948
(as Livermore, J. with Kaplan, L.) Treatment of patients with punishing super-egos. *Journal of Social Casework,* 29:310–316.

1953
(as Livermore J. with Eiduson, B.) Complications in therapy with adopted children. *American Journal of Orthopsychiatry,* 23:795–802.

1956
(as Livermore, J.) A schizophrenic child reviews her own treatment. *American Journal of Orthopsychiatry,* 26:365–375.

1960
(as Livermore, J.) Identification of teenage girls with Mexican-American minority. *American Journal of Orthopsychiatry,* 30:630–636.

1966
(as Livermore, J.) On conjoint therapy: A discussion of a paper by A. Rogawski. *Psychoanalytic Forum,* 1:326–327.

1967
Deprived children of the upper socioeconomic strata. Proceedings of Conference for the Advancement of Private Practice.

1968
Multiproblem families of the upper socioeconomic strata. Proceedings of Conference for the Advancement of Private Practice.

Cultural traditions as codeterminants of goal setting. In: *The Course of Human Life,* ed. C. Buhler. New York: Springer, pp. 296–326.

1969
Implications of adolescent heterosexual behavior for ego development in young women. Proceedings of Conference for the Advancement of Private Practice.

1973
(with Shor, J.) Leading ladies and gentle men. *Clinical Social Work Journal,* 1:67–77.

1974
Eight ages of a clinical social worker. Proceedings of Conference for the Advancement of Private Practice.

(with Shor, J.) Erotic provocations and dalliances in psychotherapeutic practice. *Clinical Social Work Journal,* 2:83–95.

(with Shor, J.) Women in transcendence: Clinical pathways to change. *Clinical Social Work Journal,* 3:55–60.

1975
Therapists in competition and cooperation with exorcists: The spirit world clinically revisited. *Clinical Social Work Journal,* 3:286–297.

(with Shor, J.) Age games in play-mating: Some clinical cues to qualities of intimacy between lovers of widely disparate ages. *Clinical Social Work Journal,* 3:187–200.

1976
On our clinical fantasy of reality. *Clinical Social Work Journal,* 4:245–251.

1977
The California Institute for Clinical Social Work: Conception, birth and early development. *Clinical Social Work Journal,* 5:316–327.

1978
Vulnerability to supernaturalism in children and their parents: A psychodynamic appraisal. In: *The Child in His Family: Vulnerable Children, Vol. 4,* ed. E. J. Anthony, C. Koupernick & C. Chiland. New York: Wiley.

1979
Gentlemen bountiful: Repairing the patriarch. *Clinical Social Work Journal,* 7:62–74.

(with Shor, J.) *Illusion in Loving: A Psychoanalytic Approach to the Evolution of Intimacy and Autonomy.* New York: Brunner/Mazel. Penguin Paperback.

Review of *Mothers, Fathers and Children: Explorations in the Formation of Character in the First Seven Years,* by S. Brody & S. Axelrod. *Social Work,* 24:438–439.

1981

Editorial in each issue of the *Clinical Social Work Journal,* 1981–1996.

1982

Partings and impartings: Toward a non-medical model of interruptions and terminations. *Clinical Social Work Journal,* 10:123–131.

1987

Theories, therapies, therapists: Their transformations. *Smith College Studies in Social Work,* 57:75–92.

Creativity and the constructing of the self. *The Psychoanalytic Review,* 74:263–279.

The illusion of sexual equality: Progress or regress? In: *Psychosocial Studies,* ed. H. Caroff & M. Gottesfeld. New York: Gardner Press.

1989

(with Alexander, J., Kolodziejski, K., & Shaw, R.) On final terminations: Consultation with a dying therapist. *Clinical Social Work Journal,* 17:307–324.

The play in supervision. *Smith College Studies in Social Work,* 59:157–169.

1990

Primary trauma: Work, love and play toward repair. *Journal Smith College School for Social Work,* 18.

Review of *Handbook of Creativity,* ed. J. A. Glover & R. A. Reynolds. *Readings: A Journal of Reviews and Commentary in Mental Health,* 5(3):28.

Discussion of sexual mate-swapping: A comparison of "normal" and "clinical" populations, by L.A. Chernus. *Clinical Social Work Journal,* 8:120–130.

1991

The Playground of Psychoanalytic Therapy. Hillsdale, NJ: The Analytic Press.

Review of *Wisdom and the Senses: The Way of Creativity,* by J. Erikson. *Child and Adolescent Social Work Journal,* 8:431–434.

1994

On the vicissitudes of the love affair between social work and psychoanalysis. *The American Psychoanalyst,* 28:17–19.

Review of *The Child's Path to Spoken Language,* by J. L. Locke. *Readings: A Journal of Reviews and Commentary in Mental Health,* 9:30.

Review of *The Metaphor of Play: Disruption and Restoration in the Borderline Experience,* by R. Meares. *Clinical Social Work Journal,* 22:236–241.

1996

Notes toward a history of the independent psychoanalytic societies in Southern California. *The American Psychoanalyst,* 30.

La Crisis del Psicoanálisis. *La Peste de Tebes,* Buenos Aires: La Asociación Psicoanalítica de Argentina.

(with Edward, J.) *Fostering Healing and Growth: A Psychoanalytic Social Work Approach.* Northvale, NJ: Aronson.

Review of *In Search of Dreams: Results of Experimental Dream Research,* by I. Strauch & B. Meier. *Readings: A Journal of Reviews and Commentary in Mental Health,* 11(4):24–25.

1997

Philosophical considerations in analysis. *Clinical Social Work Journal,* 25:19–25.

On the crisis of psychoanalysis. *Council News,* Council of Psychoanalytic Psychotherapists, November.

Review of *Children At Play: Clinical and Developmental Approaches to Meaning and Representation,* ed. A. Slade & D. P. Wolf. *Clinical Social Work Journal,* 25:121–127.

Review of two books: *The Analyst in the Inner City: Race, Class and Culture Through a Psychoanalytic Lens,* by N. Altman; and *Reaching Across Boundaries of Culture and Class: Widening the Scope of Psychotherapy,* ed. M. P. Foster, M. Moskowitz & R. A. Javier. eds. *Clinical Social Work Journal,* 25:371–375.

1998

Transcending gender stereotypes: Eluding the Eva Peronista position. *Gender and Psychoanalysis,* 3:175–211.

Review of *The Origins and Psychodynamics of Creativity: A Psychoanalytic Perspective,* by J. Oremland. *Clinical Social Work Journal,* 25:450–455.

1999

Humor and play. In: *Humor and Psyche,* ed. J. Barron. Hillsdale, NJ: The Analytic Press.

Meaning making and playing in psychoanalytic therapies. *Smith College Studies in Social Work,* 69:509–523.

In Press

Review of *The Psychoanalytic Mystic,* by M. Eigen. *Journal of the American Psychoanalytic Association.*

The Social Work
Psychoanalyst's Casebook

∞

Overture

The Editors

This book began as an ode to Jean Sanville, who has devoted her life to developing her several overlapping professional identities—scholar, social worker, writer, editor, and psycho-analyst—in the service of community, organization, institution, and individual. Our authors celebrate Dr. Sanville's outstanding contributions to both social work and psychoanalysis. She has forged a place for herself in the larger analytic community and in so doing has helped to pave the way for other social work analysts to take their place in American psychoanalysis. You will meet her in the interview with which we begin.

In the process of collecting these contributions honoring Dr. Sanville on her 80th birthday, we've discovered that our ode has become a symphony of polyphonic analytic voices, echoing the diversity of current theoretical perspectives and the widening popula-tion of analysands. The chapters illustrate a unity among these clini-cians that derives from their common social work background. Especially do we see how a basic social work principle—to begin where the client is—finds its way in some form into each of these treatments. So age-old and so fundamental is this concept that one no longer knows its orgins.

In each chapter, the clinician searches first to discover where the analysand is and begins to build a relationship based on respect and empathy. The conviction that it is important to begin where the client is leads to a degree of flexibility in the arrangements of some of these analyses that may be thought unusual by some psychoanalysts. Time arrangements, use of the couch, and other so-called parameters are seen as alterations in the service of adapting to the unique needs of particular patients.

For clinicians raised on the teachings of such early social workers as Mary Richmond (1917) and Virginia Robinson (1930), following contemporary analytic theories is like reading old music scores. Richmond, who wrote the first textbook on social work, for example, stressed the importance of self-determination, individualization, and the development of a reciprocal relationship between client and worker. Virginia Robinson echoed these thoughts, giving added emphasis to the significance of the relationship between caseworker and client in the practice of social work.

Readers of this volume are offered an opportunity to learn, among other things, how the theoretical conceptualizations of these analysts have contributed to their understanding and interventions; how countertransferential issues have affected their treatment; how their efforts have facilitated their analysands' intrapsychic changes and, at times, changes in themselves; and how they bring their social work experiences into their analytic sessions.

The perspectives and therapeutic approaches described reflect the widely divergent theoretical outlooks and clinical approaches that characterize psychoanalysis today. There is also variation in the way these analysts understand and apply the theories that guide them. None of the analytic duets is exactly like any other. The uniqueness of each treatment derives not only from the particular perspective of the analyst but also from each analyst's and analysand's individuality as well as the particular way the two participants relate to one another. On the whole, the analysands in these cases appear to be a more traumatized and troubled group of patients than those whom earlier generations of analysts were accustomed to treating. Many of them would once have been described as "hard to reach," or "difficult to treat," clients with whom social workers have long been familiar. This has had a large impact on the treatments elucidated in this volume.

The contributors to this book, like Jean Sanville and most other social work analysts, have for the most part traveled long and frequently difficult paths in order to become analysts. Although psychoanalysis has had a profound influence on the practice of social work since the early 1900s, social workers have had to deal with opposition from other psychoanalysts and from analytic institutes, as well as with resistance from their own colleagues (and sometimes from within themselves) in order to train and practice as analysts.

Freud's delivery of his famous lectures in 1909 at Clark University in Massachusetts was for many social workers the beginning of this journey from social worker to analytically informed social worker and then to social work analyst. Those lectures of Freud's deeply impressed the social workers who heard them or learned about them. The theory of mind Freud proposed offered a way for social workers to understand why so many of their clients failed to respond to advice and environmental manipulation, interventions common to both social work and psychiatry prior to Freud. Those early caseworkers began to see how the psychosocial problems they were dealing with could stem from inner pressures as well as outer ones, from unconscious as well as conscious forces. Most important, Freud directed case workers' attention to the person who had the problems rather than simply to the problems themselves.

In 1918, nine years after the Clark Lectures and the same year that Jean Sanville was born, a small group of social workers who had become acquainted with Freud's ideas and saw their potential value for social work founded the Smith College School of Social Work (Sanville, 1996). Although there were many social work schools at the time, Smith was the first to base its teachings on Freudian concepts.

Other training programs followed. The application of Freudian theory was, however, carefully restricted by schools and agencies. For the most part, social workers were encouraged to understand the unconscious but were cautioned not to deal with it. Even after social workers had begun to treat patients, Florence Hollis (1964) specifically advised her students and colleagues not to elicit dreams. If clients related their dreams spontaneously, then social workers were to confine their focus to what was preconscious or conscious. While such caution was intended to protect clients against the misuse of analytic theory, it tended to leave the impression that the unconscious was "off limits" for this group of clinicians under any circumstances. This attitude has to some extent lingered on in the minds of some social workers as well as in the minds of some of their non-social work colleagues.

At the start, mental health treatment was solely the responsibility of the medical psychiatrists, even in social agencies. For the most part, social workers were responsible for collecting data for the psychiatrists, helping with discharge planning in mental hospitals and working with families of children in treatment in social agencies. The physician was the lead singer with agency and staff the supporting chorus.

After World War I, however, an increase in the number of persons needing help and a scarcity of medical analysts to treat all the agency clientele forced the assignment of clients who needed psychotherapy to social workers. By the 1930s, social workers were providing treatment and agencies were hiring psychoanalysts to supervise them and to conduct inservice training programs.

During the 30s, 40s and 50s, social agencies had a unique opportunity to offer inservice analytic training. European analysts fleeing the Holocaust and its aftermath emigrated to America and sought work in this country. Many were not physicians and thus, with a few exceptions, were not permitted to analyze adults in America. Among the immigrant nonmedical analysts who became consultants to social agencies were such social workers as Fritz Redl, Oskar Sternbach, and Rudolf Ekstein. Dr. Ekstein may have been the first social worker to be accepted as a member into a medical institute, an exception to the rule. Some émigré medical analysts, like Viola Bernard and Margaret Mahler, also helped to train social workers. Dr. Sanville's interview indicates that caseworkers interested in the analytic approach frequently sought field placements and positions in those agencies where they could gain access to these and other highly skilled clinicians. It was such an effort on Dr. Sanville's part that enabled her to work with Margaret Mahler and Marianne and Ernst Kris.

As analysts were helping social workers gain greater insight into the inner world of their clients, these social workers were bringing their heightened appreciation of the outer world to the analysts they were working with. It is difficult to assess how these exchanges may have affected those analytic consultants and supervisors. One wonders, for example, whether Viola Bernard's deep interest in community psychiatry, which led her to organize the American Psychoanalytic Association Committee on Psychoanalysis, Community, and Society in 1968, had something to do with the fact that she taught for many years at the then New York School of Social Work and also supervised and consulted with graduate social workers. We do know that at least one collaboration between analysts and social workers led to an important advance in analytic understanding (H. Parad, personal communication, 1999). We think here of the joint work of Eric Lindeman and Gerald Caplan, both physician analysts, and Howard Parad and Lydia Rappaport, social workers, in the development of crisis theory. Their work followed the Coconut Grove Fire in 1942 and began as an effort to prevent the sudden-grief syndrome associated with that disaster.

The influence of psychoanalysis on social workers, however, has been the more apparent consequence of the association between the two disciplines. Social workers were so impressed with their introduction to analytically oriented treatment in their agencies that some began to seek further training in psychoanalysis. A number of them sought out analysts outside of agencies to study with. Private study groups began to develop. Paul Federn appears to have been the first to organize such a group for psychologists and social workers. Among his pupils was Martin Bergmann, a well-known nonmedical analyst who later developed seminars that included social workers.

Among the social work analysts who studied with Bergmann were Gertrude and Rubin Blanck, who went on to develop an interdisciplinary psychoanalytic psychotherapy training program themselves. Similar seminars began to form throughout the country, under the direction of both medical and nonmedical analysts. For several decades these seminars, along with personal analyses and private supervision, became the major training resource for nonmedical clinicians in the United States.

But these opportunities for learning did not fulfill the need some therapists experienced for more formal training programs. When Theodore Reik started what some historians regard as the first nonmedical training institute in New York City in 1948, the National Psychological Association for Psychoanalysis (NPAP), it was enthusiastically welcomed. Reik was one of Freud's nonmedical colleagues in Europe. When Reik was charged with a breach of an Austrian law against "quackery," which made it illegal for a person without a medical degree to treat patients, Freud intervened on his behalf. "The Question of Lay Analysis" (Freud, 1926) was part of this effort. Arguing that psychoanalysis was not a specialized branch of medicine, Freud advanced reasons why it was desirable to train nonmedical clinicians as analysts. Speaking of the treatment of neurotics, Freud suggested that "medical education, however, does nothing, literally nothing towards their understanding" (p. 231). Peter Gay (1988) notes that Freud thought that medical training was likely to be a handicap. All his life, Gay points out, Freud was intent on preserving "the independence of psychoanalysis from the doctors no less than the philosophers" (p. 492).

Reik later fled the Holocaust and came to America. When he found himself unwilling to accept the demands of the New York Psychoanalytic Society that he agree not to practice or to play a prominent role in the Society, but instead limit his activities to serving as a control analyst, he established NPAP. Joel Shor, Jean Sanville's late husband, was a prominent member of that group. There is, though, some disagreement about the origins of this program. Emily Ann Gargiulo (1998), a New York social work analyst, insists that Reik did not establish the institute but, rather, was willing to let a group of social workers organize a program around him. According to Gargiulo, these were social workers who had received certificates in psychoanalysis from the Washington School, which, first having accepted social workers, then excluded them once the physicians and psychologists returned from World War II.

Over time, an increasing number of interdisciplinary training institutes for nonmedical analysts began to develop. By 1964 there were some 30 such training centers in the New York area alone (Wallerstein, 1996). In 1970 the Los Angeles Institute and Society for Psychoanalytic Studies became the first interdisciplinary group on the West Coast to accept psychologists, social workers, and nurses as candidates. Dr. Sanville was one of its founders. That institute now includes marriage and family counselors and research analysts. In time, nonmedical training programs began to be formed in other cities across the nation.

In the course of all of this, social workers were acquiring increased analytic skills and experience. By the 1950s, a few had ventured forth to open their own private practices in psychoanalysis. In a talk he gave at a Memorial Service for Rubin Blanck, Martin Bergmann (1995) described the paths by which social workers began to identify as psychoanalysts in their own right. One way, he noted, was to marry a psychiatrist. Even if psychiatrists were opposed to social workers doing analysis, it seemed that once they married social workers their opposition to nonmedical therapists seemed to diminish.[1] Other social workers came to analysis as a result of being referred certain patients who physician analysts felt needed preparation before they could analyze them. The idea was that, after three or four years of working out their external problems with a social worker, these patients would be ready to return to the referring analyst. After working together and forming a relationship, some social workers and patients did not see the point of such an interruption. They thus continued to work together after the so-called preparatory period.

As social workers began to practice therapy privately, particularly psychoanalysis, they, like other nonmedical practioners, were often disapproved of by the analytic establishment. Unlike their European colleagues, American psychoanalysts, anxious about their status in the medical community (Richards, 1999), were insistent that psychoanalysis remain in the hands of physicians. They were remarkably successful in insuring this. Nevertheless, as we have noted, some were willing to teach and supervise social workers. Those who

---

[1] While beyond the scope of this volume, a consideration of the influence of the many social workers who have married medical analysts, whether or not they be analysts themselves, on the analytic outlooks of their mates would be interesting to explore. In England, both Balint and Winnicott were married to social workers. The impact of Enid Balint and Claire Winnicott on their husbands work has long been acknowledged. As a matter of fact, Claire Winnicott's inviting Jean Sanville to come to England to edit those of Winnicott's papers which had never been published is one example of his wife's intimate involvement with his work.

did so, albeit often in secret, braved considerable opposition from some of their colleagues and organizations.

It took several major occurrences to effect a change in the situation. The first was a lawsuit brought by the American Psychological Association in March 1985 against the American Psychoanalytic Association (APA) and the International Psychoanalytical Association (IPA) as well as two of its affiliated institutes in New York. Jean Sanville testified for the plaintiffs in this suit for an entire day. A negotiated settlement was not reached until October 1988 The second event, also a result of the lawsuit, was the passage in 1986 of the Gaskill proposal by the Executive Council of the American Psychoanalytic Association. This proposal stipulated that component societies of the American could accept into training any individuals who have achieved a professional identity as human caretakers through therapeutic clinical activities of demonstrated excellence (Cooper, 1990, p. 177). No degree or clinical training was specified. The Gaskill proposal opened the door for full clinical training in psychoanalysis to psychologists, social workers, nurse practioners , and others—although it has taken time for social workers to gain full access.

Social workers are now, however, eligible for American Psychoanalytic Association fellowships and are being admitted as candidates to many American-affiliated institutes. These moves by The American reflect the organization's attempts to develop a more open, inclusive, democratic attitude (Margolis, 1998) and in part are a response to pressure from their own affiliates as well as to the reality of a declining number of medical candidates.

The lawsuit also resulted in a change in the bylaws of the International Psychoanalytical Association to permit psychoanalytic societies in the United States that were not part of the American Psychoanalytic Association to apply for direct membership in the IPA (Cooper, 1990). This step has furthered the movement of social workers into the analytic mainstream as more independent institutes and their members have been able to join the IPA.

Out of these multidisciplinary groups a confederation of Independent Psychoanalytic Societies of the United States (IPS) was formed. Its purpose is to represent nonmedical independent psychoanalysts around the world. Among its members are a growing number of social workers. Dr. Sanville served as copresident from the West Coast from 1992 to 1996. She was also a Delegate from the North American Region to the House of Delegates of the International Psychoanalytic Association.

At the same time as social workers have sought to gain opportunities for training and inclusion as psychoanalysts, they have faced a struggle for acceptance within their own profession. It was not until 1980, when Crayton Rowe, a prominent social work psychoanalyst, founded the National Membership Committee on Psychoanalysis in Clinical Social Work, Inc., under the auspices of the National Federation of Societies for Clinical Social Work, that the idea of social workers practicing psychoanalysis gained some legitimacy within the profession of social work. Today that organization represents social work analysts in a consortium of analysts of various disciplines who are seeking to establish overall standards and to insure the viability of psychoanalysis in the 21st century.

The opposition that continues within social work itself is complex in origin, involving principles, prestige, and finances. The profession is faced with the task of granting its own members the opportunity for individuation and self-determination that it seeks to insure those whom the profession serves. It will need to pay attention to this fast-growing group and make room for diverse activities if social work analysts are to be assured of their place in the profession. It is our hope that this issue will be resolved, for today more than ever social work needs all its voices singing together.

Thus, 73 years after Freud (1926) proposed that some American benefactor "might spend a little money to get the 'social workers' of his country trained analytically and to turn them into a band of helpers for combating the neuroses of civilization" (p. 250), social workers are entering the analytic community through both the APA and IPA, as well as by other avenues. They are becoming full-fledged members, although without the benefactors Freud envisioned. Indeed this book is a testimony to that accomplishment

The question now for many of us is whether the social work analysts of the 21st century will continue to identify as social workers or whether they will leave their social work background behind. Will they feel pride in their social work origins, as our contributors do, or will their roots in a profession that has historically been regarded as of low status lead them to abandon their past? Will their long exclusion by an analytic establishment that some perceive as only reluctantly admitting them, as well as the critical stance taken against them as analysts by some members of their own profession, keep them from acknowledging their social work background? Will they then simply use their social work credentials as the legal context for professional practice, or will they retain their dual professional identity, as do psychologists today (Perlman, 1994)?

The analyst we honor in these writings, Jean Sanville, clearly retains her identity as a social worker, as do the editors and contributors to this volume. We enjoy the polyphony that combines and adds our social work experience to the enrichment of our analytic voices. Many of us also find it deeply rewarding to apply our analytic knowledge in the traditional pursuits of social work, such as prevention, community work, advocacy, and social action. Jean Sanville is an outstanding example of a social work analyst who brings the offerings of each domain to the other. We think too in this connection of Selma Fraiberg, who like Dr. Sanville, remained throughout her life firmly connected to social work and to psychoanalysis , combining the best of both worlds (Fraiberg,1987).

Social workers have long known how much they owe to psychoanalysis in their everyday practice of social work. With this book we hope to show what analysts with a social work background can contribute to analysis itself. We envision a future when social work analysts will find their worlds enhanced by each other and when the analytic community will discover psychoanalysis to be enriched by the contributions of their social work colleagues.

References

Bergmann, M. (1995), *A Memorial Tribute to Rubin Blanck 1914–1995.* Presented at Fifth National Clinical Conference, National Membership Committee on Psychoanalysis in Clinical Social Work, New York City.

Cooper, A. (1990), The future of psychoanalysis: Challenges and opportunities. *Psychoanal. Quart.,* 59:177–196.

Fraiberg, S. (1987), *The Selected Writings of Selma Fraiberg,* ed, L. Fraiberg. Columbus: Ohio State University Press.

Freud, S. (1926), The question of lay analysis. *Standard Edition,* 20:179–250. London: Hogarth Press, 1959.

Gargiulo, E. A. (1995), *A Memorial Tribute to Rubin Blanck 1914–1995.* Presented at Fifth National Clinical Conference, National Membership Committee on Psychoanalysis in Clinical Social Work, New York City.

Gay, P. (1988), *Freud: A Life for Our Time.* New York. London: Norton.

Hollis, F. (1964), *Casework: A Psychosocial Therapy.* New York: Random House.

Margolis M. (1998), The American Psychoanalytic Association, A decade of change: Prospects for survival, growth, and unity. Plenary Address. Presented to American Psychoanalytic Association, New York City, December 18.

Perlman, F. T. (1995), The professional identity of the social work-psychoanalyst: Professional affiliations and future prospects. *J. Anal. Social Work,* 2:31–84.

Richards, A. (1999), A. A. Brill and the politics of exclusion. *J. Amer. Psychoanal. Assn.,* 47:9–28.

Richmond, M. (1917), *Social Diagnosis.* New York: Russell Sage Foundation.

Robinson, V. (1930), *A Changing Psychology in Social Case Work.* Chapel Hill: University of North Carolina Press.

Sanville, J. B. (1996), Ferenczi and Psychoanalytic Technique. A discussion of André Haynal's paper. Presented to Federation of IPA Societies, Los Angeles, January 13.

Wallerstein, R. S. (1996), The identity of psychoanalysis: The question of lay analysis. *Bull. Menn. Clin.,* 60:515–535.

Chapter 1

Playing in Time and Space
An Interview with Jean Sanville

Interviewers: The Editors

Would you start by telling us how you were originally drawn to social work?

The simplest answer would be that I became a social worker as a route to becoming a psychoanalyst, but of course there is a longer answer. While still in high school, I found on my father's bookshelf Karl Menninger's *The Human Mind*. Being a bit worried about my own at the time, I read it cover to cover and was really turned on by psychoanalysis as he portrayed it. It looked as though the route would be through medical school, which did not appeal to me. But I was transfixed by some paragraphs that described a budding new profession, psychiatric social work. Menninger was declaring that it was no longer possible even to think of evaluating personalities broken by their efforts to adapt to their environments without considering the nature of the environmental factors. He advocated psychiatry's turning to "young women" who would be especially trained to evaluate those factors. Moreover, he maintained, training in psychoanalytic principles would also "reanimate social work."

I knew only one social worker, a friend of my mother's from Goucher. Like most social workers of that era, she worked in a public agency offering services to the poor, and, in the course of telling me many stories about her cases, she declared that there were two prerequisites to being a social worker: "strong legs and a stout heart." I did not doubt that I possessed both. But I missed something: her stories dealt abundantly with factors outside the person, and I could not see her clients in my mind's eye so well as I could Dr. Karl's, for his stories included the insides of his patients' minds. Dimly I began to glimpse some possible combination of the socioeconomic and the psychological.

I went off to college assuming that the best major for me would be psychology. Alas, it was the era of operant conditioning, and each course was more disappointing than the last. We ran rats in mazes with no knowledge of their psyches other than that they would behave in ways that got them the rewards. Frequenting the library, I discovered the works of Margaret Mead and was fascinated with her *Coming of Age in Samoa* and *Growing Up in New Guinea*. And there too was George Mead and his *Philosophy of the Act* and his *Mind, Self, and Society*. They wrote of real people, in different environments and with minds as well as behaviors. So I changed my major to sociology and actually ended up with a double major, though with decided preferences for sociology and anthropology.

In my senior year, through my library explorations, I learned of the Smith College School for Social Work and its psychoanalytic orientation. The school had been founded just a few years after some social workers who had heard Freud when he visited Worcester decided that his theories were the underpinnings that social work needed. I was excited to discover that something of which I had dimly dreamed actually existed: a profession that attended both to psyche and to social surround. I applied and was granted a scholarship and went there immediately after graduating from the University of Colorado at Boulder.

My teachers of theory were mostly psychoanalysts from the East Coast cities, and they were male physicians. I was stimulated by them, but ambivalent, for they often talked as though they had powers of divining the innermost motives of us students, entirely women at that time. To some extent, the casework teachers, all women, emulated their methods and often engaged in blank-page approaches to interviews, with an air of owning secrets not to be freely imparted. What saved us students was, I think, the incessant communication among us about ourselves, about the faculty, and about what we were learning and how. And we "got even" every summer by enacting skits in which we played one or the other of them, joked about their ways, their ideas. About the latter, we made up songs that to this day can come back to me. In short, we survived—and thrived—giving a humorous perspective to what was an immersion experience during those three summers.

Smith's program has always been a "bloc" one; that is, between those summers in academia came nine months of field placement. My first was at Worcester State Hospital. Bernard Malamud and the psychiatrists were in charge, and we, the social workers, were their handmaidens. I lived with two other Smith students in the hospital, and our jobs entailed getting acquainted with patients who were deemed sufficiently well to go home on leave and to visit them subsequently to ascertain how well they were doing and what further help we might be to them. Here the "environmental" was clearly important. In those home visits, I realized the truth of needing "strong legs" and learned how complicated and difficult life could be for patients and their families; a "stout heart" did come in handy. But within this teaching hospital itself there was broad and deep learning to be had, particularly in the regular staffings of all patients and the discussions among all of us who had anything to do with them. The orientation then was mainly psychoanalytic but did not preclude attention to the part possibly played by the organic and by the sociocultural surround. There was ongoing research aimed at compre-hending causative factors in schizophrenia. The library was excellent, and I read extensively in the analytic writings available.

My second year's field work was in Family Service of Cincinnati, which was also strongly analytically oriented. There the social workers were in charge, and they brought in analysts to consult with us. We learned how to "take case histories" and to present them in staff meetings so that the analysts could be maximally helpful to us. I loved that setting, with its opportunity to work with persons in much better shape than those psychotic patients at Worcester and where social workers were the ones to have all direct contact with clients. We were the therapists and drew on psychodynamic theory in their treatment.

What was your pathway to becoming a social work psychoanalyst?

My first three positions were in family agencies. I started in Pittsburgh, where the attraction for me was that the agency was Rankian, a point of view scorned by the Freudians up at Smith, so I wanted to see for myself what it was. That year I concomitantly took a postgraduate course at the University of Pittsburgh, with Ruth Smalley as my teacher. She, who got her original training at Smith, enabled me to respect much of what the "functional" school had to offer. It differed, she thought, in its psychological base, operating not from a psychology of illness but from a psychology of growth, with an emphasis on the creative potential of the person. The client rather than the social worker was seen as the center of the relationship. The professional was to lend herself to the client's growth purposes, rather than estimate the degree and kind of sickness he or she suffered. The Rankians explicitly defined the purpose of social work as social rather than individual. Smalley and her colleagues were critical of us in the "diagnostic school"; they claimed that we took too much responsibility for the cause and cure of social problems and ignored their complexities. Social work's special contribution was the alleviation and prevention of social ills through participating in the forming of social policy, through the development and modification of social welfare programs, and though the use of its distinctive methods. I did quite a bit of debating with my teacher as to how real these differences were from what I had learned at Smith. I did not then foresee that the profession might eventually split, with one segment holding a philosophy somewhat akin to that of the Rankians, and the other, a clinical one, emphasizing the individual and the intrapsychic. I suspect that my year with Smalley rendered that split unlikely in my professional psyche!

After that year, I went to New York, where I accepted a position at the biggest "diagnostic" family agency in the country, the Community Service Society, on condition that they offer me psychoanalytic supervision in work with children. They did, and they gave me as supervisors Margaret Mahler and Marianne Kris, with Ernst Kris an occasional resource too. Mahler was then interested in autism and childhood schizophrenia, and I had child patients who qualified for such diagnoses. So I was getting closer to my dream.

My next move was to the West Coast, to a job with Los Angeles Family Service. Now I had a supervisor, Janet Nolan, who was also a graduate of Smith but who, unlike me, had had years of experience before undertaking graduate study. I also had an analyst as a regular consultant, Sam Futterman, still in Army uniform when he first began with us. In time, he moved on to be the Director of the then new Veteran's Administration Mental Health Clinic and invited me to be a member of his staff. It was an offer I could not turn down, for nearly every analyst in town was serving there. We worked with patients with service-connected emotional disabilities, a lot of what we now call posttraumatic stress disorders. French and Alexander were prominent theorists in that period, and our whole staff experimented with implementing their "corrective emotional experience" and discovered both its possibilities and its limits. The clinic was a hotbed of analytic thinking. Enthusiasm and excitement were at a high pitch. Everyone from the top down was supervised; there were regular staff conferences; most of us were doing group as well as individual therapy.

So much did I love working there that I was almost sorry when Frederick Hacker, looking for someone to serve as head of child therapy in his clinic, somehow found me. He well sensed that the one thing not pleasing to me in the VA job was that no children had managed to become veterans! A big factor in my move was that Beverly Hills would be nearer to my home, and I wanted more time to be with my own child. Moreover, the Hacker Psychiatric Clinic was an outgrowth of the Menninger Clinic in Topeka, and Karl Menninger was a regular visitor, so it did seem as though fate had somehow decreed this! After some initial reluctance, in 1947 I took the position and stayed there for over a decade. In that clinic too everyone was a supervisor and everyone had a supervisor. Psychoanalysis was in its heyday; the demand was great. I got to design my own playroom, and I saw all kinds of children—some of the sort that Mahler had taught me about, very disturbed, long-term cases; others who could be treated with relatively brief therapy. And I saw adults, too, usually in intensive treatment. The clinical experience was rich; but, in addition, when I was made Chair of the Hacker Foundation for Psychiatric Research and Education, we brought analysts from all over the world to lecture and do workshops with us, and from them I kept broadening and deepening my knowledge of psychoanalysis.

For the first time, I could afford to seek analysis for myself. One obstacle had been that there were as yet relatively few analysts around, and, with most, I had worked or sought supervision, or both, or sat at their feet in workshops, or had treated members of their families, or had socialized. So when Milton Wexler moved to Los Angeles from Menningers', I became one of his first analysands. I was somehow pleased that he was not an M.D. but that he was so outstanding that the American Psychoanalytic had awarded him full membership. (Some of my analyst friends made cracks about this entering into my choice.) To this day, I feel it was a good choice, and I am grateful to him. As we ended that analysis, he facilitated my separation-individuation not only from him but from the "family" at the Hacker Clinic.

In 1958 I left the clinic and went into private practice. But it was to be nearly another 20 years before I became an analyst. And those were full years: teaching at UCLA, founding the California Society for Clinical Social Work, founding and playing Dean to the Institute for Clinical Social Work, getting my own doctorate from International College. Then, in 1978, I joined with a group of psychologists who, frustrated by the fact that the American Psychoanalytic continued to refuse other than M.D.'s for training, formed the Los Angeles Institute and Society for Psychoanalytic Studies, the first group on the west coast to accept non-medical candidates. We had all been powerfully involved in psychoanalysis and had obtained our own training the "bootleg way," each along somewhat different pathways. We simply appointed ourselves the training analysts and proceeded to develop an excellent training program.

But for recognition on the broader scene some aggression was necessary. In 1988, when the American Psychological Association sued the American for its policy of not admitting other than M.D.'s to training, I, as then President of LAISPS, was requested to testify in a fancy law office in downtown Los Angeles. I was cross-examined all day by an attorney for the American as to how I and others had been disadvantaged by the American's exclusionary policies. As is now known, the case was ultimately settled out of court, and we were at last free to apply for membership in the International Psychoanalytical Association. That involved many site visits from the IPA. They examined our files, including the CV's of us training analysts and the kinds of records we kept on candidates. They interviewed us individually too and met with all other members and students. They watched us in supervisory sessions and in our teaching. And, according to their own rules, they first awarded us provisional membership and then, in 1995, at the 39th International Congress in San Francisco, LAISPS was made a full constituent member of the IPA.

In what ways do you see your social work training and experience having affected your practice of psychoanalysis?

As mentioned, from my reading of Karl Menninger at age 14, the two were from the beginning linked in my mind. Because of my choice of Smith, with its strong analytic orientation, social work was psychoanalytic social work. When Joyce Edward and I gave a subtitle, "A Psychoanalytic Social Work Approach," to the book we edited together, one colleague wrote inquiring whether we were inventing a new profession. For me, it was never otherwise. Although the analysts who taught me, both in school and later in agencies, emphasized the intrapsychic, the teachers in casework classes and the social work supervisors in the agencies showed me how what is outside gets inside and vice versa. And, in case I had any doubts, my experience with patients and clients regularly demonstrated the interaction between internal and external. I am pleased to report that I never succumbed to the notions once prevalent in the mental health world that schizophrenogenic mothers *caused* childhood psychosis. I could see that what was *in* certain children exerted adverse effects on parents; insides could also affect outsides. When I moved into the realm of child therapy, there was no question but that either a colleague or I would need also to work with the parents of the child/patient.

There is reason to think that psychoanalysts over the years learned a lot from the social workers whom they supervised. Good social work theory has always been bio-psycho-social, and there is reason to believe that analytic theory is moving rapidly in that direction. At the conjoint meetings of the IPA House of Delegates and the Executive Council in Buenos Aires in 1998, it was seriously proposed that analytic training needs a "fourth leg," education about the importance of the sociocultural surround in which people are born, grow up, and now function.

Who are the persons who have had the most influence on your outlook on life in general and on the ways you practice psychoanalysis?

To begin with, there were my parents. Because of the sociocultural surround and perhaps the time in history, I had not only a mother but a father who played as central a role as she from my infancy onward. I grew up in a small community in Pennsylvania where my father was the only physician. His office was just a walk down our backyard to the next street. So, except when he was off delivering babies or making home visits to sick patients, he was home for meals, and, when he was not with patients, I could often be with him. That was not only desirable but necessary, since my mother, who had been a teacher and school principal, was frequently herself busy with her own activities—on the local school board, on the boards of various colleges in nearby cities, or managing some properties that were hers. So I often accompanied him when he had to visit patients in the surrounding county area, and I was sometimes privileged to witness his conversations with them. I could see that his patients respected him, even loved him, and I suspected that healing ensued not only from the medicines prescribed, but from out of the special relationships he formed with them. He and I had lots of opportunities for talking, too, on those trips, and I think he communicated both love and respect for me, perhaps sometimes giving me credit I had not yet earned for an intelligence beyond my years.

But the result was that this important other who was my father imparted to me a confidence that came in handy in life, a confidence that, although I might not know, I could learn. Dr. Bovard loved learning. He read avidly, not only about medical matters, but about everything, and he enjoyed discussing what he was taking "inside." He spoke often of the miraculous ways that bodies tend to heal themselves, and of his job being to facilitate that spontaneous mending. I came to believe that psyches too tend toward self-healing and that the job of a clinical social worker or a psychoanalyst is to foster that "reparative intent," as Joel Shor and I later labeled it.

My mother too had a love of learning. From early on I heard stories of her courses at Goucher College and of her ongoing friendships with women she had known there. It was she who, on finding that social work was of interest to me, invited a former roommate to visit us and tell me about that field. Her own interests were very much in education, and her many teacher-friends came frequently to visit and to talk with her about their problems, sometimes with students, sometimes with the system. I heard many of those conversations and could see both her identifications with them out of her own experiences and her ability also to offer an "outside" view. In recent years, I have been impressed with the importance of a focus not only on empathy but on alterity and have guessed that I witnessed samples of that dialectic in her way of helping her friends. Mother too liked to read, and dinner table conversations often included exchanges about what stories were preoccupying one or another of us at the moment. So from both parents I inherited a love of learning and an inclination to turn to books for knowledge.

I would mention too my maternal grandmother, who had also been a teacher. I attribute a lot of my own playfulness to having identified with her way of being in the world. Her husband, my grandfather, was an earnest and strict man, and yet she never seemed to experience any constriction within herself on account of him. I remember no dissonance between them; indeed I knew that love and respect went in both directions. But, confident that grandfather could fend for himself for a month or so, grandmother also did her own thing, for example, packing up my cousin and me and taking us in the summers west to Colorado, where resided three of her Swedish sisters. She had a great capacity for pleasure, and it was because of those fun-filled experiences with her on those trips that I fell in love with the Rocky Mountains and chose to go to the University at Boulder.

My supervisors at Smith also had a profound influence and during both years I also had abundant opportunity for consultation with analytically oriented psychiatrists, such as William Thomas Barton, and with analysts, such as Lewis Hill. After graduation it was possible in those days to choose jobs on the basis of the quality and quantity of supervisors and consultants who would be available. The most influential of these persons were not those who tried to have me emulate their ways of working, but those who skillfully enabled me to develop my own ways, as Ruth Smalley certainly did, and later Sam Futterman, Eugene Mindlin, and Frederick Hacker. I found myself with professionals who had no trouble discovering and respecting my apparently innate allergy to dogma; they put forth little that I experienced as authoritarian. Because I was blessed with such sensitive helpers, I probably did come to practice in their ways!

You have treated both children and adults. How might doing so have affected your analytic approach?

One of the main differences in working with children is that therapy is seldom just a two-person situation. The child usually does not refer himself and—depending on his age and cognitive development and how the parents have introduced the idea of therapy—he may or may not understand who this new adult might be and how she could possibly be helpful. He may or may not experience his symptoms as troublesome, or perhaps he sees them problematic mainly to his parents, in which case he may have some sense that the therapist is aligned with parents. It is clear that, from the start, the child therapist is working in a social context. Parents are involved, siblings, sometimes school teachers, physicians, others who have to do with the child's life. I would say that, for me, there was almost infinite variability in the patterns developed for working with different cases. As a child therapist, one may have contact with any or all of these persons who influence and are influenced by the child.

The experiences both during my Smith years in Worcester State Hospital and later with children and their families impressed on me the importance of the surround, the environment into which one is born and reared and where one now lives and functions. The intrapsychic cannot be understood apart from the interpersonal context in which it unfolds and continues to unfold. In work with adults who are not psychotic, one is less likely to have direct access to the others who are central for the patient, but those of us who have treated children are keenly aware of their influence. The child therapist also learns however, that we are not all created equal and that some children are much more difficult than others for parents—and indeed may be for their therapists too. The opportunity for direct work with parents could render us immune to the notion that parents are to blame for all the problems their children manifest. Parents too had childhoods, often experienced deprivations and trauma themselves, and so need empathy and compassion. Yet I knew many therapists, even some clinics, that have developed occupational prejudices against mothers, inevitably handicapping their treatment approaches.

Play and playing, of course, are a part of therapy with children, and, as Winnicott put it, when the patient is unable to play, it is the job of the therapist to bring the person to a state of being able to play. It is dismaying to find that not all children can play, for example, those who suffer severe autism. I began my *Playground of Psychoanalytic Therapy* with a chapter on the importance of play in childhood, followed by a chapter on Katie, a child who could not play. It described the intensive and extensive treatment of a child from the age of two-and-a-half until twelve. Eye-to-eye contact was slow in developing, as was speech. Whatever was akin to play was at first repetitive and not communicative. Before age eight there was nothing like symbolic play. I experienced the mother as a cotherapist, and we learned together how to make contact with this insulated and isolated child.

My next chapter was about a child who could play, a "contemporary Little Hans," and effective treatment was very brief because of his very active involvement with me and with the playthings available. Here too the mother was constructively involved, actually present in the therapy hours. And Rickie was most verbal and imaginative. He "worked" hard to understand his problem, and it was in play that he could deliver his unconscious fantasy and begin to harmonize it with the external world.

Of course, there were many child patients whose language skills were not so well developed; for them the language was of the body and of playing, of actions rather than words. But I never was as impressed as some therapists with *what* the children were trying to say in their play actions; that was often open to a wide variety of interpretations. I was more struck by the very capacity for playing and by how, if the child and I could establish a safe playground, it could facilitate eluding the fixities that were interfering with growth and repair. Inasmuch as my readings informed me that the capacity for playing was characteristic of the whole mammalian species, I felt that Freud had neglected a basic instinct!

However, he did offer a glimpse of how the dynamics of playing enter into adult analysis when he put forth the idea of "the transference as a playground." But perhaps because of the intellectual ambiance of his day, he could not safely develop this keen intuition. It was with the intent to explore this metaphor and to discover whether what I had learned from children about the role of playing could carry over to the treatment of adults that I wrote *The Playground of Psychoanalytic Therapy*. It seemed clear that what Freud had in mind was that, to constructively use the transference, the patient has to be capable of a certain make-believe, a kind of double vision, *feeling* the analyst to be a version of central figures in her past but simultaneously *knowing* that he doesn't exactly fit her template. The two participants have to be able to create together the sense of safety that enables the analysand to experience the setting as an "intermediate region," both real and imagined. Only then can she use it to test the transference, her own previously automatic assumptions, and in time transcend former patterns of interpreting the data of her relationships.

So I have seen it as one of the instrumental goals of analysis to awaken the playing child in the adult. In the playing of the child and in the words and dream images of the adult are clues not only about what has gone wrong but about what I believe to be the ubiquitous reparative intent—the wish to make things better. The child portrays both in the scenes he constructs with the materials in the playroom and in the dramas he may enact with the therapist. Most adults employ words, albeit with varying degrees of skill. But these are comprehensible only in context and are understood not only in their literal meanings but in the *ways* they are put forth. Interpretations are, in my view, best conjointly made by patient and analyst, not pronounced by the analyst in ways that connote authority or finality, since that would discourage using the interpretations as playthings. As the child may build a tower with blocks, only to then knock it down and build another that pleases him more, so we hope the patient may use language proper to keep emending and extending his theories as life brings new challenges. As the role of positive emotions in promoting growth and development is being emphasized by infant researchers, so analysts are also seeing room for recognizing the patient's self-healing aspects, including what Freud noted as the symptom itself being an attempt at cure.

Are there other influences that have made play come to occupy such an important place in your own life and in your analytic approach?

I think I was lucky to have a lot of quite playful people in my early life, as I have mentioned, and I probably connected creativity and play early on. My father's cousin, Margaret Williams, was a vibrant person, an artist, and a professor of art in Grove City College in Pennsylvania. Having studied in France for a year, she was profoundly influenced by the Impressionists, and her studio in her home was full of that color and light that we associate with them. My parents loved her work and had her paint a mural on one entire wall of their cottage on the Allegheny River, and I watched her at work on that. But when I visited with her and her sister, as I often did, I never accepted her offer to try painting myself. Instead I'd go off to the town library, bring back piles of books, and read and read. Much of my own early play was in the realm of language, not image. It was not until many years later that I discovered something of the potential artist in myself, and my medium was not Margaret's but consisted of "found objects" on the beach where my husband, Richard Sanville, and I kept a house for weekend retreats. There I became virtually enchanted in playing with stones and driftwood and shells. I put them together in various ways in what I later learned were called "assemblages" and usually forced these dead things to portray something alive. Obsessed with this activity, I made hundreds of different combinations. When a colleague and friend, Corinne Sturtevant, told an art dealer in Beverly Hills that he should see them, I was totally surprised to find myself in an art show, for I'd never seen myself as a "real" artist. After the Bel Air fire a few years later destroyed my home and all that I then had left of those created objects, my obsession with that form of playing diminished, and I returned to words instead of images. I look back on that period of making assemblages as a kind of vacation from words, which were my first love. And words were, incidentally, Richard's medium; he was a film writer.

How does your philosophy and approach to play relate to Winnicott's?

I feel very close to Winnicott's thinking. I became attracted to his writings sometime in the 1960s, and when he came out with *Playing and Reality* in 1971, I knew I had found a soul mate. Like a good clinical social worker (and his wife, Clare, was one of us), he emphasized the importance of the "holding environment," as it is originally created by infant and mother and, later, by therapists with patients. When it is favorable, it makes for "potential space" for playing and hence for movement away from repetition compulsions and their fixities. This British analyst did not get stuck with the polarities of "inner" and "outer" but posited "intermediate space" and cultural experience as in direct continuity with play. He declared that it was time for psycho-analysis to pay attention to this "third area" of culture itself. He would have applauded current proposals that our institutes should teach courses on what he called "the location of cultural experience," the interplay of inner and outer. I very much agree that ideally psychotherapy is a subspecies of play and that, when playing is not possible, it is the task of the therapist to enable the patient to play. That is where the work comes in!

For Winnicott, interpretation at its best was related to playing; it should be far removed from authoritative statements that are close to indoctrination; it should emerge from conjoint process. That philosophy is congenial to the social worker in me. Clearly, Winnicott treated many patients akin to those whom we social workers have traditionally treated. These are not persons with whom interpretations lead quickly to good results. He once wrote of how it appalled him to think of the deep change he had prevented in some patients by his personal need to interpret. Patience is required, and he believed that, given time, the patient would arrive at understanding creatively and joyfully. So, he said, he interpreted mainly to let the patient know the limits of his own understanding.

Would you give us an example of what you regard as a playful encounter in the treatment of an adult?

With a relatively healthy neurotic analysand, the playful may make its appearance in dreams. One such patient, a mental health professional, was generally earnest in her sessions, diligently trying to understand herself, especially in relation to her practice. In her dreams she found the potential space that seemed in short supply in most of her waking life. Those dreams delighted and astonished her with their unexpected creativity, and she invited our playing together with these otherwise private playthings. On one occasion she brought in two dreams. The first, she admitted, had occurred before our last session, but she had "forgotten" to tell me (and there is a bit of humor in that, for we both know under what circumstances such forgetting tends to occur). "I am with my older daughter. She is very pregnant, and I have the deep conviction that it is *our* baby." The second dream, from the night before, was: " I am in that daughter's car, looking for a place to buy myself a drink, some liquor. I drove the car up over a curb near a liquor store, but I realize I have to have a pistol to obtain a drink. I have no pistol, so I drive on. The scene is repeated, and I search the car thoroughly, but there is no pistol."

Associating to the first dream, she repeated what she has often told me, of her distaste for that daughter's husband, how she prefers vacations with just the daughter and the grandchildren, without that son-in-law. Associating to the second dream, she observed that the daughter will drink with her as much wine as she herself regularly drinks, quite a quantity. She was mystified by the idea of a gun and humorously said she guessed she was "after a shot." Further thoughts came, and together we got around to seeing the gun as symbolizing what she does not have in order to make the wish in the first dream a reality. But we also observed that in the dream, in contrast to the way she lives, she "violates boundaries," drives "over the curb," and that in her eagerness to do things properly, in real life, she suffers some sense of missing aggressive potential in herself. These dreams also led to deepening and extending her insights not only about her elimination of men, but about even excluding from her sense of self some qualities she deems masculine and that might be essential to the altered state of consciousness she desires!

What about patients who cannot play?

In my experience, the most unplayful patients rarely report dreams, and the free association that we try to encourage in analysis is hard to come by. They are literal-minded, do not easily comprehend the symbolic. Their bodies often have to "speak" because their psyches cannot; so psychosomatic symptoms abound. The consequence is that the transference is no playground. One such patient manifested intense discomfort upon entering the room at the beginning of each hour and could not bear lying down where she could not see my face.

Sitting so that she could see me did not help much, but it did make it possible for her to continue treatment. Our attempted interpretations about how I seemed to be like her felt-to-be unwelcoming, unloving, unsatisfactory, and even frightening mother went nowhere. I asked her one day what I might do that could help her to overcome these profound discomforts. Her answer was that I could take her hand and offer her milk and cookies. With my background in child therapy, I could lightly and humorously have played this theme out. She could not follow her own prescription, however, because for her such motoric regression could not be experienced playfully. Nevertheless, she began to use it as a metaphor, which is in the direction of a kind of verbal playing that was absent from her usual concrete mindedness. I wish I could describe a dramatic breakthrough, but I feel that what is indicated is very intensive and extensive treatment that will involve the "regression to dependence" that Winnicott felt to be necessary when the patient has lacked the maternal provision that frees the otherwise innate impulse to play.

We are also aware of the importance you place on creativity. Could you share some of your thoughts on this topic?

Closely connected to playfulness is creativity, which I see not as a gift of the gods to a chosen few, but as distributed quite widely. Certainly some people manifest more creativity than others, and the unplayful ones I have just described are least likely to manifest the capacity for making something new, original, or inventive. But there is an innate epistemophilia. Babies are born to be theory makers, to construct propositions about self and world, to make meanings. And they hope that those meanings will enable them to negotiate the inevitable conflicts between becoming unique individuals and maintaining esential connections with others. Each of us solves those conflicts in characteristic ways, most awarding priority to one or another line of development, a few comfortably oscillating between self and relationships, capable of enjoying both illusory fusion with loved and admired others and illusory autonomy. Neither can be exactly "real." Therapists who best foster the innate creativity in each patient tend to respect the symptom itself as an attempt at cure; their interpretations are least likely to be narcissistically wounding, for they are seldom made by the analyst to the patient in absolute ways, but rather are conjointly constructed and always open to further emendations.

Language appears to be another of your loves. We should very much like to know how this has evolved.

I seem to have had the same intense love affair with words as for "found" beach objects. My mother used to tell with some amusement, how, in my preschool period, I used to ask, "Do I know all the words now?" I vaguely remember putting forth that question in order to find some words I did not yet know, somehow like seeking for new transitional objects with which to play. My parents complied by habitually reading me stories at bedtime. So it perhaps was not surprising that by the time I was in school, I often silently told myself stories before falling asleep, sometimes virtual novels, with new episodes each night. After I learned to read, that too was a major preoccupation—to the extent that my parents often felt it was too much and tried to persuade me to do more active things as well. By high school years, I was also addicted to stories on radio, especially those by Norman Corwin, who in my adulthood became a dear friend.

Richard Sanville's world was also that of stories and language, and he was a fine writer. For some 20 years we were members of a poetry reading group. It started as a UCLA extension program, but eventually a group of us continued it on our own, meeting monthly to discuss agreed upon readings. We read and discussed many contemporary poets, but, for some of us, Wallace Stevens was the favorite, and we'd return to savor his work again and again. We were the originators of what has become the Wallace Stevens Society; it now publishes *The Wallace Stevens Journal.* I have quoted Stevens in many of my published articles, since he is a part of how I think. Just now I am newly excited to realize some parallels between his thoughts about thinking and those of Matte Blanco, who wrote *Thinking, Feeling, and Being.* So I cited him in a presentation at a recent conference on the work of that Chilean analyst. I essentially pointed out that, at best, our theories will be "Notes Toward a Supreme Fiction" (the title of one of Stevens's best known poems). To qualify, they must be abstract, must give pleasure, and must change. All three highlight the relation of poetry to play.

Are there certain patients that you have worked with over the years who stand out for you, and, if so, can you tell us about them and why they have remained significant?

There are many, and of some I have written. One of my earliest published articles was about a little schizophrenic girl who, after a few years, began repetitively to review her own treatment. She taught me a lot about what it is to be schizophrenic and so young, and her mother taught me what it is to mother such a child, especially if one also had an older, hospitalized psychotic daughter. Many years later I wrote of a decade of treatment of an autistic little girl, Katie, and from her and her family I learned how that was different from schizophrenia. Both cases showed me that I had to cultivate a capacity for patience and for perseverence if we were to accomplish anything. I needed those two to find out what I had learned from Margaret Mahler and to realize the need for infinitely more learning.

In my 1991 book I featured therapy with fairly difficult patients. I sometimes write to find out what I think, and to make peace with the fact that I am in a career where I can never know enough. Nora was a kind of grownup Katie, autistic and unplayful, and the work was to construct a playground. She confirmed for me the ubiquitous wish to make things better, and how, when her hopes were aroused, it could entail outbursts of hostility, which I must survive. And then there was the antianalytic patient, who had somehow missed the "dialogues from infancy" and for whom the task was the "rerailing of dialogue," as Spitz had written. There was the woman born so prematurely that we hypothesized "primary trauma." And Clare, who ended her analysis so creatively that I had to preserve the account as being of aesthetic value. As I review these cases, I realize afresh how often I write as a way of learning from the patient, hanging on to that, and noticing how much more I would like to know.

There were, of course, many more who come back in my memories. Once in a while some patients from long ago put in an appearance, and it's a rich experience to learn how they experienced their lives after therapy, how they may have integrated what they learned, or what they see as the tasks yet ahead.

If you had not been an analyst, what might you have been?

Now you invite my fantasy. Perhaps I'd have become a storyteller, a writer, like my Richard. Indeed, the appeal of psychoanalysis perhaps had to do with the sense, since validated, that it would give me the opportunity to live vicariously many lives besides my own—as indeed did the novels I read as a young person. Menninger had affirmed that he found patients and their stories more interesting than those of so-called normal persons, whatever those might be. Certainly I began fairly early in my career to write, and my CV is many pages long because it lists all the writings I've done over the years—many just oral presentations at conferences, others published in various professional journals. But journals do not pay their writers, and I will never know whether I could have made a living with another kind of writing, overtly fiction.

So, the most likely alternative would have been a career as an academic. I seemed to veer away from aspirations to teach, perhaps not wanting to be just like all those other women in my family who made that their calling. Actually, when I succumbed to the invitation of Dean Donald Howard to be on the faculty of the then new School of Social Welfare at UCLA, I found I loved teaching, but I never wanted to do it to the exclusion of practice. In fact, I could not imagine doing what some others in faculties of schools for social work did: teach about practice without actually doing it. And so, I continue to play with teaching as a supplemental activity, from which I do not derive my primary professional identity, but from which I keep learning.

You wrote a paper 25 years ago entitled "The Eight Ages of a Clinical Social Worker." Can you tell us how you view the stage you are in now?

I heard Erikson outline those developmental stages at a lecture in Santa Barbara before his book was published, and I had subsequent opportunities for dialogue with him about his ideas. We participated together in a number of UCLA conferences, and Joel and I were for a while on the faculty of the Erikson Center at Harvard. Erikson himself used to humorously declare that he had run out of stages. Perhaps because of the enormous sociocultural changes in the last half-century, we may have to create some new ones.

At this stage, I still do not contemplate complete retirement, although most of my age-mates have by now given up practice, and I sometimes wish I had the time that they have for other pursuits. I consider myself fortunate that the profession I chose so long ago has been even more fully rewarding than I could have imagined, affording me a richness and diversity of experience for which I am deeply grateful. A certain redesigning of life, both personally and professionally, at different intervals, and in response to both internal and external factors, has characterized each of my so-called stages. At the close of the eighth decade of life, I, like others, have lost many dear ones and know well what it is to be in mourning. I am glad for the friends who are still around and for the opportunity to see patients, to read, to continue to learn, and to teach and write.

My age has catapulted me into an interest in something seldom reported in published case stories: the relative ages of therapist and patient and the effects of those similarities or differences on the playgrounds of transferences and countertransferences. A dear friend and colleague, Bea Sommers, and I have developed some presentations about this for conferences of the California Society for Clinical Social Work. And last year, at the International Psychoanalytic Congress in Barcelona, I presented a paper that took a look at analysis when both participants are in their eighth decades of life. It included the interplay of gender and aging—another topic about which I have been thinking a lot.

Joan Erikson would include in the attributes of wisdom "acceptance of the cycle of life from integration to disintegration," that is, into old age and death. I agree with her that acceptance is not necessarily passive resignation if somewhere along the way one has also developed a humorous perspective about the inevitable. Among the many friends who are close to me in age I find this attribute present in abundance; together we can muster light amusement even about our losses of physical and sensory capacities, while not denying that we resent those losses too. It is, Joan has said, akin to the playing child's refreshing sense of humor: healing, enlivening laughter that keeps human feet firmly on the ground (*humus*). We could say that shared humor generates that intermediate space in which the experience is not one of just going gentle into the underground!

You have done a great deal of work in the community over the years. How have you brought your analytic understandings to bear on these activities?

I have always had a sort of restiveness that drives me to see whether what I have learned clinically might be of value in other situations and to learn more about the sociocultural surround that clinical social work has always taken into consideration. While I was working with the Hacker Foundation I was in charge of designing courses and seminars in which we could share what we knew with those of other professions that worked with people: doctors, nurses, teachers, police, lawyers. I was for a while the "expert" on a twice-a week CBS television program, "Know Your Child." It was, I think, one of the first "talk shows" and consisted of dialogues, mostly with parents, about their children. For some five years, I was a consultant to the teachers in the Day Care Centers of Santa Monica, which served so-called high risk children—offpring of working mothers, usually single, often minority, poor, living under many tensions. We took children at 2 years 10 months, and many of them had had by then enough ongoing trauma for a lifetime. But by the time we sent them on to kindergarten, they were so ahead of their peers that teachers in the public school had to design new approaches. At the end of those five years, the Lincoln Child Development Center was chosen the model program in the nation by the White House Conference on Children.

For some years I was sent by the New York-based Caribbean Federation for Mental Health to consult with governments in some of those nations about their mental health programs. Experiences varied, from that in some of the small islands, which were not sure what they wanted to do with me and where I had to structure my own activities, to Guyana, a nation that had just achieved its independence from Britain and knew exactly what it wanted: that I conduct workshops for the various groups that deal with people—not unlike what I had done some years before in Los Angeles, although with people with different cultural backgrounds. At least in those countries, their language was mine. One summer I was invited to consult with a family service agency in Kyoto, Japan, one that, perhaps surprisingly, saw itself with a psychoanalytic orientation. It was run by a social worker trained in the United States but who had spent her life in the Orient. I knew not a word of Japanese and was totally dependent on the wife of the President of Doshisha University, who served as translator. The experience left me with many thoughts about mother tongues and the ways in which differences in original language might affect therapeutic discourse.

Here in Los Angeles I have been a coleader, with Nancy Hollander, of an intercultural study group, sponsored by the Los Angeles Federation of IPA Societies, composed of analysts interested in meeting together regularly to share ideas gleaned from readings and from clinical experience and to hear from invited guests about interactions between the culture of psychoanalysis and the myriad cultures in our metropolis. I submitted a proposal to the Planning Committee for the July 1999 41st IPA Congress in Santiago de Chile for a workshop on Intracultural and Intercultural Dialogue in Psychoanalysis. It has been accepted, so Nancy and I will have an opportunity to explore with analysts from other nations a topic dear to our hearts.

As one of the founders of the first free-standing, degree-granting Institute for Clinical Social Work, you have become well known for your strong views on models of education. Please tell us something about your educatonal philosophy, the process of its evolution, and the ways in which you have implemented your ideas?

It was back in 1974 that the California Institute was founded. We who believed that clinical social workers needed to have available possibilities to study for a clinical doctorate had failed to persuade the existing universities in California to establish such programs. Ours had to be a school-without-walls, highly individualized if it was to meet the needs of students of diverse ages, experiences, and interests. We had to find ways for candidates to learn in and from their practices, and to integrate that learning with curriculum content. In the beginning we accepted only quite advanced scholars, who had already shown themselves to be "autodidacts," and in the first year the topic of study was clinical education itself. We believed that teaching was itself one of the best ways of learning, so each student was in effect also a teacher. What other schools called professors, we called "animateurs," persons skilled in promoting the enthusiasm and the dialogue that help students to realize their goals. A basic assumption was that "as the twig is bent, so the tree will be inclined," so we aimed at enabling, not indoctrinating. I had by this time taught for years at UCLA, but because Ph.D.s in the clinical field were rare, I'd done it without a doctorate. So, as I agreed to play dean the first two years, I also enrolled in a doctoral program at International College, with John Seeley as my mentor. He had been part of the experiment in an alternative mode of education at the University of Chicago, so was ideal for my project. I did my dissertation on "The Play in Clinical Education." That document, plus articles in the *Clinical Social Work Journal* over the years, will be useful to those who want to be more familiar with how our ideas began and how they unfolded.

Writing too has been a long-standing interest of yours. You have written extensively, have taught workshops on writing, and have encouraged others to overcome resistances to writing. You served as Editor of the Clinical Social Work Journal *for 15 years. How do you reflect on your work in that arena?*

Often people who do not write entertain a fantasy that we who do simply sit down and turn out publishable manuscripts. So, workshops on writing usually have to begin by dispelling such notions. Participants must drop their convictions that they should do it perfectly in one sitting; they must commit themselves to writing and to sharing that commitment with other members of the group, who, in turn, learn how to give constructive feedback. I believe that, during my 15 years of editing the *Journal,* the members of its editorial board became increasingly skilled in offering feedback. Relatively few articles are accepted just as they are first sent; most authors are asked for some clarifications, emendations. It is a very deep satisfaction to me that, during those years, social workers became better writers, and the *Journal* has played a part in that.

We are aware of your deep concern about the current "crisis in psycho-analysis" and your involvement in efforts to deal with it. Can you share with us your understanding of what is taking place and the solutions that you envision?

I do think there is a crisis. The word comes from the Greek verb meaning to decide or separate. The noun we have made of it designates a serious state of affairs, a turning point when something must undergo material change or terminate. So there are advantages to our doing what we hope to enable our analysands to do when confronting crisis in their lives—to admit that a crisis exists, try to understand why, and take appropriate actions about it. Who can deny that there are far fewer patients requesting psychoanalysis, fewer applicants for analytic training, a paucity of persons willing to be control cases, even at reduced fees, fewer academic appointments open to us? Medically trained persons can make more money by prescribing pills, and psychologists want to do that too. Third-party intrusions threaten privacy and confidentiality, demand endless paper work. Managed care organizations dictate the mode of approach, frequency, and duration. There is emphasis on short-term treatment, so these organizations do not knowingly accept psychoanalytically trained *providers*. But young persons coming into the field need referrals from such sources, and so they have to learn a new game, less interesting than the old one.

Some factors in the crisis are the result of growing social and economic problems beyond our influence, but we have also been slow to reach out and share what we know with those who try to address social problems. Psychoanalysis has earned the reputation of being an ivory tower profession, available only to the well-to-do. Few of us have reached out to pool our knowledge with that of others who address causes and consequences of poverty, homelessness, racism, gangs, violence. So our critics declare us irrelevant for today's world.

We have lost most of our toehold in academia, and part of that loss may be because, until very recently, we have been philosophically behind the times, reluctant to move away from the philosophy of positivism, reluctant to relinquish the notion of the analyst as objective observer, who can point out "reality" in interpretations. There is a certain "petrification" (Otto Kernberg's term) in our institutes. In this country for years psychoanalysis was a field closed to all but medically trained persons, and that constraint may have made for a kind of thinking that ran into severe limits since dialogue with other professions was in short supply. There were unfortunately many analysts who came close to dogma, who could not bear thinking that challenged their basis beliefs. They failed to see the wisdom in Rene Spitz's old adage that life begins with the dialogue and that psychopathology may be seen as derailment of dialogue. If one seeks the "inner" causes of some of the crisis, this is one place to look.

In this country, psychoanalysis may ultimately benefit from the consequences of the suit against the American Psychoanalytic Association, which was finally settled out of court partly, I think, because there were also many forces within that organization already moving it toward change. The doors of training are now open to other mental health professionals, including social workers. We can foretell a certain "feminization" of psychoanalysis, which may entail some basic and needed shifts in theories and practice, and in how we educate, rather than train, in regard to both.

As I have mentioned, it was affirmed in the 1997 meetings of the House of Delegates and the Council of the IPA that psychoanalysis does need to integrate a "fourth leg" into its educational programs: the sociocultural surround and its import for mental health or psychopathology. It would be sad indeed if, when psychoanalysis is moving toward what social work has always seen as essential, social work education were to move away from psychoanalysis. Fortunately there are schools such as my alma mater, Smith College School for Social Work, that not only maintain a psychoanalytic base but are open to all that is new and exciting in analytic theory and practice.

Psychoanalysis is currently deeply involved in its own soul-searching, drawing for help on the allied professionals who are now its members, and inviting some of us from outside also to advise. I have been asked to be a consultant to the Ad Hoc Committee on Graduate Education of the American Psychoanalytic Association, and I look forward to serving with this group of seasoned clinicians from both social work and psychology as they ponder how to breathe new life into existing Master's and Doctoral programs by the inclusion of contemporary analytic thinking.

I am optimistic about the future of psychoanalysis. There is no more interesting theory, and it promises to be even more valuable as we incorporate and integrate the burgeoning data both from the inner and outer worlds: the neurobiological and the sociocultural realms.

Chapter 2

The Opening Phase of the Analysis of Mr. B
A Dramatic Transference Phenomenon

Kerry Leddy Malawista
Peter L. Malawista

There is a bit of analytic apocrypha in which an exceptionally short, brilliant, and playful senior analyst opens his office door and watches (as if in a Lewis Carroll dream) a new patient unfolding in his waiting room to a height of seven feet or so. He gapes for a moment, contemplates that this is to be the first of what may be hundreds of hours he will spend with the giant, and mutters, "Oh [pause] well, come in anyway."

We use this anecdote to underscore how the analyst's spontaneous and genuine expression of countertransference demonstrated to the patient at the time, and to us today, a necessary capacity to do the work that lay ahead. In those first moments, the patient was implicitly invited (in a manner we assume he was not expecting and that thereby got his attention) into a therapeutic setting where analyst and patient could together explore, among other things, the outer–inner phenomenon of body height. The analyst intuitively recognized the potential usefulness of his own outer–inner reality of tall–short in the treatment of a man so absurdly tall. *"In her response to the patient, the therapist sets about to create herself as part of a scene in which playfulness can occur, a safe outer-inner space, a playground in which the patient will not be so earnest, but relax and be able to communicate . . ."* (Sanville, 1991, p. 248, italics added).

In this chapter we explore the opening phase (the first four months) of the analysis of a troubled but exceptionally shrewd, ruthless and expansively effective scientist and entrepreneur who is certain that he is smarter and more aggressive than virtually everyone. Mr. B's unusually powerful aggressive drive and intellect are fused into what has become both a productive reality and a hot bed of narcissistic fantasy. His self-concept is grandiose, yet he feels acute discomfort in his psyche; similar perhaps to the discomfort we imagine the tall analysand and the short analyst felt in their bodies. But, just as we assume that both the short analyst and the tall patient have distinguishing attributes other then height, Mr. B is unusual not just in the magnitude of his aggressively driven intellect; but also, despite obvious signs of intense intrapsychic conflict, in his capacity for clear and forthright self-perception. He demonstrates this capacity in the first moments of his relationship with his new social worker analyst, moments in which she not only notes and respects his ability to perceive and communicate his immediate reaction to her, but in which she demonstrates her capacity to surprise, to remain actively neutral, to react counter to his expectations (whether anticipated, desired, provoked, or despised), and to provide opportunities for change.

The Analyst's New Patient

On opening her office door, the analyst encounters her new patient. Self-referred on the basis of her office location as listed in his health insurer's directory of preferred providers, he has come for routine evaluation. He enters the office and almost immediately mutters, "Oh [pause] no [pause] I [pause] don't think this will work."

He is a tall, strikingly attractive youthful, 45-year-old man, casually but precisely dressed, bristling with aggressive energy. He speaks fluent English with a pronounced French accent.

Analyst: "If you wish [pause] that's fine [pause] but, while you're here, could you tell me more of your thoughts about it [pause]?"

The analyst, is 36 years old, of English-Irish Catholic stock, is often mistaken for younger on first meeting, face to face or by phone, She is the mother of two young children whose existence is apparent to any perceptive person coming to her home office.

> The patient, having arranged the appointment, enters the office for the first time and notes both consciously and unconsciously its atmosphere furnishings, [etc.]—and its occupant, the therapist—sex, age, appearance, manner, voice, and whatever other qualities feel relevant at this moment [Sanville, 1991, p. 247].

Mr. B proceeds to express his perception that the analyst couldn't possibly have "enough life experience," be neither smart nor confident enough to help him: he would "run right over" her. He described his mother sitting on the far side of the sandbox when he was little because she was not able to tolerate the constant complaints about his aggressiveness with other children. He told of kicking a fifth-grade classmate in the stomach over an issue of pride and his subsequent shame that the other boy was hurt so badly that he required hospitalization. At the end of the hour he concluded, "Maybe you can help me [pause] You weren't defensive when I criticized you. [pause] I'll try it."

Mr. B returned and over a period of about three months engaged in a twice-weekly, face-to-face exploratory psychotherapy. He quickly became an unusually intriguing, provocatively paradoxical object of clinical interest to the analyst. She found him charming and attractive, intellectually nimble, often cannily perceptive; but at times disingenuous and self-serving. While his chief complaint concerned the quality of his marriage (specifically his wife's rages and brittle emotional instability), he gingerly circled the topic while speaking engagingly about other topics: his relationship with his son and daughter (ages six and eight); his enormously lucrative entrepreneurial enterprises; and the vicissitudes of culture and politics in Europe and between Europe and the United States. While Mr. B's wanderings felt defensive to the analyst, they seemed not so much avoidant as they did an expression of protectiveness of his wife and marriage. Prior to Mr. B's first consultation with the analyst, he and his wife had gone for marriage counseling, which his wife found "too stressful" after only a few meetings. He went back to the therapist, who recommended that both Mr. B and his wife find individual therapists. She would remain available if and when they wanted to resume. Mr. B followed through on the recommendation; his wife reportedly refused. Several months later, after Mr. B's analysis was underway and he became somewhat more content and companionable toward his wife, the wife accepted a referral from the analyst and tentatively began an analytic psychotherapy of her own.

During the exploratory work Mr. B often bantered with the analyst about psychoanalysis. He was intrigued by the couch and the idea of free associating to an other who is out of view. The analyst felt he would be a fascinating analysand. With the ego strength demonstrated in his entrepreneurial successes, his apparently stable, long-term friendships, and his demonstrated ability to make use of the analyst, she believed he had the capacity to make good use of analysis. She also felt that analysis was probably necessary if he was ever to get any real relief from his compulsive need to adversarially dominate the women in his personal life. Historically, he had apparently brought to his intimate relationships much of the same ruthless competitiveness as he had to his business dealings. While the analyst fundamentally thought of Mr. B as a well functioning, neurotically compulsive man, she carefully monitored her countertransference for indications of the extent and malignancy of his clearly evident narcissistic character pathology. Although she could see how his internal conflicts were significantly hindering the quality of his interpersonal life, she was impressed with how adaptively he had yoked and harnessed them together with his aggressively inquisitive intellect in the service of work.

Mr. B played with the idea of entering analysis as a treatment and as a business deal. He expressed his perception of the analyst as a salesperson who, like himself, got a "charge" out of outsmarting the other person and convincing him he needs more than he bargained for. He said he mistrusted her and reiterated the idea that he was "too much" for her. But he also acknowledged a familiar fear of disappointment he "always felt" when he got too close or put "too much of himself" in collaborative projects. Despite his protests, his investment in the treatment progressively deepened, as did his faith in the analyst.

As he became more engaged, he increasingly relaxed his adversarial posture both physically and psychologically. The analyst noted that as he did, he began to produce progressively more exaggerated yawns and somewhat odd, spastic movements of his arms and legs.

Session 24: The Last Exploratory Therapy Hour

One day Mr. B was expressing his worry that, when the analyst was quiet, he had lost her in some way. He said he was working to be charming in order to hold her interest, but punctuated the observation with a yawn and a series of twitches. Midway through the hour he said, "I worry that the time is gonna be over. [pause] I hate when it's gonna end." He talked of feeling "stuck," not making progress, not having much to say. The analyst commented about the possibility of seeing progress in the act of observing himself feeling "stuck." After a long silence and with much evident difficulty, he began:

Mr. B: "I feel like [pause] I worry [pause] I worry now that you're more focused on yourself. Hard to say it. So [pause] I worry that you think if I'm not making progress I'll stop. So, you're thinking more about yourself than about me."

Analyst: "Your reaction was to my comment? My reassurance that you are making progress?" [pause]

Mr. B: "Yes, I think you said that because you're worried. I felt angry when you said that. It's not like you."

This last, "It's not like you," felt to the analyst like something very new, "unlike" Mr. B. It seemed to represent a sudden deepening of the intimacy between them.

As Mr. B continued to describe his experience of the exchange, he began to shake until his whole body was contorted with spasms. He grabbed his coat and held it tightly against himself in an effort to control his shaking. He looked to the analyst like a terrified small child clutching a blanket, desperately trying not to fall to pieces. She felt a decidedly maternal urge as if she had come across a lost toddler, an urge to comfort him until his own mother could be found. She felt certain that the spasms were psychogenic, again something akin to a small child struggling, perhaps trapped in a night terror. But she also noted that another observer might perceive his spasms as the onset of a true seizure. She wondered in passing if she ought to be more concerned, but was not.

As the convulsive activity subsided, he began to explain that this was an involuntary reaction that followed his sudden discovery that he could tell her negative, critical thoughts without reprisal. This was demonstrated by her immediate understanding that his previous silence had been in reaction to her reassurance that he was making progress.

Mr. B: "You didn't respond defensively or back away from me. [pause] Maybe people lay on the couch for analysis so as not to fight. Because I wanted to fight."

Analyst: "It wasn't clear if you wanted to fight me or have me hold you."

Mr. B: "Yes, I actually had an image that scared me [pause] in it I went over and held on to your legs [pause] like a child."

Analyst: "Perhaps you're interested in lying on the couch."

Mr. B: "Yes [pause] think I am [pause] may I?"

[Analyst nods and extends her hand to the couch. He goes to it and lies down.]

A Dramatic Transference Phenomenon

Mr. B's attacks evolved progressively from yawning to full body paroxysms, heavy breathing, and strangulated, guttural sounds. Most often they followed the analyst's interpretations, which Mr. B felt were accurate, which affirmed that she understood him and had not become alienated. Mr. B's subjective experience was of raw emotion while his body moved as if of it's own volition. "Fear" was the emotional part, "shaking" the body part. "Every time you take the initiative I'm terrified [pause] whether it's about sex, anger, or fear itself [pause] and then I shake." While he remembered experiencing mild precursors of this "shaking fear" in his early 20s, when he had briefly participated in a peer counseling program, he could otherwise think of no precedent. He was amazed by this phenomenon, which occurred only in the analyst's office. During the episodes, he experienced no subjectively or objectively apparent alteration of consciousness. He observed the attacks freely, usually continuing to speak, curious and embarrassed. Overall his reaction to the phenomenon seemed appropriate and proportional. His absence of concern that the fits could be a harbinger of a more debilitating illness seemed congruent with the analyst's own perception.

By this time the analyst had further background information about the patient's family. Mr. B described his mother as a homemaker, his father as a high level bureaucrat. The family lived primarily in France but spent a few years in Chicago when Mr. B was a toddler. He was the first born of three children, his brother and sister being three and five years younger, respectively. He hinted that he had been mother's "little prince" and that there was more to her then the embarrassed, ineffectual woman who had disowned his aggression in the sandbox. After the analysis was underway, his ubiquitous perception of mothers as disapproving and critical, alongside his emerging fantasies of scary and exciting, literally phallic women, suggested that she was probably more powerful than he liked to think. As a child he was apparently aggressive, precocious, and arrogant and was often taunted by his peers. He had yearned for intimacy and proved himself capable of forming enduring friendships.

Analysis Begins

Both Mr. B and the analyst understood clearly after his brief first excursion on the couch that an analysis had begun. The negotiation of administrative details (scheduling, fee, etc.) was straightforward. There was none of Mr. B's earlier tire kicking, haggling, or deal making. The only difficulty was the reality of Mr. B's business commitments, which included a weekly commute by air to another city where his company had established new offices. They agreed to meet in twice-weekly, two-hour sessions, a compromise allowing four hours of analysis a week and accommodating the demands of his work. To the analyst, this deviation from standard technique was not a "parameter" in the sense defined by Eissler (1953), but a pragmatic solution to a reality-based need. She noted her feeling that these negotiations were reassuringly collaborative, not at all adversarial.

Analytic Session 40/41

Mr. B was talking about work, difficulties with a merger he was planning and, hesitantly, about his pleasure in it.

Analyst: "You seem embarrassed by your excitement, and pleasure."

Mr. B: "Yeah, being alive and engaged. A friend said my cheeks are red with recognition. [pause] I go back and forth, wanting recognition and embarrassed by it. I enjoy the bargaining. I'm having fun. But 'it ain't over till it's over.' [severe shaking] It's so addictive. [second spasm] I don't understand, but it seems like I feel apologetic. I feel guilty for enjoying myself. And now I feel afraid to do the final strike, the 'coup de grâce.' I remember [describes a sixth-grade race where he let others pass him at the end so as not to suffer the recognition of winning] I'm embarrassed to do the big win. [spasm] I don't know what it is. But in the big picture maybe it's not so important."

Analyst: "Must be some reason you think of stopping yourself, even now as you say it's not so important."

Mr. B: "Yes. It's all very confusing. One thought is that it can all happen without me. I can back out. This guy called me a 'double dipper' because I sold the company once and then I bought it back later for a lot less and then sold it again for much more. Said I can't do that! [triumphant laugh] I'm *so* competitive!"

Analyst: "He's not gonna tell you!"

Mr. B: "I can be a triple dipper if I want! [said with obvious pleasure]. He's not gonna tell me what to do. I thought to myself when he was saying it, "I'm going to win!" It's embarrassing. But it's like sex. Male dominance and winning—like sex. All related. Almost the same satisfaction as beating an opponent. Same satisfaction. Getting aroused by someone, conquering her and seducing her. (flirtatious laugh) I'm not sure I deserve to win. My wife says 'go for it.' I'm good at selling, knowing what the other person wants."

Analyst: "Are you doing that with me now?"

Mr. B: "Not sure. Think part of me always does it. Here I'm trying to be open. Be a good patient. Not hide my feelings and to make you feel good by making progress. Be sensitive to your being American. People at home think Americans are so . . . bottled up, so . . . politically correct. . . . I'm trying to be sensitive to that. Your being American, combined with your basic vulnerability. [laughs] I really have to be careful. It's unbelievable how rigid American culture is, constraining, unforgiving. Everyone has to be so polite. As soon as you break one of the invisible rules, you're shit. Happened to me more than once—and apparently when I drive I'm too aggressive. Once you transgress, they run you down. Americans are intolerant."

[sudden shift from flirtatiousness to contempt. He is cool, distant.]

Analyst: Seems you were talking about seducing women, flirting and being charming with me, then you go on to these ideas of how we could never fully connect because I'm American [pause] and you're not.

Mr. B: [pause] "Yes [pause] embarrassingly, it goes together. In these sex seduction scenes there was always this hangover. [pause] I was afraid of the closeness after and would always pull away. I suddenly remember two dreams from last night. Sex dreams. In one I was with someone who looked like my cousin when she was younger. When I was younger I did have sexual feelings for her [pause] of course, we all know she was my mother, a sublimation."

Analyst: "That last part, for my benefit?"

Mr. B: Yeah. [laughs] But in my dream I knew it was my cousin and also really did know it was a mother substitute. We were dancing. I put my hand on her breast. Then we danced and there was an incredible scary feeling. But pleasurable. [laughs] And then her vagina was moving back and forth. [pause] I don't think this is possible, [pause] but she was masturbating me [pause] like her vagina was a hand and I said to her, 'I never met a woman who can do this. Wow!' Very arousing and pleasurable. I thought in the dream I was ejaculating and when I woke up I thought I had. But fortunately I hadn't. Woke up and thought about my cousin/mother. Do you want to analyze this?"

[In this last comment she heard an echo, "Do you want to dance?" She knows now that Mr. B finds her comments exciting, sometimes even scary, Apparently he's feeling that he's "never met a woman who can do this."]

Mr. B: "I'll tell you the other dream. Scary! I was having sex with a woman, but then I see she has a penis. I thought, 'I'm having sex with a man.' Felt like normal sex. But [pause] she has a penis, I thought, 'not a "she," a "he".' Then I woke up with the alarm."

Analyst: "Alarming dream!"

Mr. B: "Yes, they both were [pause] the dancing and the super vagina. [laugh] I felt I was having sex with my cousin *and* being seduced by mother. [severe spasm] I've stayed away from my mother because of this, she was always just *too* interested in me. As a kid I thought that my mother and sister were both too interested, sexually interested, and I think I was interested too. Fear kept me away. [pause] I distance myself in general. Afraid of being engaged. Sorry I'm rough today. [laughs] Go up against your *American* sensibility."

Analyst: "Keeping your distance from me too, and whatever *my* interest might be in all this."

Mr. B: "Good. You're smart. I can keep going."

[This "compliment" felt more hostile than flattering, He's merely looking for the inevitable "neither smart nor confident enough," which he described at their first meeting and now anticipates, desires, despises, provokes.]

Mr. B: "I remember a line in a movie: 'I feel like a walking dick.' His whole body was a dick! Walked around feeling embarrassed. It hit a nerve. It's about my timidity. That my whole being is phallic and masculine and I'm ashamed of it. A walking dick. What do you think? I want to know what you think. How do you understand this? I pay you. [pause] I just realized I want to push your limits, like a kid."

Analyst: "Several times you said you worry about offending my sensibilities and now you're wanting to push my limits. [pause] What do you think about that?"

Mr. B: "I feel like I expose myself to you. Then I want to provoke a struggle. I want the upper hand."

Analyst: "Who's on top, like the dream . . .?"

Mr. B: "Yeah, yeah. [pause] Now what do I do with all this? [intense, insistent] All I feel is more fear. Tons of it." [spasm] I'm so capable in many areas, but so hampered by fear. Fear of closeness. Fear of hurting others. Fear that if I'm as good as I can be it'll be intimidating and also somehow humiliating. People don't want you to succeed. [pause] I lack empathy. Like I can't be good without thinking others are bad. I always add a competitive spin. Attracts so much fire. At university people didn't like my having success. At the company people are intimidated by me. [Talks about how he doesn't talk in meetings.] Pull the cover over me. [laughs] A dick with a condom!"

Analyst: "I was thinking back to the dream and wondered when you said you woke up and were glad you hadn't actually come."

Mr. B: "Uh, practical reasons [pause] But [pause] well something else . . . scary. Another fact: I didn't masturbate 'til 17. First sex was even later. But in about 7th grade, not sure what you call them in English [pause] a dream where you come. Woke up confused and scared. I never masturbated."

Commentary

Throughout this and other early analytic sessions, the analyst's only conscious technical goal is to remain openly available to receive Mr. B's communications and to pay close attention to the interpersonal process in the room. Her experience of Mr. B is two-fold. On one hand, he seems engaged in playful exploration of their relationship. On the other, she is continuously aware of his insistent need to find her deficient. He doesn't want to need what she offers; he expects (desires, fears) to eventually "run right over her," the only question is when.

While the analyst's comments are congruent with Lawrence Friedman's (1984) description of "close process monitoring" in that they are all intended to elucidate moments when the flow of the patient's associations shift in tone, content, quality, etc., she makes no intentional effort to selectively focus on analysis of defense (Gray, 1994). Her only specific goal is to consistently convey her interest in receiving and understanding her patient's communications, especially so in the context of immediate experience in the room (Davison, Pray, and Bristol, 1990).

At several points in this session Mr. B erupted with spasms and guttural moans: twice when he was talking about the pleasure–fear in his aggression, and once in relation to his dream-fantasies of attraction–repulsion to his cousin/mother. The analyst could easily have become interpretively seduced by Mr. B's "epileptic body language" but waš not. She observes the phenomena and notes their apparent correlation with conflicting, paradoxical, or ambivalent affects; but she is taking conscious care not to interpret prematurely or even highlight the fits until some meaning they contain is clear enough to her that when she gives it voice, there will be reason to expect that Mr. B will be able to make use of the observation: recognize in it something new of himself. The analyst has not yet perceived any meaning in the seizures which Mr. B would not have already noted, and she feels that to voice these predictable observations would only serve to reinforce their defensively distracting, histrionic component.

Analytic Session 46/47

During this session the analyst makes her first direct comment about Mr. B's "seizures." She attempts to introduce the idea that his fits are related to his associations. Mr. B's reaction is intense but ambiguous as to the effect of the interpretation on the symptom itself, or on their understanding of it.

Mr. B is speaking about his fear of being evil. He remembers his pleasure as a little boy teasing and frightening the girls, and how he still fears people being mad at him. For the first time he acknowledges that he sometimes intentionally provokes his wife's outbursts. He continues his mixed bag of praise and criticism of the analyst, the latter more and more consistently expressed in the form of displacements to "mothers" in general. Then his thoughts move from hatred of female authority to appreciation of his own maternally tinged pleasure in his children.

Mr. B: "I realize I never talk about my kids. [pause] I'm in charge of their showers at night. When they were little, I started carrying them around in towels. We developed a game, it translates into 'flying turtles.' [Laughing, he describes how he carries and flings them around in the air.] I maneuver them around in the corridor. So much fun. Recently we improved the concept, so now it's 'flying mouse.' [describes the change, more laughing] So much fun. You know, life isn't all bad. Last night we had such a funny thing. [pause] Matt was hitting me with a towel. He was laughing, and I ignored him awhile. Then I made this scary sound. [demonstrates] I'd never done it before. Actually as I just did it, I realize it's the sound I scared the girls with in kindergarten. Matt got a little scared, and Patrice laughed so hard that toothpaste came spitting out of her mouth. Then we all laughed and played more flying mouse. That could only happen when my wife's not there. She can't bear our horseplay. [pause] I think my not telling you about that 'til now is part of my regimented life. I adopt different personalities in different situations. Maybe you're like my wife, a mother. A mother would disapprove of my pleasures."

Analyst: "Can't tell me your pleasure. Mother's will say you're out of control. Like not masturbating. And with Matt, going from exciting to scary."

Mr. B: "Yes, yes [pause]. I just had a sexual thought. [laughs] I'd tell you, but I wish I didn't have it. We finally got cable; we can watch HBO in our bedroom. I saw this show with two women nude in a tub, washing each other. When they got out of the water, they both had dicks! Real sizable dicks! [nervous laugh] Pretty surprising. But I got turned on pretty bad by that. [laugh] I'm not sure by which part of what. But I was certainly turned on. Confused and threatened. So maybe its like what you said about pleasure and control. I was certainly taken by surprise. And I wasn't turned on when it was just two women, sort of mundane. But there's something about these women with dicks."

Analyst: "They have it all?"

Mr. B: "Yes. This is pretty scary. [pause] Is this O.K.? After all, you are a *mother*."

Analyst: "How much you worry about how I'm reacting."

Mr. B: "You could be offended. But it's true, pleasure and being out of control are related. And this thing from my mother. Very deep in her from her father. Has to do with the scariness. It's *not* O.K to show you're happy or content. It will invite envy, the evil eye. Better to look miserable. My father is only about showing and bragging what he has. And I'm stuck between the two! [begins to shake] Showing pleasure, showing contentment is dangerous. Better to look disconnected. [body contorts vigorously as he continues to talk normally] Looking miserable is essential." [spasms worsen, grunting and loud breathing]

Analyst: "Something is scary and you do look miserable."

Mr. B: "Yes. Strange [still shaking] so disconnected. I was just talking, not feeling anything, while this other thing is going on with my body. Disconnected. My thoughts were fine. My voice was O.K. Yet something was terrifying. Don't know what happens."

Analyst: "It was as though what you were describing was also happening at the same time: showing your powerful feelings, and also disconnecting from them."

Mr. B: [angry] "No. No! That's not it! [silence] I don't know why I needed to say "No" like that. Then I wind up seeing that what you said is right. For some reason I just said "No" and felt angry. It's almost like I blacked out. But I didn't. I can't even say exactly what I was saying when it started. [silence] I was thinking how my style at work is to show misery, too. But then I do what I want. I think I express misery to manipulate people. I probably do that with my wife, too. [deep breaths, obvious effort to calm himself] Not easy to admit this. I feel so happy doing this. It's so important to me. [sweetly] Thank you for helping me do this. It's so important to me . . . I'm doing it again! [renewed spasms] Here we go. Not showing pleasure, not losing control, using displeasure to manipulate. All linked . . . if I walked down the hall at work happy. So basic. But it feels *so* dangerous." [spasms subside]

Analyst: "Before you felt pleasure with me, then you felt angry."

Mr. B: [hand starts to shake] "You're definitely touching a nerve. So scary! To acknowledge I . . . *yiyi!* [whole body in spasm] feel pleasure with you. 1 need to go to the bathroom. [still shaking]. Oh, my *God!* You might have a dick! [renewed spasms, brushing himself frantically as if to rid himself of bugs] Why is it so much more frightening if *you* have a dick then? [intense shaking continues] Is this some fucking incest fantasy!? *Hiyyaa!* [calms self] First the corridors at work, then whether you have a dick! [laughs] Is it that simple? Fear of intimacy? [big breaths] This is scary."

Analyst: "Frightening, the idea that I have a dick. Because maybe like with the HBO show, it would be so much excitement."

Mr. B: "Now I remember that dream I told you! Sex with a woman who had a dick. Shit! Not homosexuality! Do we have to do that? Talking about my homophobic father? I never had sex with a man. But in the Scouts I wound up bunking with this guy who I thought was gay. Slept in the same bed. He had a tense mouth, and I thought because he'd sucked too many dicks."

Analytic Session 54/55

During this session the analyst comments further on Mr. B's psychogenic seizures as a behavioral expression of affect related to the content of his associations. Again his response is intense, but while new material emerges it remains unclear whether any modification of the symptom or further elucidation of its meaning results. The analyst's consistently close monitoring of the interpersonal process in the room does appear to be producing a generalized loosening of the strictures on Mr. B's self-perception. He is apparently beginning to explore new ways of experiencing his characteristic mode of thinking, perceiving, and relating (Chused, 1996).

Mr. B: [talking about being very engaged and emotionally identified with his son, who plays soccer, how he has recognized that he used to keep himself disengaged in order not to feel too much] "It was painful, painful to lose. Sad to see him lose his stamina, give in to hopelessness. [tears, holds hand up limply] I disengage to reduce the pain. [gives examples] I keep my hand up to keep the feelings away. Too much suffering. Except suburban, upper-middle-class Americans."

Analyst: "Like me"

Mr. B: "Yeah. You don't suffer enough. [continues to think about whether his family should go back to France or not] There is always this terrible combination of pain and fear. And all I do is try to not feel it. [sobs] I don't want to feel *bad* anymore. [Sobbing he puts a tissue on his face, accidentally breathing it in.] Suffocated by a tissue on the psychoanalytic couch. [laughs] Occupational hazard? Malpractice? I'm starting to get back my humor. It's been buried a long time. Now I'm funny again. My wife's problems have added to it. Yesterday she threatened violence in front of the kids. I actually felt scared; sometimes I feel she could do it. Really see her picking up scissors and stabbing me. It's embarrassing. To have the mother of my children act this way. I oscillate between feeling hopeless [pause] to maybe I'll weather through it. As long as I'm here, I'll hope for change. No point in making decisions in ignorance. And I am suffering less with her. [veers off into discussion of a scientific book related to his business he's reading and ideas for new research and development] In some ways I think my interest with new things is to disengage from my company, in case it gets killed in the merger. It's not a real death. Not real danger. [sudden violent spasm] Excuse me."

Analyst: "Do you know what the thought was that started you shaking?"

Mr. B: "Just fear. [catches his breath] Funny. Came so fast and unexpected. Just felt like intellectual understanding, and then out came all that other stuff. Something about saying it's not death. Last time I was talking about death. I've said before, you can be involved in the game, like soccer, and it's *not life or death*. But that feeling came from below."

Analyst: "I'm reminded of other strong and unexpected feelings you've talked about. How exciting it was, for instance, when the women stood up and had penises."

Mr. B: [angry] "That doesn't fit. They're not related. Like you just brushed away these other feelings. But I just had this memory of when I was young. Could be related to how I move my feet when those fits . . . happen. [several deep breaths] I was "X" legged, not sure of the English word. [shows knock-knees with hands] It was real bad when I was three. They said if I didn't wear braces it would be a bad problem. My feet turned outward. Braces for my whole legs. Make my legs straight and my feet. [feet tremble] Think I was three—before I was four because we were in the U.S. I remember the device. Remember my father's stories about it. [spasm] They put it on me. I hated it. Fought it. And was I a fighter! [laughs] They gave up after two or three days. When I was shaking my legs before, it reminded me. Maybe it's related. I was wanting them off. I remember finding the brace a couple years later. Then it was tossed out I guess. Another memory. Not really a memory, another story I heard. I didn't get a haircut until I was two and a half. I had long, beautiful, curly hair. When I got to the States people kept asking me if I was a girl. So they finally took me for the haircut. My father says I fought and fought. They had to hold me down, paralyze me to cut it off. And I remember something else. Older, maybe seven or eight [sudden spasms] with my grandparents, I had a toothache. They took me to some strange provincial dentist. I didn't trust him. He came with his [imitates drill sound]. I didn't want to open my mouth; my father forced my mouth open. I was moving, and the dentist slipped and scratched my front tooth. Again, my father forcing me into a dangerous situation. All three, actually. I know what you're thinking."

Analyst: "What's that?"

Mr. B: [sarcastic] "Whatever horrible thing my father did to me, we will discover. The fear of the unknown. So say it. I *do not* want to be some damn *textbook* case."

Analyst: "*You're* not going to he forced into some prescribed treatment."

Mr. B: "Yes! Yes. So what can I do instead?"

Analyst: "These memories seemed to follow your feeling that I was wrong with my comment."

Mr. B: "Maybe [pause] I can't accept it as Freudian. Jungian maybe. It's in all of us. That it's not my fucked-up personal history, but the history of my people. There's this feeling of [pause] paralysis. [silence] Even exploring it I don't want. It's scary. I don't like to think of myself as a little boy with long curls. I remember it was said, but I never really thought about it, never pictured it. All three memories. All three about my father forcing me with a blunt instrument. [laughs] Something to this. And my father was *not* a touching, physical man. Always made him uncomfortable. Even now if he gives me a kiss or a hug he pushes away. I see it with him and the kids even. I'm different. I like to hug. I'm more like my mother that way. [silence]. I don't feel right. I've got a headache and I'm dizzy and I have to go to the bathroom. [silence]. Another time, maybe 10, I went to Scout camp for five days. Got home and had a big bellyache. They brought me to a doctor who said I was constipated. Told my father to buy—can't find the English word—one of those bottles with liquid they put in your rectum. They did this to me. what is the word?"

Analyst: "Enema."

Mr. B: "Then I pooped. This is not good. I'm going forward, not backward. [laughs] About that same time, they asked me what I wanted to be when I grew up. I said, 'Scientist because then my work won't depend on anyone else.' " [long pause]

Mr. B: [somber] "I think I'm trying to leave you out of this. Ignoring how you react to me. Afraid of what I'll find if I press too hard. If I probe deeper, I'll find you're not smart enough or too timid or something. I'll protect myself from finding the real answer. I'm afraid you can't understand my real problems. Afraid to lean on you with my full weight. But I have leaned pretty hard so far, afraid you will push, just fall over. You're behind a curtain. Hides your problems. If I encounter you as equals afraid you couldn't stand the test. Afraid you're not trustworthy, solid as I need. [pause] But I'm tagging along, hoping for the best." [suddenly cheerful]

Analyst: "And being careful not to look too hard, afraid of what might be seen." [She is careful in her comment not to specify who is looking at whom, who is afraid, or what might be seen.]

Mr. B: [mildly scornful] "Yes, afraid the cardboard wall will crack under pressure. There's something in your intonation that's not confident. That raises my fears. Nothing you can do about it; it's your voice. I wish you were stronger and I could abandon all control and you could fish me up from down under. Can you stand the weight if I push a little on the cardboard? What's the word for this?" [points to the wall].

[Mr. B's request for "drywall" emerges in the midst of a mixed metaphor that menacingly uses the wall of the consulting room (the literal analytic environment) as an analogue for the expected (provocatively wished for, despised) deficiencies in the analyst and her "Freudian" analytic process.]

Analyst: "You ask me the English words for things at times. I think maybe to give me back some power."

[She sees now that sometimes she has decided to give Mr. B the English words he requests. Earlier she felt that to interpret his requests for help finding words would interfere with communication. At this juncture her feeling is that Mr. B's need to make the request is itself the essence of this communication.]

Mr. B: "Yes, I think when I say those things, questioning you, it's like I'm testing my parachute before my next dive. Like my conviction that I wouldn't depend on anyone anymore. At work now I'm completely dependent on others for what happens. Every time I try to achieve something new, unique, special, it gets in the way. A repetitive career pattern. I'm always trying to coerce the establishment into doing what I want. I'm the young rebel, never the adult. No matter how old I get. People say I even look younger than I am. Something scary about finally being an adult. Not wanting to become the oppressor. I identify with the oppressed. My wife says it's just that I refuse to accept responsibility. Something basic in that [pause] not being an adult. [violent spasms] Scary. There's a seat for the adult, and I can't move to that seat. I'm barred from it."

Commentary

Mr. B's technique of "giving the analyst back some power" by asking for English words apparently has something in common with those he uses at work to 'coerce the establishment' (by all indications, something he is very good at). What his wife reportedly calls "refusing to accept responsibility" he thinks of as "identifying with the oppressed" and "testing his parachute before the next dive." All could be understood (and interpreted plausibly) as manifest features of false-self personality organization (Winnicott, 1960): a precocious ego formation crystalized in the first years of life under the premature, structuralizing press of mother's inaccurate efforts to meet his needs—"greater than optimal frustration" (Tolpin, 1971), "excessive breaches in expectancy" (Stechler and Kaplan, 1980). Mr. B's "refusal to depend on anyone anymore" could then be understood as a residue of failure to achieve basic trust (Erikson, 1950). On the other side of the coin, his transferential representation of the analyst as yet another mother (his own, his children's) who is expectably not trustworthy, not smart, strong, or confident enough to let him "abandon all control and be fished up from down under" (something clearly requiring basic trust).

Interwoven with the preoedipal themes just highlighted, the same material begs classic oedipal observations of body damage and castration anxiety. After describing his inhibited adult role functioning and fear of "death in the merger," Mr. B convulses. When invited to explore the fit's antecedent as similar to previously discussed "strong and unexpected feelings," he becomes angry and produces a cascade of "oedipal" memories, screen or otherwise: At age three, Mr. B struggles as his father (like Laius?) forces him into ultimately unnecessary leg braces. When he is two-and-a-half, his father pins him down ("paralyzed . . . to cut it off") for "the first haircut"; and again at seven or eight for the provincial dentist's drill; at 10 for the prescription enema (not incidentally, the last English word he will successfully flush from the analyst). After eliciting the analyst's help with the enema, he returns to expressions of basic distrust: his wish to need never depend on another.

When the analyst links Mr. B's requests for English words to his doubt that she can ever understand *real* problems (bear their "full weight"), he produces yet another affect-laden bloc of material temptingly baited with opportunities for "interpretation" in the sense (often attributed to analysis by new patients): "To translate," or to "say what it means." (Mr. B: "Do you want to analyze this?" "How do you understand this? I pay you . . .") Oedipal or preoedipal, whatever one's theoretical bent, there is something here for everyone. But Mr. B's overt contempt for "textbook" treatments and "textbook" afflictions unmistakenly signals his *expectation*, his *provocative desire*, to receive (and *despise*) just that from the analyst. He arrived at the analytic door well prepared to scorn anything that might remotely suggest a "textbook" approach. From "fear of annihilation" to "ambivalent competitive strivings," he remains enthusiastically prepared for triumphant disappointment.

During this early phase of his analysis, Mr. B, like many (if not all) sophisticated new analytic patients, is expecting some form of identifiable, predetermined "analytic technique." Where he is overtly ready to resist, another might be overtly eager to submit. Submissive or oppositional, both are similarly "interpretation resistant." Some, and Mr. B seems a likely candidate, remain so throughout their analysis.

While some patients may gain an impressive intellectual self-understanding, many do not achieve any substantive structural or behavioral change. Chused (1996) likens these patients' resistance to interpretation to the difficulty children have "listening" to their analyst's words. She contends that, like children, these patients do not need "better interpretations but the opportunity to make their own observations and alter their perceptions autonomously" (p. 1050).

The analyst can provide these opportunities by offering what Chused refers to as the "informative experience":

> Informative experiences arise out of those analyst–patient interactions in which the anticipated, the consciously or unconsciously desired or provoked reaction, does not occur, and what does occur is so jarring and discordant with expectations that action and thoughts are derailed, and expectations become suspect [p. 1050].

Mr. B's analyst, in her distinctively gentle way, has responded to her challenging and interpretation-resistant patient with few formal "interpretations" but instead has consistently provided opportunities "informative experience": from her opening request to hear his critique of her in their first meeting; her immediate understanding during the last exploratory hour that he had heard her reassurance as disingenuous and self-serving; her consistent calm in the face of his dramatic (involuntary? exhibitionistic?) convulsions; to her empathic (and strategically well-timed) refusal to further feed his defensively artificial appetite for English words.

Analytic Session 58/59

[Mr. B talks animatedly about a satisfying business trip to the West Coast, Felt on top of things. Describes chaos at home. Last-minute preparations for the departure to France later today, a long-awaited, month-long visit with family and friends.]

Mr. B: [after a long silence] "I'm tired. [pause] Came in on the red eye. Feel bad. Like I've come unprepared for class. [silence] Last night I felt afraid of going downstairs. I'm embarrassed now saying it. Imagined someone sneaking in. As I went to lock the garage, I imagined someone hiding. They'd come in the house and do something."

Analyst: "What would happen if they came in?"

Mr. B: "Violence. Guns or knives. I stop them before they get to the kids. They're black. Maybe just easier to see them as outsiders. But even my wife, I'm afraid of her being violent, take a knife and stick it in. As a kid I was violent. And now all this inhibited aggression in me. On this trip I joked with a competitor. I was waiting for a taxi and he got out of one. I said, 'I'm gonna steal your taxi, steal your customers, steal your business: Then you die!' Couldn't believe I was being so openly aggressive. Not just with him, but in front of a whole audience of other business guys. First it felt good. [spasms] Then I felt real bad, guilty. Afraid he'd retaliate. Poor him. I didn't mean to make him feel bad. Same way in sports. I never felt comfortable crushing the opponent. But maybe I shouldn't credit myself with compassion. [laughs] I was thinking of my wife . . . she brought home five green bathing suits to try on."

[He continues on about how he enjoyed having her go over the details with him, how he usually hates this sort of thing when she "obsesses," but this time he found her funny and engaging. Then he remembers a recent incident at a restaurant where he dealt well with a problem with his son, how good he'd felt, how he'd really been a good father to the boy. His description of the interaction impressed the analyst. Mr. B had apparently been closely attuned to his son. He'd refrained from becoming overidentified or narcissistically invested in the outcome. He had done well and seemed appropriately pleased with himself.]

Mr. B: "All of a sudden I feel this [pause] flexibility [pause] in my abdomen. [He is moving his hips up and down on the couch.] Somehow a sexual connection. [laughs] Think somehow my rigidity is tied to a lack of sex. Thought that with this moving my abdomen. This here [points to hips] what's the word?"

Analyst: "I think there must be something more to not knowing that word."

Mr. B: "Right. It's hips. I think even the word was blocked, just like the movement. [violent spasms] Fear comes from my feet. [pause] They're shaking. [He momentarily confuses words for feet and legs; spasms shake his body.] I think I'm moving them in feet and legs: [spasms shake his body.] I think I'm moving them in an overtly sexual way. [continues to shake] Don't know why I'm having this. I just want to move my hips. [laughs as he moves] Hope you're O.K with it. It's about my inflexibility. Scary. Worried you'll think it's sexual. Feels like basic freedom, to move your hips freely. [gyrating continues] Is it OK?"

Analyst: "You worry so how I will take it."

Mr. B: "That you'll be concerned. Scared. It's probably aggressive. [violent spasm and grunting] So weird. The bottom of me feels sexual and the top of me, aggressive. [moaning] Very strange. [shaking and noises continue] *So Scary!!!* [yelling] Don't know why this is so scary. Really is. Taking some expression and the fear associated with it. [shaking continues] Sexual, aggressive, scary all at the same time. Like different parts of my body, two separate pieces. [still shaking unbelievably] Embarrassing. So below my cognitive level. Wish I could stop. It's like I'm watching it happen." [more yelling sounds, spasms continue]

Analyst: "Sounds scary."

Mr. B: "Yes. Sorry. [violent spasms start up again] Your husband will think you're doing voodoo in here. This is new to me. [laughs] My wife asks me what I do here. [ironically] 'Oh, I move my hips and scream.' Strange! I think I told you, I didn't masturbate during my entire adolescence, nor have sex. This is exhibitionistic. [pause] You're seeing me do this."

Analyst: "I'm watching you."

Mr. B: "I apologize, but not to you directly. More like you're an audience. Like other people are watching. Not one on one. Normally I'm so inhibited. I walk rigid. I imagine with my posture that I pull my penis back. I think I keep my butt and hips pulled in. Keep my penis back. Now like this attempt to put it out there."

Analyst: "Like with the taxi, in front of an audience."

Mr. B: "Yes! Yes, same idea. First time I've been right out there and showed my aggression. Always hold it back. My freedom to walk out in front of a taxi and audience with my penis out. I usually fear being offensive. This is new. Exposed, not hidden. Is this kosher? What we're doing? Is it allowed? [laughs] Well, if nothing else, it will be better for my back, which often hurts. Probably the way I walk. [body starts heaving again, hips moving up and down] This thing of moving my penis. *Hiyyaa!* Well, I guess it's legitimate back exercise. But I shouldn't have to pay $2.00 a minute to do it! [violent spasms, yells] Don't know what's going on!"

Analyst: "You were saying how you always hold yourself back. But maybe the aggression came out there with me too, about $2.00 a minute. Slipped it in."

Mr. B: "Yes, I think you're right. That was hostile. I'm afraid if I open the window further all my aggression will come rushing through. Was a quick little attack. Yes. I think all my aggression repression as a kid turned into sexual repression. As a kid there were lots of people busy curbing my aggression."

Analyst: "You've connected these sexual feelings with me."

Mr. B: "After my inhibition, there was a point that I enjoyed seducing women. For the conquest. Getting them to have sex. Sales is similar. I enjoy it. Zero in on your target and make them do what you want. I get a lot of satisfaction from sales. This talk of my sexual relationships. Too politically incorrect. Feel I can't tell you. You'll disapprove. Think ill of me. And maybe too much intimacy between us. Funny. I worry I'll hurt you. If I hurt you, then you can't help me."

Analyst: "I think maybe you also want to hurt me *because* I have helped."

Mr. B: "Yes, 'cause then I want to take that away. Even though you have. As soon as you say it, I want to take it away. Say, 'Don't think you're so good.' Feels offensive the way I feel about you. To tell you these thoughts. [silence] Hard to admit it. Afraid you'll be offended. I'm critical of everyone. I try to keep it down. That I'll make you feel bad. *Crush you, Shatter your confidence!* [intense] The crux of the barrier between us is in these thoughts. I keep them from you. Afraid if I talk about my relationships with women it gets close to this. My perception of your lack of confidence as a woman. Have to cross that bridge. I guess I've already told you. I picture you growing up an unconfident girl. I'm sure you've dealt with that. Not sure you were attractive—and still not sure. I see people's vulnerabilities. Everyone's. It's written all over them. In their eyes and hands. I suppress it. Try to look like I don't know this."

Analyst: "I think there's some pleasure in the knowing, and in the telling."

Mr. B: "Yes. [laughs] There is, too. Like being mean to the girls in kindergarten. When I first told you about that, I felt bad. And you said, 'No, you don't!' I laughed and laughed 'cause I'd never admitted how much I enjoyed it. Loved it! But it's aggressive to show other people's weaknesses."

Analyst: "There is the worry about me. But also I think about how vulnerable you were feeling earlier today and I think there's also a way you want to turn it around and make me the vulnerable one."

Mr. B: "Yes . . . I think you're right. I do that. And I was feeling very vulnerable. Yes."

Analytic Session 64/65

In the middle of this session, Mr. B had a mild spasm and then covered his face, saying he couldn't help it but he was making terribly ugly faces and didn't want her to see.

Mr. B: "Almost like if you saw me you'd want to get away from me. I look like Quasimodo. You'd be repulsed and want to get away from me." [He continues on this theme. reporting for the first time how his mother had told him he was such an ugly baby.]

Mr. B: "Unbearably ugly. She said it took her months to get over it. [pause] When I was making faces before, it reminded me of when I was making faces at the girls in kindergarten to scare them. But this was also like freedom to move my face. I've kept my body so rigid and stiff for so long. But I worry if you see it. So I covered my face." [He curls up on his side, facing the analyst so that she can see his face looking like a young child's. He lies there for about ten minutes of silence, seemingly totally relaxed.]

Mr. B: "Is this O.K.?"

Analyst: "Whether I can tolerate seeing you and you not talking?"

Mr. B: [making various distortions of his face] "It's like I'm trying things here I could never do before." [Lying on his side, he sticks his legs straight out so that they extend off the couch. He begins to laugh. He pulls them back, pushes them out, repeats the cycle several times, much like a two-year-old delighting in a simple repetitive game.]

Mr. B: [big smile] "I guess I'm seeing what the boundaries are here." [He continues laughing and playing with obvious pleasure until the end of the session.]

Summary

This chapter chronicles the early work of a well-matched, if unlikely, analytic dyad: a powerful, foreign-born, expansively narcissistic male hysteric, and a young female American social worker/analyst who met his needs by not meeting his expectations.

When Mr. B expressed disdain that he could resemble a "textbook case," he did not know that "epileptic reactions" much like his own had been described by Freud (1928) some 70 years earlier; or that others (Fenichel, 1932; Kardiner, 1932; Power, 1945; Menninger, 1955; Arlow, 1959; Rangell, 1959) had further studied the interplay of psyche and soma in psychogenic seizures. All, following Freud's lead, conceptualized the phenomenon as a transference symptom representing condensed unconscious fantasies and conflicts (with some presumed communalities from case to case): another compromise formation to be understood in the context of a transference neurosis.

This discussion covers only the first phase (about four months) of Mr. B's analysis. We have consciously avoided any attempt to conceptualize Mr. B's psychogenic seizures as symptoms of any kind, let alone begin any speculation about their genesis or meaning. They have been left as simply *transference phenomena:* nonverbal, psychosomatic correlates of strong emotion. All that is known at this juncture is that they occur only in the presence of the analyst (thus the "transference" modifier) and that they most often seem to occur when Mr. B feels "understood" (in his experience, a feeling that is exceedingly rare, almost unprecedented, consistently jarring).

Rather than focus on interpreting Mr. B's flamboyant seizures or puzzling out a metapsychologically sound diagnostic formulation for him (seductively attractive intellectual playgrounds, difficult to resist on paper or in the room), we have instead attempted to use the opening phase of Mr. B's analysis to illustrate a technical approach that may be generally useful with a diversity of uninitiated but intellectually sophisticated analysands, a category likely to include many (if not most) patients new to the couch. We felt this approach to be particularly well illustrated by this very difficult and challenging case precisely because of its complexity. Diagnostically, Mr. B is a briar patch of intrapsychic conflict. His seizures plead to be interpreted as "conversion fears" of oedipal conflict, *and* of primitive annihilation. His routine interpersonal life is punctuated with blatant and compulsive repetitions of murderous rivalry; his sexual life, dominated by frighteningly powerful, literally phallic women (or by their wished-for but despised stand-ins: prudishly insecure intellectually limited "mothers"). Unlike Henry Higgins, Mr. B thinks he knows exactly "why a woman can't be more like a man." But his limited insight into this ubiquitous, stale old male wish does nothing to assuage his fear of women more powerful than he. When having male genitals and having been castrated are not mutually exclusive, woman can become lethal predators, and fear of castration can become fear of annihilation. But despite it all, he works at an extremely high level, has several very long-term and apparently genuinely close friendships, and so far seems to be a fairly consistently good-enough father to his two young children.

Rather than get caught up conceptualizing the nuances of an initially inscrutable case like Mr. B (or of a simple one, if such a thing exists), at the outset assume rhetorically that a new analytic patient is "interpretively resistant" and proceed accordingly (Chused, 1996). The rationale for this approach is driven by common sense: for analysis to succeed, a new analysand's curiosity must be aroused such that he can become for himself a newly discovered object of compelling interest. The first phase of an analysis that actively presents opportunity for new and independently conceived self-observation will invite shifts in perceptual frame which by turns can become the essential precursors for real psychic and behavioral change.

A new analytic enterprise must be sustained by the intrinsic rewards of exploration and discovery, not (least so at the outset) by an *extrinsic* holy grail of symptomatic relief or analytic enlightenment. If the analyst can focus on the active interpersonal process in the room and can consistently react to the patient in a genuine way which is also counter to whatever she can discern to be anticipated, provoked, wished for, feared, or despised by the patient; he will be intrigued, energized, engaged, or provoked. Something new will be experienced; the experience will inform; and, with luck, the basis for a viable analysis will emerge.

References

Arlow, J. (1959), Masturbation and symptom formation. *J. Amer. Psychoanal. Assn.*, 7:45–58.

Chused, J. F. (1996), The therapeutic action of psychoanalysis: Abstinence and informative experience. *J. Amer. Psychoanal. Assn.*, 44:1047–1071

Davison, T., Pray, M. & Bristol, C. (1990), Mutative interpretation and close process monitoring in a study of psychoanalytic process. *Psychoanal. Quart.*, 59:599–628.

Eissler, K. R. (1953), The effect of the structure of the ego on psychoanalytic technique. *J. Amer. Psychoanal. Assn.*, 1:104–143.

Erikson, E. (1950), *Childhood and Society*. New York: Norton.

Fenichel, O. (1932), Outline of clinical psychoanalysis. *Psychoanal. Quart.*, 1:292–342.

Freud, S. (1928), Doestoyevsky and parricide. *Standard Edition*, 21:175–196. London: Hogarth Press, 1961.

Friedman, L. (1984), Pictures of treatment by Gill and Schafer. *Psychoanal. Quart.*, 53:167–207.

Gray, P. (1994), *The Ego and Analysis of Defense*. Northvale, NJ: Aronson.

Kardiner, A. (1932), The bio-analysis of the epileptic reaction. *Psychoanal. Quart.*, 1:375–482.

Menninger, K. (1955), Psychological aspects of the organism under stress, part II. *J. Amer. Psychoanal. Assn.*, 2:280–310.

Power, T. (1945), Psychosomatic regression in therapeutic epilepsy. *Psychosom. Med.*, 7:279–290.

Rangell, L. (1959), The nature of conversion. *J. Amer. Psychoanal. Assn.*, 7:632–662.

Sanville, J. (1991), *The Playground of Psychoanalytic Therapy*. Hillsdale, NJ: The Analytic Press.

Stechler, G. & Kaplan, S. (1980), The development of the self. *The Psychoanalytic Study of the Child*, 35:85–105. New Haven, CT: Yale University Press.

Tolpin, M. (1971), On the beginnings of a cohesive self: An application of the concept of transmuting internalization to the study of the transitional object and signal anxiety. *The Psychoanalytic Study of the Child*, 26:316–354. New Haven, CT: Yale University Press.

Winnicott, D. W. (1960), Ego distortion in terms of true and false self. In: *The Maturational Processes and the Facilitating Environment*. Madison, CT: International Universities Press, 1965, pp. 140–152.

Chapter 3

∞

No-Body's Baby
A Psychoanalytic Creation Story

Gail Sisson Steger

We create and recreate the self as long as we live. What is involved is a dialectic spiral between imagined mergings and imagined self sufficiency [Sanville, 1987, p. 267].

One's capacity to locate a recognizable and ongoing sense of self may become severely impaired when an "imagined merging" leads to a fusion, and the sense of "me" is annihilated. Similarly, when imagined self-sufficiency is defensively constructed, it may lead to a loss of objects, followed by painful feelings of abandonment. Annihilation anxiety, the terror of the loss of "me-ness," and abandonment anxiety, the anguished fear of isolation, are the miserable, infinitely painful extremes of the dialectic spiral described by Jean Sanville.

Agonizing episodes of either annihilation anxiety or abandonment anxiety lead to innumerable problems in relationships and in thinking and feeling. One patient may cry out in horror,"I've lost myself," while another is panicked as she feels she is falling into a dark void, no longer attached to anything or anyone. Although the fear either of annihilation or of abandonment predominates, a person may well experience both, but at different times.

Through the successful work of an analysis, patients who sustain primal terrors are able to live life, with all its vicissitudes, and tolerate different, even contradictory, intense affect states. This chapter is the story of one such patient.

"Beth" chose her own name for this chapter and, with particular generosity, has given me her whole-hearted support to describe her analysis. I have disguised this account only as necessary to protect her anonymity.

Beth: History, Evaluation, Recommendation

Beth was born 38 years ago to Mr. and Mrs. M, who had immigrated to the United States before World War II but who subsequently had also endured terrible losses. She has an older brother, Alex. When Beth was six months old, her maternal grandmother died, leaving her mother inconsolable. Mrs. M was unable to eat, rise, or perform household chores for several months. She told her daughter that "when you were two I tripped over the vacuum. I had a concussion, but when I awoke you were still playing with your toys, as if nothing had happened." This anecdote suggested that Beth was callous and unloving, certainly not a caretaker.

Beth's memory of her misery began when she was six. She and her family had gone to visit relatives. Beth awoke from an afternoon nap and did not feel well. In terror, she realized that her mother had left without telling her. She began to vomit. An uncle, hearing noises, rushed into her room. She was not fully dressed and felt terrible shame. From then on, Beth always tried to keep her mother in sight; otherwise she was flooded by anxiety.

Mrs. M considered Mr. M to be in a class beneath her and the children. Beth loved her father but did not feel he understood her. She did not feel she was safe alone with him.

Mrs. M rarely left the house. She might spend hours preparing to go out, but when the time came she found one reason or another to stay. Often Beth became the reason, peering into her mother's eyes, looking thin and wan, faint, nauseated, ready to vomit. Mrs. M "understood" and communicated her attunement to Beth with a flick of her eyebrow—the two were in "perfect," nonverbal communication. Mrs. M would say, "Dad and I will stay home," never mentioning the reason. Sometimes she might say, "Let's take Beth with us." To sustain the myth of this perfect harmony, Beth had to hide her anxiety from everyone else. *No one was to know—not even Beth herself*—Just how anxious and ill she felt. In this situation, Beth was fully merged, fused with her mother's fears of abandonment as well as Mrs. M's narcissistic needs always to be recognized as a competent mother with a happy child. These fears became Beth's. This merger led to repeated traumatic experiences of the annihilation of her sense of her self. Sometimes her mother was able to go to a social event, leaving Beth and Alex at home. However, dramatic good-byes took place on such occasions. Photos were even taken, and Beth feared that these could be final pictures. She would never see her parents again.

On occasion, Mrs. M would try to keep her leaving a secret. As a result, Beth became a spy. She noted critical details: her mother's hair style, high-heeled shoes worn under the housecoat. Early in the analysis I experienced Beth's scrutiny of me—checking to see what, if anything, was different. A new pair of shoes on my feet was tantamount to my wanting to sneak away from her or to my going to a dangerous situation where she would lose me.

Inevitably, Beth suffered severe separation anxiety. She never joined in class field trips and her rare attendance at other children's birthday parties was "in order to appear normal for my mother's sake."

At 18 Beth took a part-time job. One day she felt sick, became frightened, and talked to a senior coworker. This woman seemed kind and understanding. But, as soon as the conversation began, Beth felt frantic, began to flail her arms as her mother had done when she had had attacks of heart palpitations. And then Beth fainted. Mrs. M was called and took her out in a wheelchair as a crowd of coworkers watched. Beth did not leave the house for months. From that time her fears of separation increased and expanded; numerous psychosomatic disturbances began to appear. We came to understand that Beth panicked first at the act of separateness, which then lead to her fear of abandonment; and then she merged with her mother (flail as Mrs. M did), leading to her terror of annihilation (disintegration, fainting).

When Beth married, it was to the first man she dated, a shy soldier on leave who had been introduced by a relative. Their relationship was carried on mainly by mail. At the time of her marriage she seriously considered living with her husband *and* her parents but finally settled on living just a few blocks from her parents. Mother and daughter were in telephone contact many times a day.

Beth treated her husband as she had treated her mother. He, also, was to be obeyed; his safety was to be protected by Beth's thoughts. In fact, she went with him or followed in her own car when he had an appointment out of his office. In spite of her outwardly normal appearance, a marriage, and the birth of two children, she rarely left her house except to go to her job, which was within walking distance of her home, or to go to her parents' house.

Beth first sought therapy to help with her own parenting. She also used her first therapist to begin to disengage from her mother and her husband. These, she learned, were important steps if she wanted to be a good parent. Both Mrs. M and Beth's husband, not surprisingly, were at war with her therapy. But Beth fought as she had never fought for anything in her life. Her motivation was to raise children who were confident and unafraid, and this could happen, she realized, only if she could grow up. She actually threatened divorce if therapy were cut off. But threatening divorce from her husband or disagreeing with her mother felt like mortal danger. Beth lived in nightmarish panic and frequently called her therapist.

The therapy, which had offered such a hopeful beginning, the basis for change and relief, now itself became a problem: the therapist needed to leave unexpectedly for lengthy, unspecified amounts of time. Beth grew very frightened during these absences, and the psychotherapeutic work was sorely damaged.

After four years of psychotherapy, Beth and her therapist discussed her transfer to a new therapist because of the lengthy hiatuses and because Beth sought fundamental changes in herself. Although there had been many positive shifts in Beth's outside world, she now wanted more—she wanted to feel that she would not have to die if her mother died, if her husband died. Later, she said she wanted to count on herself, and, still later, she wanted to be able to be counted on by others. I was carefully interviewed for the job. Underlying the many questions that Beth posed was whether I could fully comprehend the gravity of her situation, the tenuousness with which she felt she held on to life, the potential for panic and suicide. I saw her three times a week for the first four months, at which time she began a five-times-a-week analysis.

Beth urgently questioned how she would reach me by phone, how she would get to me if she felt very anxious or suicidal, and who covered for *me* when *I* went away on weekends. When I told her that I covered for myself, she became even more alarmed—questioning me with obsessive, even delusional, intensity about the details of how she would be able to reach me or how I would be able to get to her to prevent her death. The exact physical space between us could mean life or death. I came to understand that increasing physical distance between us paralleled an expansion of frightening psychological space, if there were too much space she could not be inside my mind/ body, contained by me.

"If you are somewhere," Beth said," I am here. If you are nowhere, where am I?" This striking, raven-haired woman peered deeply into my eyes; her tall, slim body shook, her face blank with dismay. She could not imagine locating herself without first locating me. She continued in a low despondent voice," I am *nobody's baby.*"

I found myself concretizing this idea of "*no-body's baby.*" I pictured a baby whose mother takes up total psychic space but is represented internally by absence, unlike the sensuous, containing mother of a securely held baby. No-body's baby is in constant terror of fusing with her mother and thus of not existing as herself: she is in danger of becoming quite literally *no body*. Alternatively, Beth told me, she must be able to run to her mother—later she could turn to surrogates, to her husband, or to me when she felt frightened or she feared the terror of abandonment. She felt so frightened that she feared she would have to kill herself. If she was not with the other person's physical body, she herself had no body. Killing herself seemed preferable to the disintegrating image of annihilation, experienced so frequently in the fantasy of fusion with her mother.

The baby gains access to herself through her inner experience of a well-accepted place in her mother's mind and body. This normal developmental experience had been pathognomically disturbed in Beth. Her continuous questioning whether I would remember her or she me during a weekend absence and other transference manifestations led me to believe that her mother could not experience her in an ongoing way. Beth's life became a purgatory because she could not hold on to her mother (and thus to any sense of safety); she felt completely abandondoned, each morning wondering how she would get through the day. She used to say that "if my mother dies, I die. If my husband doesn't answer the beeper call I make I become dizzy, my breath short, I walk in circles, I panic. I'm terrified of those panics. I feel then that I must kill myself."

Beth's fantasy of "*nobody's baby*" could lead to utter atomization; her unstable unity could burst into chaotic, random fragments. I often was witness to Beth's terror, so palpable that when I first experienced it my countertransference image was of a Roman infant left on a hillside to die. Later, Beth described feeling herself at sea—no land for thousands of miles. She existed for no one; no one existed for her.

In answer to her question, I said, "I will tell you whenever I am more than two hours away by car. I will always be on call for myself unless I inform you in advance."

Thus, in response to her action fantasy (a fantasy that implicity threatened action if I did not do something), "I will have to kill myself," I gave her what I would term an *action interpretation*. My response, an unorthodox enactment, bound my life out of the office to hers; it was also a message to Beth: I was convinced of her terror just as I was hopeful about our therapeutic progress.

Beth suffered from a pathology of the ego, including pathognomonic internalized self- and object representations, which led to rigid, repetitive, unrelated, dissociated self-states. When she did not experience herself as able to get to her mother, she first dissociated. At those times she functioned as an automaton. And, if she suddenly became aware of her state of separateness, she panicked. Only when she felt safely able to get to her mother, or to her mother's seemingly omnipotent surrogates, could she function at a high level, with the strength of the omnipotent mother she imagined, believing she could run to this mother at any moment. (See *Epilogue* to this chapter for a discussion of self-states.)

Beth always perceived herself as sick and disgusting, a burden to her mother, her own feelings without value and unwanted, themselves a part of that burden. Thus, driven by a pathology generated by Mrs. M but interpreted by Beth as her own "badness," Beth experienced any strong feeling or perception as inevitably leading to a sense of herself as differentiated. She felt certain that she had separated from—and therefore killed—her mother. And, in the peculiarly powerful logic of such undifferentiated thinking, with her mother dead, she too had to die. The initial feelings that generated this circle may even have been good ones ("I feel good today. I feel whole and happy,"), but they quickly and inexorably led back through a remembered cycle of feared separation or annihilation of her mother (of whom she was a part) and thus to the fear of her own death. Bad feelings about herself were certainly preferable to states of feared annihilation when she could not think and her feelings were fragmented and unrepresentable. Her object relations consisted of part-objects, largely persecutory, which she controlled through projective identification and through magical, omnipotent acts.

I suggested analysis as the treatment of choice because I believed that only through an analysis of transference and countertransference, with the intensity and commitment of a deep, ongoing, and *new* therapeutic relationship, could Beth tolerate primitive self-states. She had the strength as well as the determination to involve herself in the most demanding—but also for her the most effective—of treatments; I believed that eventually she would be able to experience the differentiated thinking and feeling involved in ambivalence and paradox as well as other complex, mature states and that Beth would be able to re-create predictable oscillating selves of imagined merging and of imagined self sufficiency, firmly grounded in her own body: constants to which she would return, alive and of this earth, not forever stalked by death and abandonment. Above all, Beth had an unwavering desire to get well, which I thought would sustain her in the analysis even when it became terrifying. During one session, several years later, she told me that she had walked down the street and the sky looked bright and clear and, for the first time in her life, she did not feel like an alien. Soon after, she no longer needed to know when I was more than two hours away by car.

Psychoanalytic Treatment: The First Two Years

For self- repair to be maximized the patient may be enabled to play at a sort of regression, seemingly opposite to the "wish to grow up," but perhaps necessary to profound self repair. If creativity is the "capacity or activity of making something new, original, or inventive, no matter in what field" (Greenacre, 1959, p. 556) then psychoanalysis and psychoanalytically oriented psycho-therapies at best facilitate creativity in the arena of emending patients' formerly held schemas, no longer felt to be good-enough [Sanville, 1991, p. 22.].

I became an immediate, if interchangeable, replacement for her first therapist. Some differences were noted, but we were sufficiently alike in Beth's fantasy to be the same and thus able to afford her magical protection. My words were indeed magic—Beth made them so. Magical thinking reigned during our first two years. She hugged her husband to keep him safe on the freeway. She told me everything before the weekend break to put it in me to keep her safe when we were apart. In this way, she fantasized being inside me, an omnipotent container. When she began to experience anger, she wondered whether her angry thoughts would kill me. Would her newly aroused sexual fantasies for other men cause her husband to die? What might now give her an anxiety attack, and how could she shield herself? She used my words literally to hold herself. It was a terrifying world.

Beth felt that, to stay alive, she needed to possess me (be able to reach me at any moment); and in turn she dreamed of being possessed by me. The first two dreams of Beth's analysis were 1) "I carefully chose two tickets to a play and telephoned and got two better ones," and 2) "I am a child, very sick and lying on a sofa. My mother bends over me and says, 'Now you will see.' My mother rolls up my sleeve and gives me a shot of heroin." Beth's first associations began:

Beth: I've always worried about parents who are addicts who make their children into dope addicts in order to get them to secure dope for both of them. I was blamed for being the sick one in the family. My mother kept me that way, but she was sick as well.

Analyst: Analysis seems like yet another addiction. You worry that you will need my dope forever and that I will want to keep you that way. Then we would be the same in our mutual addiction, and I would make sure that you have no will of your own.

Beth: The TITkets are your tits. I like your tits. I've exchanged therapists. I like you better than the other therapist. I am worried that I am getting too attached to you.

Early in the treatment there were numerous phone calls on Friday afternoons after the last session of the week: to see if I could be reached; to confess some detail she might have forgotten (e.g., a fantasy about a man); to ask me to repeat some word I might have said (she seldom held on to any words on Friday and was often teary, feeling lost and alone and that her "skin could be pushed in"); to clarify a word; to check a new thought; to ask permission to have a good time on the weekend; to repeat the litany she had uttered at the end of the session ("I can reach you today, tonight, tomorrow . . . right? And, our next appointment is. . . ."). She felt that her obsessional thinking was out of control. Beth was always apologetic "about being such a burden." She warred within herself, trying not to call me and knowing that letting go was a primary issue, because she feared that if she did let go of me she would die.

I often waited for her calls, my free space about to be disrupted, my Friday afternoons controlled. Feeling controlled by her mother and by her own needs is how Beth must have felt as she waited endlessly for her mother. I wondered when I would see Beth's anger, the anger that comes with being controlled. The telephone cord became Beth's umbilical cord. At the time, understanding Beth's terror and fragmenting rage at being left by me for the weekend, I wanted to be available and to help her through this period, however long it took. My increasing understanding enabled me to deal with my negative feelings about our analytic compact.

The phone calls stopped when we had sufficiently worked through several transference and countertransference fantasies. For example, she was controlling me in order to take care of herself and controlling my whereabouts by these telephone calls, as she had controlled her mother by gazing into her mother's eyes. The calls stopped when enough time had passed for her to feel, first, held securely, and then able to tolerate her own multiple self-states, merged and separate.

The locus of our explorations and of my interpretations for two years were 1) understanding her paranoid, symbiotic attachment to her depressed and unavailable mother, as it was transferred on to, and even into, me; 2) her fear of changing the status quo; 3) her belief in the inexorable, unremitting power of others and her need to control that power; and, ultimately, 4) her terror in discovering this power in herself, in her own capacity to act. Acting meant to her the death of her mother and of herself.

Beth was almost always on guard lest I disappear. When the fear was particularly strong, she would sit up "to take me in with her eyes." Beth feared I would leave her as revenge for having unwittingly angered me perhaps; or she was in fact angry at me for my separate life. In another state, she was frightened that I would disappear if something good happened to her. "I'm afraid I will overdo—I'm afraid of too much good." Too much good was very dangerous, for it inevitably separated her from her mother (from me)—we were not needed. But what if the sick, needful person took over? This state always waited in the shadows. She feared that without her analytic mother she would also die.

As her attachment to me grew, Beth said: "Coming here is like taking a crayon and drawing it around myself." She felt "held together, distinct." She began to experiment with dressing up and feeling sexy, thus creating and experiencing a new self-state. Sexual fantasies abounded; angry feelings toward others became more clearly defined. She tried out all manner of activities, such as using the bathroom in a friend's house (she had never done anything so "personal" before) and discussing her fear of professional language. Language, always so powerful, felt dangerous. She imagined she was not supposed to know the terms of her profession. She feared that her new freedom might go too far—for instance, she feared she would fart in class.

Beth was pleased with her newly discovered social ease. Toward the end of our first year, she called to tell me how frightened she was by the good feelings she was having after she had left my office. "I felt so good I almost came back to the session. It was too much. Can I take care of myself? Do I have a self? *What is a self?* What do I do? Do I just play in my own world?"

She thanked me during the following session for my words, which had seemed magical to her. At a time when she was changing jobs, she apparently she needed my "magic" in order to be able to say a separate good-bye to each of her fellow employees. She had discovered that each person had his or her own personality. She now saw the possibility of missing them or that they might miss her. She was indeed beginning to make important external distinctions and internal separations and tolerate formerly intolerable affect states. But over the following weekend Beth scared herself. Missing people meant they were dead. My vacation was coming. Would she miss me? She had frequently talked about my smile. She recognized my smile. It seemed to return, always to be there to greet her. On the last day before my vacation, she told me she would miss my smile, she would miss me.

When we resumed work after this vacation, Beth was profoundly confused. After the first session, she called to see if I was really back. Had she actually seen me? Or was my vacation just about to start? Had we even had a session? She knew we had, but had we? "I knew the answers," she said, "to all of these questions, but the doubting thoughts were relentless and I telephoned just to have some peace."

In the next session she talked of making me disappear in my chair. A new Dr. Steger kept reappearing. She wondered how she could know that the new Dr. Steger was the one she had known before vacation.

Beth planned to leave over Thanksgiving. She fluctuated between feeling cocky about her expectations of being able to handle herself and fear that she would not be able to get back to me if she needed to. "I've been feeling so good about the trip," she said. "Now I'm getting frightened again. I am ready to show my stuff—me as myself—and I'm trying so hard to see the whole picture. It's like the leaves on the tree outside this office. I see the leaves, but not the trunk—not the roots."

"Seeing the whole picture" was a significant metaphor for Beth. Gradually we came to understand that by these words Beth meant being able to see things in their entirety—the full connection between people and between people and the objects, even the words, of the world. She was never supposed to do that. In fact, she couldn't. Not only was she unable to see the whole picture, she could not see herself as a part of that picture now or at a future moment. The idea of picturing herself as a part of a larger picture threatened anxiety attacks. And with the fear of an attack came the fear that the pain would be too great. Only death could silence that fear, that overwhelming pain. The whole picture included the loss of her mother. For, if Beth were a part of the whole, there would be no need for her mother. Then her mother would die. The whole picture would also reveal who is bad, who is good: "my mother or me. If I'm so good I've wasted my life."

Beth: I guess I'm afraid to feel too good. I get frightened if I feel too good or too bad. If I were really fantastic, I would be competing with my husband. He is supportive now, but would he be if I began to shine? I read a story about rape. Is that what I'm afraid of? I had a fantasy of visiting my father's grave. I would tell him how well I'm doing. He would say, "But your brother was supposed to be the professional. Where is he?" I would tell him that my brother still worked in the store as a manager. He would be pleased, but he would not understand why I am doing better than my brother. After I had the fantasy I had a fight with my son.

Analyst: When you were little, you needed your father's help to see the whole picture. He didn't understand how much your roots were stuck inside your mother, who had "no body." Now you are afraid that your husband and I will be like your father. It seems that, if you find your own ground, the important people in your life may want to violate you.

Beth: And, of course, my mother still thinks I should be home cleaning closets and never leave my children with a baby-sitter. They might be kidnapped. She could never stand to hear what I was doing. She had to tell me right away what she had done—it was always more and better.

Shortly thereafter, Beth sat up throughout the session.

Beth: I took the test [in graduate school]. [She sighs and is clearly upset.] The first half was multiple choice. We never had that before. I knew the answer to each question, but having four possibilities confused me. Two of the answers were "Sustained because of . . ." and two were "Overruled because of . . ." I couldn't even be sure about sustained or overruled. I felt like a sputterer, I mean to say stutterer, when I saw those multiple choices.

Analyst: I wonder if there was something you wanted to sputter that stopped you from seeing the answer more clearly. [I thought—seeing the whole picture.]

Beth: I was so angry. I had worked so hard, and now I couldn't show my stuff. It's like training for the Olympics; practicing, working harder than anybody else and on *that* day it's raining. The track's all muddy, and there I am slipping and falling.

I didn't have a chance on the test! I became frightened and overwhelmed and marked just anything. Facing the test was like facing my mother. Would my idea be sustained or overruled? I could never tell. It was like facing a wall. The test was that wall.

Analyst: You fear your mother will overrule your Olympic strivings. You confuse and deny your capacity to go beyond her wall.

Beth felt that her Thanksgiving trip had been a marvelous, personal success, but she also feared telling me.

Beth: You might say you're leaving; You might be vengeful. I may lose you in some way.

During the next session Beth turned wooden:

Beth: I feel I don't exist. I am a clone of the patient who was here. I am still away.

Analyst: When you are alive and happy you fear me and my revenge. You fear I will disappear. Even more, you're afraid of what you will do to me. If you don't think of me and, instead, enjoy yourself and have fun, you fear that something bad may happen to me. So you feel you must take your life, take your feelings away from yourself.

My responses to Beth evolved from my understanding of unity and differentiation in thinking, feeling, and experience as developed by Freud (1900) and Matte-Blanco (1988). Freud divided thinking into primary and secondary processes, and Matte-Blanco called the unity and differentiation of *thinking, feeling and experience,* "the symmetrical and the asymmetrical modes." When Beth's mode of being was what Matte-Blanco called symmetrical, that is, undifferentiated, she could not comprehend reality in any other way. I, therefore, responded symmetrically, as if we were one when I believed that was all she could accept. For example, in talking about my vacation, she felt nauseous. I said: "I vomit you and spit you out." Without a moment's hesitation, she said, "You get me out . . . rid of me." The image was angry, violent, projectile. The nausea stopped. However, poorly timed asymmetrical interpretations (comments that underlined our differences) were experienced as annihilating. At those times, Beth used to perseverate, said she didn't understand, became very frightened, felt lost.

Toward the end of two years, I planned to be away for a three-day weekend. She did not ask for anyone to be on call.

Beth: I had a dream last night. I also remember a dream when you were on vacation last summer. I was lying down with a pacifier in my mouth. I was my age. A woman came up from behind and stroked my head. I thought it was my mother. It reminded me of the time I was 16 and my mother and my father had been fighting as usual. I became sick to my stomach and went to lie down. My father understood that I was feeling terrible because of the fighting, and for the only time in my life he came and stroked my head. I never forgot it.

This dream reminds me of the dream I told you after the first few months of my analysis of my mother giving me heroin. I was missing you during the summer in a way that I have missed my father since his death.

The dream I had last night was very different: there were *three essays* and many *multiple-choice* questions on the test as well. I couldn't finish the third essay. It was a nightmare. I kept waking up a little and telling myself that I must go back to sleep and finish. Finally, when I became a little wider awake and made myself wake up, I knew I could not finish the third essay no matter how many times I'd go back to sleep.

Analyst: When I leave, you feel you're the bad one, not me. Perhaps feeling badness goes back to when your mother left without telling you. Then you fantasized that she was vomiting you out, getting revenge for loving your father because he soothed you just as I do now. And now you think I'm leaving because you're bad for feeling good.

The three essays are like the three days I will be gone. You are working very hard to make them be over, but three feels like too many "to finish." No magic, no confessional union with me can make that happen. You cannot keep me here like the heroin mother. The third unfinished essay may refer to ideas and feelings about your father. You are used to thinking in twosomes—you and your mother—and your longings for your father have gone underground. But you're beginning to find a way to ease your pain: remembering your soothing father, remembering your love for your father

Beth: I remember that when I was very little, two- and-a-half or three, my father would give me apricot juice every night. I walked quietly to his side of the bed in the middle of the night. He sensed that I was there and got up. My mother was very angry. He said, "But she's so thin and tiny." I'm glad I'm not so powerful that I can keep you from leaving and that my thoughts are not powerful enough to kill anybody if I'm busy and not thinking about them. I'm scared, but I feel I'll be O.K. until our next appointment.

Working Through

The therapist, like the good enough mother, must be flexibly responsive while remaining a private person and not vulnerable to the patient's projections of positive and negative feelings. . . . the reliving with the therapist of the emotional conflict is a self-provoked risking, an unconscious reaching for a better autonomy. The therapist is consciously intent on liberating the patient from feeling the need to expend himself in clinging or in combating, or in any other defensive manner of wasting his goods. . . . The medium of change is the process of dissolving of the patient's deeply ambivalent primary involvement by a gentle acceptance and then interpretation of the whole spontaneous transference, both sides of the regression, the magical and the monstrous, the benign and the malignant qualities in the secondary defensive illusions or phantasies [Shor and Sanville, 1978, p. 124].

Upon my return from the third Christmas break, following two years and four months of treatment, Beth reported a new sensation. She could name this feeling but did not recall ever having had it before. She had been looking forward to my return, but, as she neared the office on that first day, she also felt a kind of depression. It seemed to relate to how well she had done without me. Who would I be to her if she could do without me? This mildly depressed feeling heralded a new aspect of the transference, which, added to her recent progress, significantly expanded the arena of our work for the next four years.

Beth reported boredom and apathy with the many accomplishments that she had so eagerly sought. Her boredom existed in spite of the fact that she and her husband had become better friends; the ability to dress up and enjoy elegant restaurants, once such an impossible feat, now seemed commonplace; increased academic comfort in school and new, diverse relationships with schoolmates, at earlier times so thrilling, felt like "Is this all there is?"

She felt a mounting anger at everybody—her new friends, her husband, her professors, me. She demanded to know, "Why do I have to work so hard for what comes so easily to others? I do everything I'm supposed to. I'm tired of being so good and doing it all when others don't. Why can you go away on a vacation anytime you want and not be scared?"

Beth managed to express these feelings without shifting into an increasingly undifferentiated state, although, at the end of such a session, she would ask, "You're not angry with me, are you? You will call me back, won't you? I know you will." These words sounded like ritualized repair, but they continued to hold some magic for her.

Everyone but Beth seemed, to Beth, to have power and authority. The issue was highlighted by a question she had failed on an exam. In it an agent represented an insurance company and the question was: "Does he have the power to insure a policeman?" Beth knew the answer was "no" but said "yes" because of the word *represent*.

Beth: I just clicked into my world of words, where *represent* means *have the authority*. I never had my own authority. My power came from *representing* my mother. I remember the time she told someone I had a date to go to a football game. There I was, too tall and feeling ugly, trying to look like a popular adolescent cheerleader so *my mother* would feel normal!! Could I tell her I was quaking, terrified? Could I tell her I didn't have any idea how I could possibly go to any football game? How I could even go out the front door?

Beth quickly sensed her fear of, and also her pleasure in, her own power. One day, as I entered the waiting room, she said:

Beth: I'm putting away your magazine exactly where it came from.
[She knocked her purse into my plant.] Oh, I've knocked off
a leaf of the plant that you take care of so carefully! If I could
kill your plant, what else could I kill?

With permutations of this theme, a new strength grew, while a different, distinct and identifiable self-state emerged. It was one in which
Beth was superior and demeaning. Hostility, though still overt and
eruptive, now became more secretive. At times, Beth took what she
wanted, without concern for anyone else; she hid information that
could help others; she often experienced herself as superior to others.
She said that she captivated other women's husbands; all eyes turned
to look when she walked in or when she spoke. She was now increasingly "showing her stuff." Sometimes she thought I envied her money,
her youth, her good figure, her charm. She wondered if I needed her
money for my own support; she hated me for wanting anything from
her. In the meantime, as her airplane phobia disappeared, she
fantasized taking over the airplane if the pilot became ill. She pictured
herself attacking some killers as they pointed a gun at a judge.

It was apparent that she imagined and experienced stronger,
individuated self-states. Nevertheless, she might need to spoil a good
feeling with a punishing fantasy. For example, in the midst of a grand
fantasy she would worry that she would not be able to reach me in
time if something bad happened. These old fears, cropping up with
the addition of each new aspect of self, were now exacerbated by the
thought that, although she was able to do and feel so much more, she
had not in fact changed at all.

In her new job Beth remained in daily conflict about "showing her
stuff." For a while she hid in her office and only gradually, still not
volunteering for anything professional, began to relate to others. She
let herself be touched by their feelings and did not get lost. She said,
"I get under their skin, and I let them get under mine. I can do what
I think you do." She no longer imagined me as an unfeeling sphinx.
She felt filled and fulfilled by her experiences.

Beth handled my fourth summer vacation with ease. She did not
feel constricted in any unusual way by my absence. When we resumed,
I was struck by her cohesiveness. She seemed to be *Some Body* with
contents of her own. But one fantasy suggested otherwise. Four days
after my return she said, sadly:

Beth: I feel like an alien from another planet, like I've been asleep
for 40 years like Rip van Winkle or a ghost. It's like I arrived
and didn't know what money was and in trying to get

something someone pointed to my pocket and there was
change in it. They kindly took what was fair, and I got what I
wanted in exchange. I bumped into people. I was very clumsy.
But slowly I was shown the way. I learned what food was and
what was good, I learned to have fun and friends. I could
look people in the eye. I could feel I am really here. They
don't know I'm an alien, or a ghost, or that I was asleep for
40 years. I might have fallen in love. And I forgot what I was.
Suddenly, there is a tap on my shoulder and someone says,
"It's time to go back," and I know I won't even be remembered
when I disappear.

Analyst: When you are frightened you alienate your feelings, but
leaving them behind makes you afraid that you will forget
entirely how to feel. On the other hand, when you allow
yourself to feel, you believe you are losing that part of your
self which you recognize as "an alien."

Beth: I want to be able to be able to count on myself, but that
terrifies me. You can be counted on. I want to be able to be
counted on by others.

Beth worked in analysis for several more years, at decreasing frequency. Her motivation never waned. She, who had been afraid to
leave the house, now planned and took unusual and exciting trips.
She continued to work through her capacity to handle her feelings
and to feel real in meaningful relationships. She began to see her
mother without fear of dissolution. These contacts emerged naturally
while Beth retained her personal integrity. She took a job in which
she, and she alone, was counted on. One day she said, "I never worry
about being counted on anymore—it never crosses my mind. It's just
there."

Conclusion

Psychoanalysis is a process that takes great courage and patience.
Dangerous psychic traps are everywhere. Through the psychoanalytic
process, the experiencing of multiple self–object relations, and the
understanding of the transferences and the countertransferences, we
hope to become able to move flexibly within the spiral of imagined
mergings and imagined self-sufficiency, between the metaphors and
poetry of life and more differentiated thinking. Beth's growing ability
to create and maintain an increasingly differentiated internal
representation of me while knowing that I was still the same person

coincided with her toleration of multiple selves within the unity of herself and without losing herself.

Some selected manifestations of this process:

1. Upon my return from a first vacation, approximately one year after analysis began, she was very confused. Within a few days, however, she said that she *"recognized and remembered my smile."*
2. In her third year of analysis, following Christmas vacation, she felt depressed on her way to my office. *"She did well without me."* This idea was not met with panic or undoing. There was sadness and an acknowledgment that she and I were separate.
3. She became *angry at my new shoes and said, "You may go dancing."* Previously she had been frightened by the appearance of any new clothing, believing I would leave her. Now she could acknowledge some anger with playfulness, knowing that both she and I could tolerate it; and she allowed herself to become aware that I have a life of my own.
4. She noticed that I was wearing a sweater similar to one of hers. She liked the fact that *we have sweaters that are similar but are different.* The metaphor was obvious to both of us and there could, as a result, be a pleasurable and differentiated exchange.

Without panicking, Beth is now able to be sexual and flirtatious and receive admiration. She can be furious and differentiated from her most important relationships and still leave home and be counted on. She can be thoughtful, empathic, and loving. She must work hard at times to achieve either highly differentiated self-states (extreme excitement, for example) or simultaneous self-states (anger and love) without falling into symmetrical thinking. But when confusion and pain set in, recovery is rapid and stable.

Epilogue

I have focused this chapter on Beth's analysis and held that focus together through the deceptively simple starting quotation from Jean Sanville: "We create and recreate the self as long as we live. What is involved is a dialectic spiral between imagined mergings and imagined self sufficiency." In her particularly talented way of taking a complex and profound idea and making it available to a wide audience, Sanville has condensed for us a perception—and conception—that has always demanded understanding. At this point I would like to suggest three further ways to think about this dialectic spiral, as they have deepened my understanding of states of differentiation and fusion and the complex relationship between them in my patients and myself.

First: The study of metaphysics, combined with the study of metapsychology, leads to a knowledge of formerly unknown regions of the mind. It is especially important to include the already developed and extraordinarily rich insights of mystics in understanding the psychoanalytic situation. We are all a part of nature: simplistic, overly clear differentiations of human from animal, organic from inorganic, and, most broadly, inner from outer, are now obsolete, useless. But mystics place what is inside outside, with the overarching goal of becoming one with the outside, moving toward a state of unity with all things. Their knowledge is derived from meditation, their way of understanding the world. Through their writings, we may now infer a great deal about the mind, gleaned from their descriptions of the various levels of meditative exploration (Steger, 1994).

One such mystical conception is the Jewish Kabbalistic myth of creation. It describes an unknowable, infinite, indivisible, and symmetrical base of cosmic being called *Ein-Sof,* literally "without end," where inside and outside, cause and effect, time itself all mean nothing. However, there are also knowable portions of this cosmic *Ein Sof,* "emanations" or "*Sephirot,* "which may become known when man recognizes them as aspects of self: love, for example, or wisdom, sterness, compassion, power, understanding. These emanations are most sharply defined by their polarities, their capacity to temper one another. Within each emanation, hologramlike, the whole is contained. Several authors (Bloom, 1984; Scholem, 1987; Idel, 1988; *Encyclopaedia Judaica,* 1989; Lachower and Tishby, 1991;) are relevant to this discussion. The *Zohar* (1984) states,

> the whole world is constructed on this principle, upper and lower, from the first mystic point up to the furthest removed of all the stages. They are all coverings one to another, brain within brain, and spirit within spirit, [self within self] so that one is a shell to another [1.19b and 20a. pp. 83–84].

Second: Ignacio Matte-Blanco, a 20th-century, Latin American psychoanalyst, approaches the mind, Freud's unconscious and conscious modes of thinking, as a kabbalist approaches the Godhead. He suggests that the human experience is grounded in a sense of oneness with all others—with all matter—and he names this invariable, indivisible base "symmetry." What he terms "the symmetrical mode" encompasses everything, its dimensions infinite. Everything is equal to, and the same as, everything else. For Matte-Blanco, however, finite and distinct layers, knowable portions of the infinite world (similar to the kabbalistic "emanations") are understood as "asymmetrical strata." These asymmetries unfold from a symmetrical foundation: new asymmetrical relations, new and evolving perceptions of self and others, are constantly made, defined, and redefined throughout life.

Thus, as in the kabbalistic myth of creation but using his own version of psychoanalytic theory, Matte-Blanco expands our understanding of Freud's primary and secondary processes; particularly, he allows us to understand each in relation to the other. Germane material may be found in the work of many authors (Matte-Blanco, 1975, 1988; Rayner, 1995; Steger, 1996). Matte-Blanco (1975) said that

> behind every individual or relationship—as perceived or given in a certain manner at a given moment—the self "sees" an infinite series (sequence) of individuals; . . . If the attention of the observer remains focused on the first level, that of consciousness, then he will only be aware of the concrete individual; and if he lets himself be permeated by the underlying levels, this infinity will unfold itself before him, though in an unconscious manner. Embracing this infinite series (sequence) there is one unity: the class or the set. This in its turn, is lived as one unity [p. 170].

Third: Contemporary relational theorists advance ideas about the healthy self in a postmodern way: the self as decentered and un-unified, a paradox of a multiplicity of selves in an illusion of oneness. Challenging the paradigm of conscious–unconscious and discarding developmental markers in favor of shifting discontinuous nonlinear states on the basis of a redefined model of dissociation, they raise critical questions about the nature of individual integration, of how we may best understand ourselves and ourselves in relationship to others. Several authors (Bromberg, 1991, 1994, 1996; Davies, 1996; Flax, 1996; Harris, 1996; Pizer, 1996) are currently engaged in exploring this area. As Bromberg (1996) postulates:

> A human being's ability to live, with both authenticity and self-awareness depends on the presence of an ongoing dialectic between separateness and unity of one's self-states, allowing each self to function optimally without a foreclosing communication and negotiation between them. . . . He goes on to say that each self-state is a piece of a functional whole . . . . Despite collisions and even enmity between aspects of self, it is unusual for any one self-state to function totally outside of the sense of 'me-ness'. . . . Dissociation, like repression, is a healthy, adaptive function of the human mind [p. 514].

A deeper understanding of unity and differentiation in thinking, as in experience, enables us to comprehend Beth more fully. For example, Beth's displacements. She splits her mother into three (mother, husband, and me). The symmetrical logic is that her husband and I are treated exactly as the mother—we are, for her, all the same person. She may run to any one of us and believe herself safe. But while classic logic reveals that on the surface she sees three different, separate persons, analysis reveals that in her mind we are all one. Here, one appears as three.

Building on ego psychology, Matte-Blanco, the kabbalistic myth, and Bromberg's redefined model of multiple selves offer ways of strengthening our understanding of how the finite (the imagined unique and differentiated self) is used to define the infinite (the self imaginitively merged with outside objects.) In all, creation is revelation, a transmutation of the infinite into something redefined and newly limited (differentiated). I think that, while limited self-representations (Sanville's, 1991, "formerly held schemas") may be used to define one's whole being, the spaceless, timeless unconscious, Matte-Blanco's symmetrical being, the *Kabbala's* "*Ein-Sof,*" any Bromberg's "sense of me-ness." are all ways of describing the source for newly delineated self-representations. Emanation (revelation) is a perpetual process; just as the world is always being created, we are always re-creating ourselves. And therein lies the hope of any psycho-analytic treatment.

References

Bloom, H. (1984), *Kabbalah and Criticism*. New York: Continuum.
Bromberg, P. (1991), Artist and analyst. *Contemp. Psychoanal.*, 27:289–300.
———— (1994), "Speak that I may see you": Some reflections on dissociation, reality, and psychoanalytic listening. *Psychoanal.Dial.*, 4:517–547.
———— (1996), Standing in the spaces. *Contemp. Psychoanal.*, 32:509–535.
Davies, J. (1996), Linking the "pre-analytic" with the postclassical: integration, dissociation, and the multiplicity of unconscious process: *Contemp. Psychoanal.*, 32:553–576.
Encyclopaedia Judaica. K[abbalah] (1989), Jerusalem: Koren.
Flax, J. (1996), Taking multiplicity seriously: some consequences for psychoanalytic theorizing and practice. *Contemp. Psychoanal.*, 32:577–593.
Freud, S. (1900), The interpretation of dreams. *Standard Edition*, 4 & 5 London: Hogarth Press,.1953.
Harris, A. (1996), The conceptual power of multiplicity. *Contemp. Psychoanal.*, 32:537–551.
Idel, M. (1988), *Kabbalah*. New Haven, CT: Yale University Press.
Lachower, F. & Tishby, I. (1991), *The Wisdom of the Zohar*, I, II, III. Oxford: Oxford University Press.
Matte-Blanco, I. (1975), *The Unconscious as Infinite Sets*. London: Duckworth.
———— (1988), *Thinking Feeling and Being*. London: Routledge.
Pizer, S. (1996), The distributed self: Introduction to symposium on "The Multiplicity of Self and Analytic Technique." *Contemp. Psychoanal.*, 32:499–507.
Rayner, E. (1995), *Unconscious Logic*. London: Routledge.
Sanville, J. (1987), Creativity and the constructing of the self. *Psychoanal.Rev.*, 74:253–279.

———— (1991), *The Playground of Psychoanalytic Therapy*. Hillsdale, NJ: The Analytic Press.

Scholem, G. (1987), *Kabbalah*. New York: Dorset Press.

Shor, J. & Sanville, J. (1978), *Illusion in Loving*. Los Angeles: Double Helix Press.

Steger, G. (1994), The Cosmololgy of the Mind and the Bi- Logic of the Kabbalah. Unpub.doctoral dissertation, Los Angeles Institute and Society for Psychoanalytic Studies.

Zohar (1984), *A Translated Book*, trans H. Sperling & M. Simon. London: Soncino Press.

Chapter 4

∞

A Consideration of Constructs That Organize Clinical Data
Analytic Play, Analytic Surface, Analytic Space

Laurie S. M. Hollman

*I*n the midst of analytic controversies about theory and technique, each contemporary analyst is challenged to evaluate the therapeutic action of psychoanalysis, often on a case-by-case basis. We need to ask ourselves how to organize the clinical data we observe and how to conceptualize our technical choices. In this chapter I examine features of therapeutic actions taking place during the first year of an analysis of a severely obsessional woman.

I explore three interrelated but not apparently compatible constructs that seem particularly relevant to her treatment: analytic play, analytic space, and the analytic surface. Clinical evidence is offered to demonstrate the contribution these constructs made to my understanding of this obsessional patient and to the furtherance of her analysis. Subsequent to a discussion of the case material, consideration is given to the question of whether the metaphoric constructs—surface-to-depth and analytic space—can coexist.

Play and the Psychoanalytic Situation

The Relationship Between Analytic Play and Free Association
While the verbal discourse of adults and the active play of children in treatment seem to be distinct modes of communication, actually they overlap. Both adults and children in the psychoanalytic situation use words and actions to communicate as well as to distort communication. My therapeutic work in each of these treatment situations has led to my interest in various modes of therapeutic communication. Specific to this inquiry is my interest not only in behavioral play but

also in verbal play. For the purpose of my discussion, I define analytic play as the relative freedom of the adult analysand to associate *meaningfully* in various verbal and nonverbal forms.

The method of free association originated with Freud (1900) when he abandoned hypnosis and employed this method to investigate dreams. Optimizing free association is often a therapeutic goal in itself. How and when to discuss the "fundamental rule" (Freud, 1912, p. 112; 1913, p. 134) continues to be debated (Lichtenberg and Galler, 1987; Busch, 1997). Descriptions of free association are remarkably similar in spirit to descriptions of play: a joint enterprise in which the patient loosens "the barrier between preconscious and unconscious phenomena" (Lowenstein, 1951, p. 2) while attempting to be as free as possible to express spontaneously in words all thoughts, feelings, wishes, sensations, images, memories, dreams, and experiences without reservation (Kris, 1982; Lichtenberg and Galler, 1987). Solnit (1993) points out the relationship between play and free association. He proposes that, just as thought is trial action, play is experimental thought. In analysis, free association

> requires an ability to pretend, to suspend judgment, and to imagine much as we do in play and playfulness. It is expected that as a psychoanalytic treatment proceeds, the analysand, with the help of hearing himself or herself in the presence of the analyst, with the assistance provided by interpretations and working through, will become increasingly able to approximate . . . optimal free association . . . [and be] able to be 'playful' as an adult or to play freely as a child [p. 42].

The Relationship Between Play and Analytic Space

Jean Sanville (1991) expands on Freud's (1914) and Winnicott's (1971) notions about play in analytic work. She is taken by Freud's reference to "transference as a playground . . . an intermediate region between illness and real life through which the transition from the one to the other is made" (p. 154). This intermediate area is the region in which Freud believed the patient's compulsion to repeat in the transference could be turned into a motive for remembering. Sanville is interested in the parts patient and analyst play in this intermediate region. She turns to Winnicott's (1971) idea that psychoanalytic treatment "has to do with two people playing together" and "the corollary of this that where playing is not possible then the work done by the therapist is directed towards bringing the patient from a state of not being able to play into a state of being able to play" (p. 38). Sanville (1991) draws an analogy between the psychoanalytic situation and play—both offering "a special time and place . . . set aside . . . to constitute a sort of interlude from real life. . . ." (p. 243) in which to gain insight into one's inner world and developing self.

It is not only the play of the analysand that is in focus in the psychoanalytic situation. It is the task of the analyst to keep his or her capacity to play intact as well. Winnicott (1971) believed that psychoanalysis occurs in the overlap of the playing of both patient and analyst, which is recognizable in verbal communication through word choice, voice inflection, and a sense of humor. He emphasized the gerund playing, rather than the noun play, to accentuate the analyst's need to attend to playing itself as well as to play content.

Ogden (1985) elaborates on Winnicott's concept, potential space: "an intermediate area of experiencing that lies between fantasy and reality. Specific forms of potential space include the play space, the area of . . . transitional . . . phenomena, the analytic space, . . . and the area of creativity . . . " (p. 129). Ogden points out that the child's or adult's "capacity to generate potential space" (p. 129) can be identified in treatment by the patient's developmental capacity for symbolization, which is evident when the child or adult can distinguish symbol from symbolized and stand apart from both as a "thinker" or "interpreting self" (p. 137). This capacity is requisite for the creation of an analytic play space.

Play as a Developmental Phenomenon of Children and Adults

Play as both a form of communication and a therapeutic goal finds a common ground in child and adult analysis. Ogden's (1985) idea about developing the capacity to create a play space underscores a developmental approach to analytic work with both children and adults. Play is distinguished from other activities of childhood by several distinctive features that can also be applied to the imaginary world of adults: it consists of make-believe, symbolism, assimilation, synthesis, and fantasy. Whether these occur through action, words, or fantasy, they can still be considered forms of play (Neubauer, 1993). Play is a way to experiment with reality. Material for verbal fantasy and fantasy-play is derived from experiences. Wishes to turn passive into active, to undo a sense of unfairness or injustice, to reverse misfortune, disappointment, failure, feared loss and injury are commonly represented. The fantasy-maker, however, not only turns ungratifying or disagreeable situations into gratifying, agreeable ones. Once relieved of the immediacy of the real situation, the child also engages in play to work through an affective experience with real objects to assimilate it piecemeal for the purpose of mastery (Waelder, 1932). This is also true for adults who use fantasy to work through affective experiences. As the adult or the child plays out (in words or play-acting) any number of fantasied variations of experience, the drama is the vehicle for the expression of compromise formations necessary to resolve conflicts that emerged from the experience (Hollman, 1997).

While play may be closer to reality or to fantasy at different times, the intent is to pretend. Play is a function of the ego occurring in a state of relaxed superego control, although the conscience is still operative. Freud (1908) taught that the "child's best-loved and most intense preoccupation" is play and that its opposite "is not what is serious but what is real" (p. 144). For both children and adults, play is free from internal or external compulsion (Plaut, 1979). It provides a "resting place" from the pressures of reality testing without losing a sense of reality (Winnicott, 1971, p. 2).

The action of play is free from internal or external compulsion; its boundaries are freely chosen and are part of the play; and it has no reality consequences (Plaut, 1979). Play is interrupted, breaks down, or ceases when real consequences for the activity or behavior result (Solnit, 1987) or when the child can not initiate or stop the play at will—that is, when it is in the service of a developing neurosis (Greenacre, 1959) and becomes a phobic defense, an obsessional ritual, or the child is overwhelmed by anxiety (Peller, 1954).

Psychoanalytic Perspectives on the Analytic Surface

The construct "analytic surface" originated in 1901 with Freud's topographic metaphor about the surface of a patient's mind. In subsequent revisions, he included not only consciousness but also resistance as surface phenomena, and he alerted both analyst and patient to attend to the surface. For the analyst, he provided a technical rule: analysis starts from the surface with what is present and accessible to the ego in the moment (Freud, 1901), and interpretation is employed "mainly for the purpose of recognizing the resistances which appear there, and making them conscious to the patient" (Freud, 1914, p. 14). For the analysand, Freud (1916–17) drew attention to the surface with the fundamental rule of free association: "We urge the [patient] always to follow only the surface of his consciousness and to leave aside any criticism of what he finds" (p. 287).

Contemporary analysts recognize that there are various surfaces from which to view analytic data ranging from disturbances in the free association process, to analysis of resistance, to derivatives of unconscious fantasy. Many analysts emphasize moment-to-moment expressions of surface phenomena—experiences of disequilibrium in the analytic relationship, in a surprising, externalized drama (Levy and Inderbitzen, 1990), in the free association process (Kris, 1982, 1990), or in a time of "intrapsychic stress" when resistances to drive derivatives surface involuntarily (Gray, 1990, p. 1087). Poland (1992) emphasizes that the analyst cannot look at the surface from too far a distance. He indicates that the surface implies an affective "engagement in the immediacy of the . . . moment" (p. 385) within an interactive, dyadic analytic space, a concept that resembles an intermediate play space. While different analysts focus on different surfaces, each pays particular attention to his or her response or counterresistance to surface phenomena and, when things go well, to the patient's increased self-observation and verbal spontaneity following interpretive efforts that permit further insight into unconscious fantasies and mental states.

While some analysts highlight particular analytic moments, others concentrate on a broader picture. Joseph (1981) identifies the complex defensive organization of the personality, which, along with its emotional content, is part of one's fantasy world. She attends closely to the degree to which the analyst makes contact with the patient and achieves "real understanding, as opposed to subtle acting out and pseudo-understanding" (Joseph, 1983, p. 150). Arlow (1979a, 1987) indicates that the surface for interpretation is found as a shift occurs in the analyst's mind as he or she moves from an intuitive inner commentary on the patient's unconscious thoughts based on identification and introspection, to insight and interpretation based on cognition and reason tested against objective data in the session. Jacobs (1991, 1997) emphasizes the analyst's use of self as the analytic instrument. He pays careful attention to the interactive aspects of the psychoanalytic situation, such as postures, gestures, and movements that accompany thoughts, images, and verbalizations of both analyst and analysand. Paniagua (1991) posits multiple surface phenomena: what the patient says or does makes up the clinical surface; what the analyst subjectively decides to interpret at the locus of contact with the patient's observing ego is the workable surface.

Clinical Illustration: Mrs. A

Mrs. A suffered with a severe obsessional neurosis. She began four-times-weekly psychoanalysis anxious and demoralized about her role in life. She was a bright, well-spoken woman from the mid-West who was secure in her second marriage (she divorced after two years of her first marriage); took pride in her mothering of two achieving, friendly children (from this second marriage); had interests and friends; and maintained frequent contact with her parents. A younger brother had died from an unusual illness in his teens. Despite her abilities and support from friends and family, Mrs. A felt unable to sustain a long-term, in-depth focus on any of her interests and was particularly demoralized about how her mental conflicts interfered with completing creative endeavors she considered worthwhile. An overriding concern was an intense preoccupation with her appearance. Owing to an obsessive concern with a modicum of hair loss, Mrs. A has consulted a dermatologist, who diagnosed an unremarkable transitory condition. This clinical presentation illustrates staying close to the analytic surface as an avenue to deepening an understanding of Mrs. A's inner torment, which substantially inhibited her accomplishments and interfered with self-esteem regulation. I have chosen excerpts from four sessions, each approximately one week apart halfway through the first year of treatment, that seem typical of my way of working with Mrs. A during that period of her analysis. Taking excerpts from sessions is a way of freezing them in time in order to view them from specific vantage points. Simultaneously, reviewing these sessions over the course of a month gives life to the ongoing process. Both lenses, the moment-to-moment chronicle and the ongoing process, are retrospective, however, appearing more neatly observable than they are in the living consultation room. As Freud (1912) pointed out, even "exact reports" offer only "ostensible exactness" and "do not succeed in being a substitute for" the analyst's "actual presence at an analysis" (p. 114).

Excerpts from Session A
The session began with Mrs. A's detailing how she felt better after the dermatologist said her hair loss would stop in a few days: "I felt lighter and as close to normal as I have in a long time. I watched myself feel then—now is when something will happen—opening myself up to a real disaster." I became aware of her experience of ambivalence, a repeated pattern of relief followed by rising anxiety. I commented, "You feel better and then worse." She responded, "The next morning when I showered it was the worst anxiety I had in a long time. I put hairs in a bag and saw the total and thought it wasn't so bad. But before that I went back and forth with anxiety and a tremendous thought kept occurring to me—'I should take the bag to the doctor's office. Does he know how much hair there is?' I kept thinking—should I?"

I pointed out that the trend in her back-and-forth thinking centered on this idea of a potential disaster. She spoke about conferring with a friend who reassured her that her hair loss did not seem out of the ordinary, but her anxiety was not eased. She wanted to ask the doctor about a wig but felt she should wait out the weekend before calling. Unable to stay home with so much anxiety, she went to the library to read about cancer patients losing their hair. I connected her ideas of a disaster with her fear of cancer.

She responded, "That's where this story's going. I immersed myself in this information. It was totally consuming me. I was right there living this life of a cancer patient who had lost all her hair. I've heard of people harboring wishes of misfortune even for people they love. It's bad enough to recognize you have a mean side—a less than nice side to you—but if the thing you wish for actually happens. I was probably thinking, 'I'm glad this isn't me.' I classify that as a mean thought."

I observed that only when she began to feel mean did she start to qualify or minimize her feelings by saying she *probably* was mean. "Yeah," she said. "I was living that life. I was going to experience the same thing these people experienced. Underneath this little thought kept popping up—'That's not you.'—and I'd feel relief. But I can't easily see relief because so closely attached is tremendous guilt, sort of reminding me of the evil eye stuff."

Discussion: These excerpts are illustrative of how Mrs. A's inner world was filled with uncertainty and doubt perpetuated by defensive ambivalence, undoing, negation, and isolation of affect. I propose that free association in an adult analysand is the counterpart to play in child treatment and that, by the analyst's attending to the analytic surface, the capacity of an analysand to associate freely or to engage in therapeutic play is enhanced. Mrs. A's ability to sustain spontaneous and flexible verbal play, "a free mental space where meaningful thinking can develop" (Sodre, 1994, p. 391), was easily derailed by her obsessional mechanisms. Her thoughts, often referred to as colliding voices within her, engaged in tendentious battles. She once described herself with a concrete image that expressed this torment: "I'm lying here, a two-headed being, both heads are facing each other and screaming and trying to win out over the other."

I considered how to proceed in the presence of her formidable defensive organization. While her imaginative and vivid language was compelling, it was often affectively isolated. A blend of interventions addressing both Mrs. A's most observable defenses against drive derivatives and a surface level of emerging themes she was defending against seemed needed for me to engage her observing ego. As her treatment proceeded I expected that such interventions would enable her to become a more reflective participant in her analysis with a less isolated stream of consciousness.

The concept of play is helpful in understanding Mrs. A's pathology and my technical approach. Session A illustrates Mrs. A's defensive organization. Following good news from the doctor, she undoes her relief with her fantasy about impending disaster. Her ambivalence is repeatedly demonstrated when she believes and doubts. She recognizes her "back-and-forth" thinking when I draw attention to it but cannot yet reflect upon it; she illustrates it further with her story about seeking reassurance from her friend whose ideas she listens to and then discards. This characterological style resembles the anal play of a toddler who aggressively takes and holds on to objects that are quickly dropped or thrown (Kestenberg, 1966). Then the child anxiously awaits the reassuring retrieval of the object by the mother. Mrs. A engages others in this kind of play with her thoughts.

An awareness of the nature of Mrs. A's analytic play style enriches an understanding of how she responds to surface interpretations. Despite the push-and-pull of her associations, my comments about the connections in her manifest thoughts are heard, and further material emerges about her fear of bodily damage, specifically cancer, but she does not question her ideas. Similarly, when her conditional statement about her "meanness" is addressed, she listens but her affect is isolated. Like the toddler just described, in this session she appears to take and set aside my defense interpretations in the moments after they are given.

The similarity between Mrs. A's associations and the play of children is also seen from the way she includes or excludes me at different times. In the play of children, the analyst may be excluded from the play, given specific roles, or seen as a collaborator. By not reflecting on my comments, Mrs. A, in effect, excludes me from our analytic play space. She listens and then continues to play on her own. Her affect is isolated, and I feel as if I'm supposed to wonder if she will work with me or just alongside me. This style of responding keeps me alert to her defensive posture. Collaborative and self-observing functions of her ego become embroiled in conflict, limiting the spontaneity of her free associations (Gray, 1986).

In the course of the sessions that followed, as I commented on surface resistances—her defensive ambivalence, undoing, and affective isolation—she expressed feelings of guilt and ideas about being judged. The ongoing process demonstrated that over the course of time, despite her moment-to-moment responses (her taking and setting aside new ideas), defense interpretations were being worked through in her mind, and internalization was slowly occurring. She both knew and did not know that her fears were excessive, an example of the "strange behaviour of patients, in being able to combine a conscious knowing with not knowing" (Freud, 1913, p. 142). Surface manifestations of resistance seemed malleable enough for her to proceed in this manner. Despite the ponderous quality of her defensive organization, neither of us was immobilized by it.

Talk about cancer led Mrs. A to defend against wishes and fears about benefiting from the death of others. The next session comes on the heels of expressions of guilt in relation to ill will toward her brother.

Excerpts from Session B (five sessions later)
In this session Mrs. A described a "power struggle" with her mother over expressing grief for her brother. She felt "vengeful" toward her mother for being critical of her when she cried as a little girl and did not want to give her mother the satisfaction of seeing her feelings now, although her mother had become more open to them. She felt selfish for wanting to cry for herself, not for her brother. She noticed feeling with me as she felt with her mother: "I can hear some kind of bind I put you in. Here I've come to you for help in getting to my feelings, and I get like I don't want to." When I commented on how she spoke about her feelings in general, rather than her very specific struggle with feeling vengeful, she said she felt like stamping her feet in a temper tantrum shouting, "I'll show you!" and continued, "Vengeful sounds like wanting destruction and harm. It must have been in there. The way I was conscious of it was in a passive kind of way—'I won't do that.' I'd run to my room when I was six or so, slam the door and cry—rage really."

I pointed out that these feelings had begun after the last session. "Vengeful?" she said. "I recognized my reluctance and said to myself, 'It's so self-defeating.' I have to get beyond that, but I don't know how. I felt rising action and like putting a halt to it—that I'm not going to let the action keep rising. That's what I mean by reluctance. I'm reaching some kind of new place. [sighs] I'm afraid of putting on the brakes."

I brought her attention more closely to when she felt like "putting on the brakes"—after talking about her brother and what it was like to feel good about another's tragedy. In response, she spoke about guilt for viewing him as a burden: "I wanted to be left alone. I don't remember wanting him to die. I can hear some kind of possibility in a two-year-old kind of way. I can see, make this baby go away, and later thinking, 'He can handle stuff without counting on me.' I can see that, but it doesn't feel that way."

When I commented on how she quickly expressed and then dismissed her comments, she noted that she spoke about guilty feelings but did not feel anything and wished she could feel "this terrible weight and confess to it." Then she went on, "There's a pressure I feel squeezing on either side of my head like a vise being screwed. It's sort of like getting my back against the wall, some kind of pressure all over. I probably confused my brother's neediness with feeling my parents couldn't hear me."

I observed that, when it came to her brother, she minimized her feelings by qualifying them ("I guess," "sort of," "probably"). She responded that, even though he'd been dead for years, she still felt his loss. She then lapsed into a long silence, to which I drew her attention. She responded, "I was digesting that. I've never put it together like that. I've always been resisting the trauma of his death." She recalled an exchange with her mother and husband at the opera when she complained of his inattention. Her mother said, "It's not the right time." Mrs. A snapped back, "It never is. That's the problem." Mrs. A concluded, "There was never a right time for me, only for my brother."

Discussion: In this session, transference play came forward. Mrs. A's fantasies were being attached to me as she cast me in the role of a mother with whom she needed to clash. I was being used as part of her defensive system (Joseph, 1981). Varied attempts to qualify, undo, take back, and negate her ideas continued to be addressed. In the interactive analytic space, when she spoke about vengeance toward her mother, I silently experienced the same toward me, which was then verified when she said, "I can hear some kind of bind I put you in. Here I've come to you for help in getting to my feelings, and I get like I don't want to."

Mrs. A's isolation of affect slowly gave way as she reflected on the maternal transference emerging in the context of feelings about her brother. Derivatives of unconscious childhood wishes began to appear. Her comments often contained antithetical ideas. For example, she said, "Vengeful sounds like wanting destruction and harm, and I'm sure that must've been in there." By saying, "I'm sure," she was also saying, "I'm not sure." While saying she was vengeful, she was also telling herself, "No, I'm not." I drew her attention to her generalization about *all* feelings as a defense against her struggle with vengeful feelings. She had substituted generalized thoughts of unacceptable feelings for her violent wishes (Arlow, 1982). Her awareness was then expanded to include these wishes ("wanting destruction and harm") and previously intellectualized ideas pertaining to guilt about her brother's death came to the surface.

Thinking of her associations as a dynamic record of methods the ego used to resolve conflicts in the past (Arlow, 1987), we can see that her first repudiated idea was that her brother should die ("I don't remember wanting him to die"), and her second, more conscious idea was that she would not do anything to help him ("I didn't want to be counted on"). Consistently addressing her defenses strengthened her capacity for self-observation and resulted in increasingly spontaneous and collaborative verbal play with me. For each form of collaboration and increased focus on our work, however, there seemed to be a corresponding resistance (Schafer, 1983; Weinshel, 1984); for example, first she observed feelings of opposition (feeling reluctant, wanting to halt and put the brakes on), and then she observed how she talked about guilt but did not feel anything. The sequence of resistances shifted from a transference resistance to a superego resistance. Even as she was taking and setting aside her own ideas and feelings, however, she was also getting to know the nature of her resistances. These self-observations led to another, a concrete depiction of her oppositional feelings: "There's a pressure I feel squeezing on either side of my head like a vise being screwed."

Free association at its best may be assisted by a playfulness that is unencumbered by neurotic compromise (Battin, 1993). This quality may not only support analytic work but may also become, paradoxically, a goal of the work. As we have seen, characteristics of Mrs. A's discourse resemble various forms of play. When she becomes anxious, her freedom of association becomes constricted and her affect isolated in the manner of a child who retreats from her role play to a board game with rules only to find that the rules themselves become the object of aggression when they do not conform to the child's desires. Interpretation frees the child to play freely again. Similarly, when Mrs. A's defenses are addressed and modified, her verbal play expands again, and latent material emerges with more conviction. She returns to the next session elaborating on the material of the day before like a child dramatizing an increasingly complex story that she builds day after day.

Excerpts from Session C (three sessions later)
Mrs. A began: "I'm feeling low. I guess it has to do with taking my son to visit colleges and seeing kids so clear about what they want to do and who they are and I just feel like such a mess—feeling my life is in such opposition to that." She described her son's wanting to do some of the driving. Her envy of him disturbed her but was not yet connected to her desire to interfere with his driving. She explained that he had been doing very well at his practice driving and was very competent and successful at his endeavors, yet she felt a great deal of trepidation about letting him drive. She feared he would crash into another car. "There's something about the forces of what I represent—which is imminent disaster. [crying] I feel it everywhere."

I brought Mrs. A's attention to her defensive generalizing ("forces of . . . disaster . . . everywhere"), and she detailed thoughts about her daughter, who had stayed home to play in a soccer game. When the coach told Mrs. A that her daughter probably would not keep up with the team too much longer, her daughter took the warning in stride and was satisfied to play anyway. Mrs. A, however, reported, "I have this doom feeling—her whole life is in jeopardy, and I don't have the parenting skills to help her." When I highlighted the discrepancy between her experience of what the coach said and her daughter's attitude, her thoughts turned to her brother, who "didn't have the skills to survive." A repetitive sequence of thoughts from her children to her brother were noted and linked. Fears about disasters for her children were connected to thoughts of her brother's death and her feelings of responsibility for it.

"I feel so responsible for every single thing that goes around except that one comes and seems out of reach," she said. "I see it and it slips away. Over the weekend, looking at these kids, I felt jealousy. I thought, 'He'll [her son] get to do it [go to a private school] and I didn't.' That little bit of jealousy felt so bad. I felt like a horrible person. How could you not want someone you love to have something even though it's something you didn't have? I can't handle even little bits of feeling jealous of my brother—or envy. It's okay if the other person has it; you just want it too, but that wasn't what went on in my family. They said, 'There's only money for one.' Seemed unfair. Without him, I would've been the one."

After I noted Mrs. A's guilt-laden wishes, there was an unusual silence, and then she said, "Every time I get close to feeling it [pauses], there's so much thinking that goes on. There are voices—you know if he hadn't been there—arguing. They still would've thought what they thought about me because I was a girl. [pause] There's some kind of desire to be shouting, 'Well, what does everybody want from me?' If I do have the guilt and I did have the wish—so I had it—what's the big deal? "

We began to discuss her belief that wishes come true. Curious about her omnipotent thinking, she became more self-observant: "It wasn't just his dying but all along. When I was wishing I'd be the one going to private school, I thought he was the wrong one to send. My wish didn't come true that they'd focus on me—after he died, they got more focused on him."

Discussion: In this session interventions directed to Mrs. A's omnipotent thinking, catastrophic fantasies, and guilt in relation to her brother brought new aspects of her envy to light. When she displaced envy of her brother on to her children, envious admiration of her son contrasted with disparagement of her daughter. Feelings about being female started to coalesce for future exploration.

In the session that followed, Mrs. A discussed the intensity of her feelings. While she felt herself wanting to back away, she also felt she was getting "closer and closer to what bothers me." Looking at a picture of herself and her brother sitting together, she described herself like a motionless statue with her legs together and described him with his legs open, taking up her space. She compared his risk taking and rebelliousness with her compliance. She described herself as "flawed . . . lacking something . . . a piece missing."

Like those of a child immersed in a nighttime fantasy or a scary story, Mrs. A's imaginary fantasies took on frighteningly real qualities. Her magical thinking illustrated this well. The paradox for the analyst is how to enter into the fantasy to forestall its interruption, all the while sensitizing the patient to make-believe notions that distort reality. The very fantasy world the analyst needs to enter, to become privy to and an integral part of, she also needs to disturb. Furthermore, what may bring the patient—child or adult—into treatment are difficulties in conceiving of his or her pretend world as make-believe. Consequently, the patient's cooperation in treatment, as we readily see with Mrs. A, at times may be illusive. Isolation of affect and intellectualization are mirages for a treatment alliance and collaborative play. A question for technique becomes how to utilize resistance in the service of therapeutic change.

Mrs. A had difficulty with verbal play when she went back and forth between knowing and not-knowing the difference between wish and reality, past and present. In session A, she was not clear about the pretend aspect of her fantasies. She felt like a cancer patient ("Yeah. I was living that life."). Her fantasies did not offer relief or support conflict resolution. In session B, ideas about envying her baby brother and her readiness to blame her parents were intellectualized attempts to remove herself from the intensity of what she was feeling in the present ("I don't remember wanting him to die. I can hear some kind of possibility in a two-year-old kind of way . . . make this baby go away . . . I can see that, but it doesn't feel that way.") In session C, it became increasingly evident that her fantasies about her brother in the past were being lived out in the present. Ironically, instead of using thinking to clarify her reality, she used thinking as a defense: "Every time I get close to feeling it, there's so much thinking that goes on." Her tenacious, haranguing guilt was close to the surface. She was reliving, in the present with her son, the conflict she had experienced with her brother. As children do in their play, Mrs. A attempted to resolve conflict by distancing herself from her primary relationships through displacement of time and person. With intense guilt, she recalled past hostile wishes toward her son as a newborn and experienced present-day envy toward him as a college-age adolescent more readily than she felt such wishes toward her deceased brother. By addressing her surface resistance to these feelings toward her children (envy of her son and devaluation of her daughter), she became aware of these feelings toward her brother.

A fantasy (to be rid of her brother) that may have provided some temporary, wish-fulfilling relief from intense childhood envy lived on in the present with the consequence of nearly constant superego anxiety. Unconscious guilt interfered with her sense of reality and her capacity to make realistic appraisals. The more she approached triggers to this guilt, the more her free associations were obstructed (Kris, 1982). When the pretend aspect of her fantasy life was lost, the adaptive value of "trial thoughts and actions which belong to the area of play" (Neubauer, 1987, p. 5) were also lost. Fantasy was no longer consoling or in the service of mastery; it was disturbing. When I addressed her belief that wishes come true, realization of the omnipotence of her thinking opened the way for Mrs. A to comprehend guilt-laden envy of her son, which subsequently enabled her to approach her envy of her brother.

My technical approach with Mrs. A in the first three sessions presented was guided by her resistance. My subjective experiences of disequilibrium corresponded with her defensive modes of presentation. For example, Mrs. A's destructive images ("I have this doom feeling—her whole life is in jeopardy"), against the background of her bland, measured speech, jarred me. Her resistance to the emotions that corresponded to her words became a beacon that signaled my interventions. When I commented at the surface about the contradiction between her feelings of doom and her daughter's continued pleasure in the game, she became aware of this discrepancy, which then reminded her of the unusual sense of responsibility she felt for her brother. While the focus remained on her brother, I silently remained in touch with this strange depreciation of her actually vibrant, bright, and adaptive daughter. I suspected that her depreca-tion was a surface clue to a fantasy that would be elaborated in the future.

The analogy to play offers a guide to distinguishing actual from illusory collaboration with the analytic method. Mrs. A's vivid language and verbosity resembled the engaging activity of a child who appears to be freely playing when in fact she is subtly goading the analyst to join her resistance with interesting but misleading play that slowly takes the observer away from the area of conflict. Despite Mrs. A's defensive organization, however, there were many cues to unconscious fantasies disturbing her equilibrium. No detail was without meaning even when isolated. A technical task was to find which sequence of ideas seemed closest to an affective surface.

My judgment about our effectiveness was based on the expanding freedom of Mrs. A's verbal play, which permitted a deepening expression of her conflicts. When her verbiage became diffuse and generalized ("the forces I represent," session C), tempting me to work too hard to find meaning in her words, I was cued in to what Winnicott (1971) referred to as defensive "organized nonsense" (p. 56). Real analytic play, like an effective joke, "liberates the nonsense" (Freud, 1905, p. 31). My task at those times was to stay closely attuned to her *playing*, to the form, not to the content of her associations.

Just as empathic, playful parents mediate the pace with which their children come to terms with reality (Moran, 1987), analysts mediate their patients' expressions of unconscious fantasies. When analysts attempt to bypass the analytic surface, like parents who demand that fantasies become more realistic, analytic play is interrupted, defenses are bolstered, and the very efforts to reach too quickly to latent material hinder its unfolding.

For Mrs. A, resistance interpretations highlighted incongruities between her words and her emotions. However, I did not hold too strictly to a microanalysis of defense that could have limited my ability to observe and experience the larger defensive organization (Joseph, 1981) and the sequential flow of latent material (Arlow, 1987). I not only did not want to limit my understanding, I also did not want to interrupt the patient too frequently with defense interpretations that could heighten intellectualizing tendencies or inadvertently obstruct her capacity for playful, imaginative self-observation (Josephs, 1997). Mrs. A was incrementally internalizing various approaches to the surface of her material. She began to report "familiar surface distur-bances" (Levy and Inderbitzen, 1990) in her self-analysis between sessions. She became better able to recognize how her mind was working ("Here I've come to you for help in getting to my feelings, and I get like I don't want to") and her capacity to participate in analytic playing was enhanced. She more easily took note of "surface signs" (Paniagua, 1991, p. 681) of deeper material on her own.

In one more session, Mrs. A's relative freedom of association and deepening capacity to express derivatives of unfolding unconscious fantasies confirmed my choice of "workable surfaces" (Paniagua, 1991, p. 680) within the analytic space (Viderman, 1974; Poland, 1992).

Excerpts from Session D (four sessions later)
Mrs. A began the session: "The stuff about my hair is making me crazy again. I have flashes of words saying to me maybe I'll never be able to relax about my physical being. I went to a talk about breast cancer. The room was filled with women. Two doctors spoke about progress they'd had with the disease. I was aware of how agitated I was. I presumed all the women had the disease or like me were touched by it in some way. I found myself looking at other women's hair wishing I had hair like that. I thought I was going into that train of thought

for a reason—that glimmer did help—but what petrifies me is being exposed—that each day I'm closer to being exposed. [long pause]"

Mrs. A had drawn my attention to her agitation as well as to her attempt to be self-observant by noting her train of thinking. It was hard for her to sustain self-reflection when she felt this way. This attempt to do so, however, contrasted sharply with the nonreflective immersion in fantasy ("living this life of a cancer patient") reported in session A. Her agitation was connected to a fantasy of being damaged. When she spoke of a fear of "being exposed" and then paused for the first time that morning, both this image of exposure and the subsequent interruption of associations by silence captured my interest. It was a moment of discontinuity in her narration that seemed to be an incomplete communication (Boesky, 1993, p. 186) at the surface. I remarked, "Exposed?" She continued, "That my hair is getting thinner and closer to having bald places, that I won't be able to pretend I'm normal. It's not even looking ugly anymore that bothers me. I used to think that's what it was—that I couldn't go out not looking good. It's been so many months like that. I started to get used to it. I don't need to look pretty, but I can't stand the idea of looking like a freak—not normal."

I knew she could detail this torment and become absorbed in talking, but she was obfuscating. She was speaking affectively when she explained she had a "glimmer" of her train of thought. This comment was directed to me and to our analytic relationship. She was telling me that my work with her had been affecting her, that she was trying to carry it out in my absence, but she could not sustain an analytic attitude at the meeting just as she could not sustain it in the session. She was trying to hold on to her "glimmer" of the make-believe aspect of her emerging fantasy. This blurring of reality was a clue to surface material, but I was unsure of how to make it workable (Paniagua, 1991). The unexpected moment to intervene came when she denied the obvious. It was then that I chose to speak. I addressed the resistance underlying her overt distress by interpreting the defense of negation: "You said, 'I *don't* need to look pretty.' That's odd to say given these constant worries."

Mrs. A responded, "It's my wish since I was 10 or so. I'd feel attractive, but having my hair groomed was a large part of it. It is odd that, if we were going out to dinner and I'd groomed my hair, it would bother me if it was frizzy, out of shape. If I didn't fear my hair falling out . . . every time I look at my shoulders—it's the same old issue. My hair being affected by rain was just a milder degree of being freakish. I got a compliment on my hair the other night. I said, 'Really? I feel like a bag lady.' I feel like my hair is a disheveled mess and everything about me is. There was a picture in the paper of a bag lady watching two society type ladies. [cries] I think that's how I always felt, on the inside, and now I feel it on the outside also. All those years I felt I was a step away from looking like that . . . it's pretty painful. It's looking like a piece of garbage—dirty and crumbled up. [crying] Like bag ladies live in piles of garbage. There must be something to that because I've been cleaning my house. I'm not famous for cleaning. I've been cleaning closets, doing laundry, wiping counters like I've never done before. It's something I've felt guilty for and can do something about, but I feel frantic about it—I've gotten away from it because I don't know a limit. If I clean one closet, I say there's another to do."

Mrs. A's frantic tone had shifted qualitatively. The space between us had a more textured, sensitive quality. Her frequent isolation of affect was absent. As she was talking, I was silently reminded of how I'd been noticing that she'd been coming to sessions looking unkempt in an unappealing, even vaguely unclean kind of way. From dismal clothes to absent makeup and unstyled hair, she was noticeably unadorned. This enactment was now being verbalized. My recall of her visual presentation supported the interventions that followed. I commented that she turned from her body to her house.

"It's not that far a turn," she said. "My body is my house for me. The feeling I get when my house is in order is pleasing and attractive. It really is deep. This process of decorating goes on and on. My husband gets aggravated about it being done. The pleasure afterwards doesn't seem to be like it is for me. I get pleasure on a visceral level. That's the same thing with my appearance. It has always bothered me—always been important that people shouldn't see this mess. For years I haven't made my bed unless people were coming over. But I began to the past few years. When I go to bed I really like it made. Seems like such a small thing to be talking about, but it took me years to ask what is important to me. When a bed is messy and rumpled up . . . it seems uninviting. Sounds like something sexual about the bed, but I think, like when you're on vacation, and the maid does the bed. Then your house is the bedroom—the first thing you see when you open the door."

Mrs. A's associations had become flexible and richer. I was experiencing a dynamic, metaphoric surface (Poland, 1992). I noted, "Your house is your body." "In disarray," she answered. "My body definitely feels in disarray. I'm far from feeling pleased about my body. I think about my skin and hair. I've never obsessed about the size of my breasts. I try to keep my weight okay. But I feel in disarray."

Discussion: Minimal interventions following an important interpretation that challenged her negation brought forth, through the use of a metaphor, derivatives of an unconscious fantasy (Arlow, 1979b) about being female. My memory of Mrs. A's depreciation of her vibrant daughter came to me as an expression of this self-representation. The slowly encroaching enactment of her messy appearance was a nonverbal surface that accompanied the verbal one within the "interactive analytic context" (Poland, 1992, p. 384). A silently portrayed fantasy about her female self-representation that could have stayed hidden in a fog of words found an entrance into the analytic space. I silently experienced and understood this enactment, not as an obstacle but as an overdetermined analytic surface, a transference phenomenon that would be explored in a timely manner. It complemented my understanding of her verbal associations.

Through her house-body metaphor, Mrs. A became able to play. She entered a mental space where she could more freely engage in meaningful, trial thinking (Solnit, 1993; Sodre, 1994). Her painful perception of her body as messy and flawed, first mentioned when comparing herself with her son (session C) and again when she was looking at a picture of herself and her brother (discussion of session C), was more fully communicated. To enable the play to develop further, I needed to respond to it and to do so in an imaginative way that would show my understanding without taking it over (Meares, 1993). The analyst's remarks are empathic when they "tend to be associative, . . . with feeling and abbreviated. They should not break up the metaphoric play" (p. 158) but somehow respond to the patient's inner life as it is represented by her metaphor. I both observed and took part in this play. A transformation occurred in which Mrs. A was able to turn from an agitated state of feeling "freakish" to a playful state of mind in which she could creatively envision a disheveled house and messy, rumpled up bed as representations of her body. This was a moving illustration of oscillating between symbol and symbolized in an imaginative and self-reflective way, an example of spontaneous, verbal free associations where words and affect resonate together.

Conclusions

Mrs. A came to treatment because she felt bound by her psychological situation. She was unable to utilize opportunities around her. She could not mobilize her otherwise excellent ego capacities to achieve her goals and to experience herself as having value. Creatively constricted and preoccupied with her appearance, she felt unable to grow and change on her own and sought analytic help to mediate the battling psychic forces within her. Expanding analytic play was particularly relevant to Mrs. A's obsessive defensive organization and overarching superego. Specifically attending to the surface maximized analytic play and the creation of an analytic play space where the interpretation of symbolic communication became possible. Various orientations to the surface were identified which emphasized both the content of moment-to-moment expressions of surface phenomena and the form of her defensive organization.

In the opening of this chapter, I questioned whether both metaphoric constructs—analytic surface and analytic space—could be used to organize psychoanalytic data. I believe so. The surface refers to what is present on the patient's mind to which each analytic participant attends. Unlike Freud's (1916–17) conception of an analysis carried out solely by the observing analyst's evenly hovering attention upon the freely associating, "unreflecting" (p. 287) patient, the focus in the material presented was on bringing the analysand into a process of self-reflective observation. The surface is not only what the analyst chooses to focus on, but also what the patient can attend to and needs a response to in order to move her analytic play forward. When the analyst questions a surface, the patient's reaction to the question and, sometimes, to the questioner becomes part of what is studied (Boesky, 1993). The surface "comes alive in the immediacy of the analytic moment" (Poland, 1992, p. 399) in the context of the analytic space. Thus, the concept of space refers to the intermediate region between reality and fantasy, the site of analytic play, and to "the affective and communicative dyadic context of the analytic process" (p. 381).

The construct of analytic space expands many of Freud's concepts, including the analytic surface, transference, and resistance. While Freud advised both analyst and analysand to attend to the surface, he did not entertain an idea of dual participation in observing and interpreting. However, he recognized the intermediate region in which both participants worked, a region where transference phenomena could be created and played out. In this way, transference can be viewed both as a resistance and as a transitional space between reality and fantasy. Transference, from this dual perspective, was exemplified by Mrs. A's enactment, which paved the way for subsequent verbalization of her female self-representation. The use of the term analytic space (Winnicott, 1971; Viderman, 1974; Ogden, 1985) captures both views of transference within the analytic situation.

Freud's orientation to the surface shifted from the topographic conception of consciousness (1901) to an analysis of unconscious resistance (1914). In the context of the construct of the analytic space, surface resistances can be understood in a more meaningful way. Interpretation of resistance has a quality of play that bridges the interactive and the intrapsychic (Loewald, 1980) in the service of structural change. Resistance is experienced by analysand and analyst.

Resonating affectively for both, it guides them to understandings that might otherwise go undetected. While resistance appears "to impede [the] informational exchange both intrapsychically and to the analyst" (Lichtenberg and Galler, 1987, p, 74), it may actually signal the potential for a more informative exchange. The construct of an analytic space provides a context for this interchange.

I have a discussed a way to formulate the process by which therapeutic action occurs: the analyst brings the analysand from a state of not being able to play into a state of being able to play. This process was illustrated by the shift in the patient's obsessive defensive organization, observed in the first session, in which there was a near absence of a "state of mind required for playing" (Ogden, 1985, p. 130) to a liberated process of free association by the last session in which such a state was present. Interventions were geared to enabling Mrs. A to play in a therapeutic and creative way. She became more able to move from "subjective creator to objective audience" like an artist of the mind crossing those bridges back and forth (Greenacre, 1959, p. 79), observing and understanding her mental activity. In a corresponding way, I engaged in this creative and developmental process of introspection along with the spontaneity and freedom of thought, characteristic of analytic play.

Modification of Mrs. A's defensive mental activity gave way to "that space between symbol and symbolized, mediated by an interpreting self" (Ogden, 1985, p.133). Her creation of her house-body metaphor—her symbol, what it symbolized, and a sense of herself as a creator of meanings standing apart from what she is thinking about—occurred in the analytic play space (Ogden, 1985). First, through her nonverbal enactment (her messy appearance) and then, through her metaphor, she was able to communicate what she had been unable to express clearly. An increased potential for more complex understanding emanated from this psychoanalytic process.

While I have documented clinical work during the first year of treatment, I suggest that there is a fluctuating progressive–regressive capacity for analytic play that occurs throughout an analysis as analyst and analysand discover and rediscover multiple workable surfaces. I hope to have stimulated an interest in these constructs so that others will investigate their usefulness in exploring the therapeutic action of psychoanalysis with their patients.

References

Arlow, J. (1979a), The genesis of intepretation. *J. Amer. Psychoanal. Assn.*, Suppl., 27:193–206.

———— (1979b), Metaphor and the psychoanalytic situation. *Psychoanal. Quart.*, 48:363–385.

———— (1982), Problems of the superego concept, *The Psychoanalytic Study of the Child*, 37:229–244. New Haven, CT: Yale University Press.

———— (1987), The dynamics of interpretation. *Psychoanal. Quart.*, 56:68–108.

Battin, D. (1993), To play or not to play. In: *The Many Meanings of Play*, ed. A. J. Solnit, D. J. Cohen & P. B. Neubauer. New Haven, CT: Yale University Press, pp. 57–74.

Boesky, D. (1993), Scientific proceedings—Panel Reports: The analytic surface. Chair, L. B. Inderbitzin & Reporter, B. J. Seelig. *J. Amer. Psychoanal. Assn.*, 41:179–189.

Busch, F. (1997), Understanding the patient's use of the method of free association: An ego psychological approach. *J. Amer. Psychoanal. Assn.*, 45:407–423.

Freud, S. (1900), The interpretation of dreams. *Standard Edition*, 4 & 5. London: Hogarth Press, 1953.

———— (1901), A case of hysteria. *Standard Edition*, 7:1–122. London: Hogarth Press, 1953.

———— (1905), Jokes and their relation to the unconscious. *Standard Edition*, 8. London: Hogarth Press, 1960.

———— (1908), Creative writers and daydreaming. *Standard Edition*, 9:143–153. London: Hogarth Press, 1959.

———— (1912), Recommendations to physicians practicing psycho-analysis. *Standard Edition*, 7:109–144 London: Hogarth Press, 1958.

———— (1913), On beginning the treatment. *Standard Edition*, 7:121–144. London: Hogarth Press, 1958.

———— (1914), Remembering, repeating and working-through. *Standard Edition*, 12:145–156. London: Hogarth Press, 1958.

———— (1916–17), Resistance and repression. *Standard Edition*, 16:286–302. London: Hogarth Press, 1963.

Gray, P. (1986), On helping analysands observe intrapsychic activity. In: *Psychoanalysis: The Science of Mental Conflict*, ed. A. D. Richards & M. S. Willick. Hillsdale, NJ: The Analytic Press, pp. 245–262.

———— (1990), The nature of therapeutic action in psychoanalysis. *J. Amer. Psychoanal. Assn.*, 38:1083–1097.

Greenacre, P. (1959), Play in relation to creative imagination. *The Psychoanalytic Study of the Child*, 14:61–80. New York: International Universities Press.

Hollman, L. S. M. (1997), Developmental considerations in female latency: A discussion of kidnapping fantasies in nine-year-old girls. *The Psychoanalytic Study of the Child*, 52:89–117. New Haven, CT: Yale University Press.

Jacobs, T. J. (1991), *The Use of the Self*. Madison, CT: International Universities Press.

———— (1997), Response to the contributors to "Essays inspired by Theodore Jacobs's *The Use of the Self.*" *Psychoanal. Inq.*, 17:108–119.

Joseph, B. (1981), Defence mechanisms and phantasy in the psychoanalytical process. *Bull. Eur. Psychoanal. Fed.*, 17:11–24.

———— (1983), On understanding and not understanding: some technical issues. *Internat. J. Psycho-Anal.*, 64:291–298.

Josephs, L. (1997), The view from the tip of the iceberg. *J. Amer. Psychoanal. Assn.*, 45:425–463.

Kestenberg, J. S. (1966), Rhythm and organization in obsessive-compulsive development. *Internat. J. Psycho-Anal.*, 47:151–159.

Kris, A. O. (1982), *Free Association*. New Haven, CT: Yale University Press.

———— (1990), The analyst's stance and the method of free association. *The Psychoanalytic Study of the Child*, 45:25–41. New Haven, CT: Yale University Press.

Levy, S. T. & Inderbitzin, L. B. (1990), The analytic surface and the theory of technique. *J. Amer. Psychoanal. Assn.,* 38:371–391.

Lichtenberg, J. D. & Galler, F. B. (1987), The fundamental rule: A study of current usage. *J. Amer. Psychoanal. Assn.,* 35:47–76.

Loewald, H. W. (1979), Reflections on the psychoanalytic process and its therapeutic potential. *The Psychoanalytic Study of the Child,* 34:155–167. New Haven, CT: Yale University Pres..

Lowenstein, R. (1951), The problem of interpretation. *Psychoanal. Quart.,* 20:1–14.

Meares, R. (1993), *The Metaphor of Play,* Northvale, NJ: Aronson.

Moran, G. S. (1987), Some functions of play and playfulness: A developmental perspective. *The Psychoanalytic Study of the Child,* 42:11–29. New Haven, CT: Yale University Press.

Neubauer, P. B. (1987), The many meanings of play. *The Psychoanalytic Study of the Child,* 42:3–9. New Haven, CT: Yale University Press.

——— (1993), Playing: Technical implications. In: *The Many Meanings of Play,* ed. A. J. Solnit, D. J. Cohen & P. B. Neubauer. New Haven, CT: Yale University Press, pp. 44–53.

Ogden, T. H. (1985), On potential space. *Internat. J. Psycho-Anal.,* 66:129–141.

Paniagua, C. (1991), Patient's surface, clinical surface, and workable surface. *J. Amer. Psychoanal. Assn.,* 39:669–685.

Peller, L. E. (1954), Libidinal phases, ego development, and play. *The Psychoanalytic Study of the Child,* 9:178–198. New York: International Universities Press.

Plaut, E. A. (1979), Play and adaptation. *The Psychoanalytic Study of the Child,* 34:217–232. New Haven, CT: Yale University Press.

Poland, W. S. (1992), From analytic surface to analytic space. *J. Amer. Psychoanal. Assn.,* 40:381–404.

Sanville, J. (1991), *The Playground of Psychoanalytic Therapy.* Hillsdale, NJ: The Analytic Press.

Schafer, R. (1983), *The Analytic Attitude.* New York: Basic Books.

Sodre, I. (1994), Obsessional certainty versus obsessional doubt: From two to three. *Psychoanal. Inq.,* 14:379–392.

Solnit, A. J. (1987), A psychoanalytic view of play. *The Psychoanalytic Study of the Child,* 42:205–219. New Haven, CT: Yale University Press.

——— (1993), From play to playfulness in children and adults. In: *The Many Meanings of Play,* ed. A. J. Solnit, D. J. Cohen & P. B. Neubauer. New Haven, CT: Yale University Press, pp. 29–43.

Viderman, S. (1974), Interpretation in the analytical space. *Internat. Rev. Psycho-Anal.,* 1:467–480.

Waelder, R. (1932), The psychoanalytic theory of play. In: *Psychoanalysis,* ed. S. A. Guttman. New York: International Universities Press, 1976, pp. 84–100.

Weinshel, E. M. (1984), Some observations on the psychoanalytic process. *Psychoanal. Quart.,* 53:63–92.

Winnicott, D. W. (1971), *Playing and Reality.* New York: Basic Books.

Chapter 5

∞

A Woman of Her Time (Or Was She?)

Samoan R. Barish

"To reconsider one's life, seeing it suddenly in a new formation, may be a tremor worth undergoing in one's later years"—Carolyn Heilbrun (1997)

This is the story of an older woman's life and of the creative use that she made of her analysis. She was able to draw on and use her analysis as a playground for reviewing seven decades of her life, while simultaneously recasting her present life.

My reasons for writing about her life and our years of work together are numerous. First, more than 30 years after the beginning of the women's movement, most of us know that so much remains the same. Although Ms. P, my patient, grew up in another era, I see young women of today struggling with similar conflicts.

In working with Ms. P, and in helping her to expand her restricted life, I was forced to grapple with my own self-imposed restrictions. In many ways, I am telling this story both from the point of view of being a witness and from that of being a participant.

A second reason I have for telling this story is that it counteracts to some degree the ageism and sexism of our culture towards older women, and perhaps even deep in our unconscious feelings about the hated and feared "old woman" (e.g., the "wicked old witch"). We know that, in the past, psychoanalysis held that older people were "unanalyzable." Here I add my voice to those of many others in recent years—for example, Simburg (1985) and Settlage (1996)—that have debunked these earlier, misbegotten views.

Finally, in recounting this story, I am in effect delivering it for Ms. P to the outside world. This was something she had great difficulty doing herself and now may not have the time left to do. By writing and reflecting on her life and her analysis with me, I hope it will also illuminate some aspects of the readers' lives and clinical work.

"Essentially, Dave, a person consists of memories."—Muriel Spark (1997)

Ms. P was born in 1920, one year after women won the right to vote and several months after the 19th Amendment was ratified. Her mother described the occasion of her birth with an apocryphal story: directly outside the hospital window, a black chorus was singing with great passion, "Your Star Will Rise." Clearly, her mother was drawing the conclusion that her daughter was destined for greatness!

The life of Ms. P, a woman "of age," demands to be understood within a psychosocial context since internal and external forces are always at play in a continual dynamic dialectic from conception to death. There is a myriad of interactive factors that affect our developing selves and contribute to determining who we become.

The patient's relationship with her mother, in tandem with the *Zeitgeist* of the time's rigidly constructed views of gender, conspired to derail her own natural spontaneous gestures toward genuine self-expression and expansiveness.

Her gender affected her view and expectations of herself throughout the stages of her life. Underpinning this chapter is my belief that gender is socially constructed. As Jane Flax (1990) notes, "Gender now appears to be a powerful and virtually all-pervasive force in the organization of many societies, in ways of thinking, and in the constitution of each person, male and female" (pp. 21–22).

Ms. P had impressive access to her rich inner world and her acute memory and interest in her past, which led to a review of her life. This life review was filled with exquisite renderings of visual detail, facts, events and feelings.

The major thrust of her/our archeological digs was not the recovery of repressed memory, but, rather, the repeated process of re-remembering past experiences with an ever-increasing range of affects and with an ever-shifting constellation of meanings that could be imputed to these experiences. She developed different perspectives of these events, as if looking at them through a multifaceted prism, with greater depth, subtlety, and coloration.

As Cohler and Freeman (1993) remind us, "Remembered events change in meaning over time, as a function both of place in the life course and the context of retelling. . . . The meaning of experience can be reconstituted on the basis of subsequent ones and the present is always coequal in determining the experience of the past" (pp. 132–133).

Indeed, part of the present was our own unique dyad and the analytic ambiance that flowed from it as a result of our intersecting subjectivities (Stolorow, Brandchaft, and Atwood, 1987). Thus, Ms. P and I were each involved in coconstructing different versions of her life history. The nature of the process she went through, in deconstructing and then reconstructing and reassembling internal and external elements of her life, held high interest for each of us and was a major characteristic of our intersubjectivity.

Patient's Background

The following is a much-condensed version of Ms. P's history and background, filtered through the overarching determining power of gender. It is difficult, however, to talk about gender even though it is fundamental to everyone's life experience, because, paradoxically, it is both prominent and elusive at the same time. In today's world, there is a loosening of the constriction of gender, compared with Ms. P's era, when there was a strict binary division. Ms. P's family lived in a staid, upper-class, conservative suburban community. Her family and community quite rigidly set down deportment, etiquette, and proper social behavior for each of the genders. Foisted upon her was a clear and unchanging view of what was expected of a girl when she grew up. Integrating any aspects of the masculine appeared to be unthinkable and entrapped in conflict. In Ms. P's words, "All my life I've lived in the shadow or been influenced by men. I've had painful feelings of the very real power of men. It's the position of choice and decision, which as I see it, men alone have had." Jane Flax (1990) tells us that, "Every culture constructs ideas about gender . . . Gender partially structures how each person experiences and expresses his or her self . . ." (p. 26).

Ms. P spent her earliest years living in the same house in a community in the Northwest. Following her mother's discovery of her father's infidelity, her parents abruptly separated when she was five years old. Her mother, frantic and agitated, took Ms. P and her sister on a tumultuous trip around the country. Ms. P remembers clinging to her mother in strange beds and towns. Then, news came from her father that he wanted to reunite, and the family joined him in the Southeast. Although they built a new home, life never went well for the family, and her parents divorced when Ms. P was 17 years old. The divorce left its lasting mark.

Her father was a distant man who had a long work commute and consequently spent much of his time away from the family. He held the special status of being the man and breadwinner in the family. Ms. P felt that he was well meaning, but that he did not understand her and became irritated with her for minor infractions of social rules. In many ways, her father could be characterized as being an absence in her life, rather than a presence. Surely she had little opportunity to identify with him (Benjamin, 1988, 1995).

Ms. P's mother, despite a rural background and less education than Ms. P's father, was intelligent and intellectually curious and also somewhat eccentric. Overall, she was a competent and resourceful woman, but lacked a nurturing side. Although regretting her divorce, she lived quite self-sufficiently for the rest of her life. She was a very harsh woman who could be unforgiving, as well as judgmental. These characteristics of her mother contributed to Ms. P's fear that she would incur her mother's wrath and would be rejected and left unable to fend for herself in the world.

Ms. P also had an older sister with whom she was not close. Apparently, the sister had an undiagnosed breakdown as a senior in high school and subsequently became markedly withdrawn. She did go on to marry and have a family, but, despite years of therapy, she remained depressed and made several suicide attempts.

While she was growing up, Ms. P's sphere encompassed her mother, and in many ways this eclipsed all else. Within this shared sphere, there was a sense of her mother's grand expectation and ownership of her. Her mother disregarded her daughter's experience and self-image. Instead she insisted on seeing her daughter as she, the mother, wished her to be.

Ms. P's struggles to separate from her mother and her difficulties stepping out on her own were many. She could not stay away at college and returned to her mother after one semester. Several years later she left home determined to find her "fame and fortune" but was unable to support herself, a difficulty she had throughout her life.

Ms. P met and married a man who seemed urbane and made a fairly good living. She became increasingly unhappy in the marriage and wanted to leave but was too frightened because she felt she could not support herself and their son. Ms. P entered therapy early in the marriage and, after about six years, her former therapist encouraged her to leave her husband. The therapist helped her through this whole period and even suggested a new man for her.

Feeling liberated following the divorce from her first husband and prior to remarrying, Ms. P used much of the settlement money to take an extended trip. She stayed away longer than planned and, as a result, lost custody of her son to her ex-husband. This was a crushing blow. After some time, she married the man her therapist had recommended, and they went on to have two children. The couple has remained quite comfortably married through the years.

During this lengthy treatment, many important life events occurred. By their very nature, they entered into the analysis and became experiences we shared. Among the key events were the death of her 94-year-old mother, notable birthdays (65th, 70th, and 75th), as well as her 40th wedding anniversary and the marriages of her two children, who went on to have children of their own. During her treatment, Ms. P had pneumonia and recovered, broke an arm and recovered, and, finally, broke her hip and decided, during a long recuperative period, to end her treatment.

Psychoanalytic Theory

In psychoanalysis, we have no grand, unified theory. Rather, we have a multiplicity of theories, from which we must choose those we feel are the most relevant to our work, to us, and to our patients. How we use our theories and whether we become their masters or their servants is a matter of ongoing interest to me, but is beyond the scope of this chapter (Barish and Vida, 1998). In Ms. P's treatment, I have drawn on a number of contemporary theories such as self psychology, feminist perspectives, intersubjectivity, and relational. In addition, my work has been informed by object relations theories, infant development, and attachment theory.

All the theories that I have called on in my work with Ms. P are imbued with the spirits of Ferenczi (Dupont, 1988) and Winnicott (1965, 1971). Ferenczi was a courageous analyst who believed that the analyst should be a real object. He recommended that the analyst be "sincere" with patients and receive them with "tenderness," in order to help the patients face the terrors and pain of the past. Further, his belief that all our therapeutic work is experimental in nature goes some distance toward buttressing my confidence when it is faltering. Many of Winnicott's (1965, 1971) ideas and attitudes about development and treatment have direct relevance to my understanding of Ms. P and to the atmosphere and style of our clinical work. His use and appreciation of the omnipresence of paradox helps orient me in my work. Further, his recognition of the importance of the holding environment and the pernicious effect of impingement, as well as his notions about intermediate space and therapy as a safe playground, serve as invaluable guidelines for me.

The latter is a notion that Jean Sanville (1991) has richly elaborated on. It has served as a beacon that has lit the playground for Ms. P and me. In addition, Kohut's (1971) early views of the grandiose realm of the self, the deficits that occur owing to faulty mirroring, and the lack of a sense of one's right to ambition have contributed to my understanding of Ms. P.

The intersubjective perspective of Stolorow et al. (1987, 1994) inform much of my theoretical base. Stolorow and Atwood (1992) direct our attention to the "intrinsic imbededness of self experience in intersubjective fields" (p. 10). They emphasize the mutual, reciprocal influence that necessarily occurs between the child and his or her caretakers, as well as between the analyst and patient. Accordingly, they view the analytic situation as a coming together of the unique subjectivities of each of the two parties.

Invariant principles arise as a result of repeated patterns of intersubjective transactions. The therapeutic situation provides the unique opportunity for an in-depth exploration of the patient's unconscious organizing principles as they manifest themselves in the transference and are co-created with the analyst.

Stolorow et al. (1987) describe two basic dimensions of transference; namely, the selfobject pole of the transference and the repetitive pole. The selfobject pole encompasses the patient's deep, unmet longings for necessary developmental experiences that were lacking or fundamentally faulty. This transference functions as a holding environment setting the context for "reinstating developmental processes" (p. 44).

The other dimension of the transference, the repetitive pole, is the source of resistance and conflict, as the patient expects and dreads "a repetition with the analyst of early experiences of developmental failure" (Stolorow and Atwood, 1996, p. 185). These two dimensions of the transference are forever in flux, alternating between the foreground and background. They fluctuate according to the patient's experience of the analyst's attunement.

Brandchaft's (1994) work on pathological accommodation, which builds on some of Kohut's (1971) earlier formulations as well as on Stolorow and Atwood's (1998) work, contributed to my understanding of Ms. P's predicament. Brandchaft tells us that when the parent cannot accommodate to the age-appropriate needs of the child, the child, being more flexible, accommodates to the parent, thereby sacrificing his or her own developing self. The child embraces the parent's primitive organization, clinging to it tenaciously because it is the only cohesion the child knows. The child is in grave jeopardy should he or she attempt to reclaim ownership of himself or herself. Every move toward self-delineation threatens the bond on which survival depends. This is an impossible paradox. Ms. P had a repetitive childhood dream, which I will present shortly, where we see this paradox in bold relief. She cannot live with her mother without surrendering her self, but cannot survive without her mother for fear she will be thrown into terrifying space and unboundedness. Truly a Faustian bargain!

The Course of Analysis:
Initial Session and Early Phase of Treatment

We met more than 19 years ago. When she came into my consulting room, Ms. P, a tall, handsome woman, appeared almost regal in her bearing, and yet there was a curious adolescent awkwardness about her movements. Her face had a pleasant but anxious look. Her fastidious physical presentation suggested that appearance was very important to her. It was almost as if she were wearing a hat and carrying white gloves.

Although she appeared to be quite self-possessed, her anguish was palpable as she responded to my query about what had brought her in. She revealed to me a painful narcissistic blow she had experienced several months earlier. She said that she had taken what was a very big step (for her) a number of years ago by returning to school, an alternative school of architecture in a neighboring state. She and her small group of fellow students were informed that they lacked some prerequisites but were given suggestions as to how to fulfill these requirements over a span of years.

Although Ms. P graduated from the program, she never made up the prerequisites and therefore was unable to be licensed in her field. Gradually, she came to see that, despite some personal connections, she would have to meet the requirements. She could not, however, get herself to do this and continued to hope that she would get special treatment. Ms. P conveyed to me how utterly devastated she was when she finally realized that no exception would be made in her case. She said that she had become very "depressed" and had come to view the demands made on her as a "rejection." She was particularly upset to see her peers "pass me by." She never acknowledged how bad she felt about this situation. "I always put up a pleasant front," she explained.

In recounting other major events in her life, she told me about another traumatic event that had occurred some 25-odd years earlier. Her son from her first marriage, who was approximately 10 years old at the time, had chosen to live with his father during a custody hearing. Ms. P briefly related some of these details in a matter-of-fact manner. She informed me that she and her son always visited regularly and had pleasant relations. I sensed that this was an emotionally laden area, bearing further discussion. I made some comment to that effect, and she mildly, perhaps somewhat reluctantly, concurred.

Another matter that Ms. P revealed in our initial interview was that she had already had many years of analytic therapy. With the exception of one woman therapist much earlier on, all of her previous therapists had been men. Also, she said that she had never chosen her own therapist before and "wanted to see a woman who could be like a sister."

My initial impression centered on Ms. P's obvious psychological mindedness and her capacity for expressing herself. She appeared to be intelligent, somewhat intellectual, thoughtful, formal, and a shade distant. But she also seemed to be in a great deal of pain, and her deep sense of shame was evident. I wondered about what it meant that Ms. P had been in analytic treatment for such an extensive period of time. I understood that she felt that talking with another in therapy was a useful and even necessary process for her. Indeed, this was an important part of her life. I knew there would be much to explore around her expectations, needs, fears, and hopes as they pertained to treatment. I felt that we had made a good connection and that we could work well together. We agreed to meet two times a week with the possibility of increasing the frequency as we proceeded, which subsequently we did.

During our second session, Ms. P shared a dream she had had in the early hours of the morning after our initial session. In the dream, there is an ugly little baby at the beach. As the baby is being pulled up to walk, it becomes apparent that she has two extra legs. These legs are undeveloped and unused, yet the baby attempts to walk on these wobbly and unsteady vestigial limbs.

Together, we looked at the possible symbolic meaning of her decision to leave her former network of referrals and to see me. It felt to me that the use of her own initiative indicated a developmental step. Little did either of us realize at that point how threatening such steps away from her internalized mother were for her.

Perhaps the ugly baby in the dream represented both her fear that she was seen as being ugly by her mother (and by me) as well as changes in her view of herself if she discovered that she could "walk on her own two feet." Speculations notwithstanding, it seemed to me that her emotional legs were somewhat atrophied from lack of use, but they did exist and could become functional. I took this dream to be a positive indicator of her wishes and capacity to resume the growth that had been stunted and derailed.

Hoping to help Ms. P resume the road toward continued growth, we began to explore the precipitating trauma. Beginning to adopt a stance of sustained empathic inquiry (Stolorow et al., 1987), I conveyed my recognition of the enormous pain and humiliation she was feeling.

This seemed to help her become a bit more spontaneous. She said, "At least I can tell you, I feel so bad. I feel like I've been demoted." And I responded, "It seemed as if your very being and identity was wrapped up with your becoming an architect."

While we were talking about her making the transition to the couch, Ms. P talked about her "difficulties making physical changes." She then recalled an experience when she was 12 years old that appeared to be a replay of the event that brought her into treatment with me. This memory and her associations to it were to become touchstones in her analysis. It linked up innumerable events and their meanings throughout her life. We were to refer to this memory of her depleted self-state countless times during her analysis.

Ms. P remembered that the summer before she was to enter middle school the other girls in her clique developed faster, were preoccupied with their bodies, and became interested in boys. She was not ready and referred to this transition as "from jumping into the pool to diving in." She experienced herself as falling from grace as she saw her friends move into new areas that frightened her. She felt humiliated and began to retreat into a haughty isolation. This defensive retreat, with its underlying feelings of great shame, became an enduring characteristic throughout her life. In her own words, "I was toppled . . . this feeling of exclusion formed my identity." The one person she turned to for some solace was her mother, whose response was to tell her that the problem was simply that she was better than all the other girls. She remembers that she felt "flattered" by her mother's opinion but did not feel that that helped her deal with the situation.

As we jointly began to engage in the process of "unfolding" and "illuminating" Ms. P's subjective world (Stolorow et al., 1987), an example of the repetitive pole of the transference surfaced. She gave voice to her belief that I was feeling annoyed with her and was probably thinking, "What! You're still dealing with this problem? What's wrong with you? Why haven't you solved it yet?" As we investigated her belief that I was exasperated with her, she said that she thought she detected a certain irritation in my voice. I was surprised by her assertion since I could not discern any feelings of irritation in me. I did not try to disabuse her of her feelings, however, but, rather, continued to discuss them. We came to see that Ms. P often expected others to be critical and contemptuous of her.

Sometime later in treatment, I noted a series of unrelated incidents involving her daughter, her husband, her hairdresser, and a friend; in these incidents she had candidly stated her position and held her ground. I said, "It seems as if an important shift is occurring for you and that you are beginning to take matters more into your own hands." Subsequently, she revealed that although she generally agreed with what I said, my statement had made her feel "uncomfortable."

Elaborating she said, "I'm worried now about what will be expected of me, and can I keep it up?" She was beginning to be able to articulate both her wishes and her fears of changing, and also how they might affect me and threaten our relationship. Various transference themes that dealt with separation and accommodation began to emerge, and we were to struggle with these throughout the rest of this long analysis.

With some reservations, Ms. P would begin sessions with a current problem that was causing her difficulty. I was keenly aware of her conflicting wishes and fears that I would tell her what to do, as her mother and former analysts had. I recognized that a delicate balance was required. For the most part, I would try to encourage Ms. P to talk out the presenting issue, and we would try to understand underlying meanings and problem-solve it together. Sometimes, I would respond spontaneously and tell her my impression and what I thought of the situation.

Gradually, Ms. P elaborated on the extent to which she had consciously withheld material from her previous analysts, as well as from people in general. Our attention then turned to the lengths she would go to in deciding what to bring in and what to leave out of our sessions, which was a mighty struggle for her.

Another example of the repetitive transference and our work with it occurred several years into her treatment. Ms. P was able to tell me that she noticed a reluctance on her part to come in and talk about an exciting experience. As we explored this, what emerged was her apprehension that talking about it would bring it to an end. I suggested that she felt that her vibrant experience put her at risk with me, as if I might be jealous and resentful. We began to piece together her powerfully held convictions that if she used her own initiative in a vital manner it would necessarily be a threat to me and to our bond. Our investigations into such constellations of subjective experiences seemed to usher in the following ongoing transference refrain throughout the treatment: "I can't have my life and my analysis, too." Ms. P took a big step when she informed me at the beginning of a session, "Something bothered me all last session, and I couldn't say it to you. You were a few minutes late, and I was worried. I thought maybe something happened. And you were distracted."

We explored the factors that had prompted her to hold back from more spontaneous expression. She used some analogies to convey her experience. Ms. P said, "Like a child with an adult who's the authority, it's not polite." I said, "So, it's as if you have to make believe that you didn't notice something when in fact you did. It sounds like you try to talk yourself out of what you're perceiving and feeling." We discussed the cost to Ms. P of feeling compelled to leave her own experience, giving precedence to the other's feelings and needs instead.

Further, she feared that, if she were to share her feelings by pointing out my lateness, she would hurt or anger me, which in turn would make her feel very anxious. This led to associations to her mother; she cited any number of incidents when she had expressed displeasure toward her mother. Inevitably such negative expressions led to her mother's censuring her in word or deed and Ms. P consequently feeling endangered and "cut off." I understood her reactions to be yet another manifestation of the repetitive pole of the transference.

Following a session in which Ms. P described her husband's giving their daughter just the push she needed to overcome her own fear, I suggested how much Ms. P must have wished that she had been given such a helpful push as a child. Ms. P said she thought about my comment and realized that "I see you as a guide, helping clear the path for me." This was a selfobject dimension of the transference, in which Ms. P showed evidence of experiencing me as a new, longed-for object who could help her find her own path (walk on her wobbly legs).

Sometime later, Ms. P shared a transference dream in which she was sitting on some pillows next to me: "You're older and have a simple, natural look without unnecessary adornments or pretense, but clearly a 'major woman.' I had brought some hot chocolate. You say, 'I have a better idea,' and bring me a roast beef sandwich with good cheddar cheese on wonderful dark bread. It was delicious, simple, nutritious, and wholesome." In her associations, Ms. P elaborated on her reaction to a comment I had made in a recent phone message that I had left her. She liked the fact that I was "simple and direct." Of course, this dream is overdetermined, and there are many ways to interpret it. But, it demonstrates the selfobject dimension in which I was experienced as providing longed-for and necessary enrichment and sustenance for her.

Middle Phase of Treatment

Ms. P began concentrating on writing about her life, and this process seemed to usher in the middle phase of treatment. She had written somewhat haphazardly about her life throughout the first part of her treatment, but gradually and somewhat imperceptibly, her writing became more deliberate and she began to take it more seriously. The writing was an aid for her in recovering and rounding out memories from her past. Concurrently, there seemed to be a qualitative shift in her treatment, with Ms. P becoming more of an equal partner in our work. Her writing seemed to be a manifestation of a soul-searching life review that she was impelled to conduct under her own steam.

We might say that Ms. P set the stage and presented the scene and I entered into it with her (Sanville, 1991). Thus, as Winnicott (1971) said, we were in another "potential space" (p. 107), real and not real, internal and external. Time and time again, I found myself engaging with her at this level of play. Something altogether unexpected began to happen as Ms. P flourished in her creative use of the treatment with me. Her writing about her life was not just an important adjunct to her analysis, it became a valued and valuable expression of her creativity. Sometimes she would read selected portions of her writing to me, others she would refer to, but much of her writing she kept to herself. She would maintain her own rights to her privacy.

Ms. P now seemed to have less trepidation and be freer in expressing her negative feelings toward me. During a session when she was more assertive about expressing her dissatisfaction with me, she connected her feelings to some recent writing. In particular, she recalled two memories, fraught with pain and bad feelings about herself: One morning, on leaving for school during early adolescence, she had had an unusually "reckless moment." She unilaterally decided to act on her own idea to shorten her skirt by hiking it up. Unfortunately, her teacher censured her by saying, "How uncouth of you to have done that!" She was flooded with shame and self-loathing.

In the second memory, Ms. P recalled going on a four-person date to a school dance late in her adolescence. She enjoyed herself immensely and said to her friends, "Let's stay for one more dance." They agreed, but she paid for her liberated sense of expansiveness the following morning when the mother of one of the other girls came to her house and complained that she had kept the group out too late. She felt that she was seen as "a bad person," and, indeed, she felt that she was "a bad person."

I suggested that she seemed to be in a difficult and tricky spot. She was now able to assert herself more directly and to tell me more energetically how she wanted me to act toward her. However, her memories pointed to times when she was more assertive and followed her own inclinations, and she would end up being severely chastised and feeling humiliated. I recognized the jeopardy she was in then and was now feeling with me. She seemed visibly moved and concluded the session by saying that, although it had been difficult for her to tell me about not liking my comment, it was not as difficult as she had anticipated.

On yet another occasion, Ms P. took an additional risky step. With an air of controlled annoyance, she promptly called to my attention the fact that I had been a few minutes late. I felt as if I were a child being chastised by a powerful grownup who was shaking her finger at me. I was convicted, with no grounds for my defense, and was left feeling ashamed and angry. I imagine that my reactions were akin to feelings she had experienced throughout her life. As we explored this incident, she said that she had barely been able to confront me. She recalled her automatic organizing principles of feeling the requirement to protect me from feeling exposed or embarrassed, as well as being frightened that I might become annoyed at her.

Many versions of this encounter occurred during the course of the treatment; each time Ms. P typically became huffy and scolding. She appeared to be overly fussy at such times, and I would feel some annoyance and shame. She was so fastidious that she would remark if she noticed a piece of thread or a paper clip on the floor of my office. Her doing so annoyed me, but I usually did not share my annoyance with her, except when she directly asked me if it bothered me. If she did ask, I would acknowledge my annoyance, and we would talk about it. This, by and large, had the effect of clearing the air.

It was during this middle phase that Ms. P wrote a lot about her parents' divorce and the effect it had had on her. To be sure, we had talked many times about the divorce, but her writing seemed to help her obtain some sense of mastery over that event. In addition, she was honing her literary skills. Writing was increasingly becoming her new craft. Further, it was during her concentrated writing phase that Ms. P arrived at a new and important realization: she became aware that up to this point she had seen her father only from her mother's point of view. She now realized that she had never thought that *she* might have other opinions and feelings about her father *distinct* from her mother's. I saw Ms. P's new awareness as an indication of her growing capacity for self-delineation.

I believe that the timing of her parents' divorce worked against Ms. P's ongoing struggles to separate from her mother. Her life was taking an upswing, which was in stark contrast to her mother's condition. Her fears of losing her secure base with her powerful mother were therefore increased. Ms. P's own words speak eloquently about her recognition of the impact her parents' divorce had had on her and her development. She wrote:

"I'd always thought I was really indifferent or untouched by my parents' divorce. I've come to see that, on the contrary, I was profoundly marked by it. I didn't want to be affected by something that was strictly speaking my parents' business. That didn't seem fair. But I now know it was an event that changed my life forever. Just as World

War II changed the world's history forever, so did my parents' divorce change mine. It was even finally filed in 1939, just after the Germans invaded Poland! I guess it was my 'London Blitz.' "

Yet another painful and overdetermined experience was her oldest son's choice to live with his father during a custody hearing. Ms. P would refer to that event with its myriad of implications throughout the treatment. Incrementally, she became more candid in sharing some of her angry and hurt feelings toward her son for his rejection. She also expressed her feelings of shame, loss, and grief in contrast to her customary old style of masking these painful feelings.

In all those years she had ostensibly maintained good relations with her son, although she kept her distance emotionally. Periodically, she would try to open up a discussion with him about their relationship, but she felt that he quickly dissuaded her. I suggested that it was as if, once again, she were the helpless child with her powerful mother. She concurred, saying that she could not push her point of view.

As her son approached his 50th birthday, he wrote her a letter surveying his life and including some oblique references to his feelings regarding the custody. Ms. P brought in the letter, as was often her style, and read it to me. She asked for my reactions, and I agreed that he seemed to be giving her an opening finally to talk about it. She knew she wanted to respond and worked on a reply to him, weighing every phrase, feeling the importance and seriousness of this opportunity.

For the first time since the event occurred 40 years ago, Ms. P was able to deal directly with her now middle-aged son. In a most remarkable manner, the two of them engaged in a series of heart-wrenching dialogues about the event and its manifold ramifications for each of them and their relationship. I recall feeling teary during some of these discussions.

Termination of Treatment

Toward the end of her long treatment, Ms. P recounted a childhood repetitive dream she had when she was approximately five years old. This dream occurred following her parents' six-month separation and her unsettling cross-country trip. In the dream, Ms. P sees a beautiful meadow, hills and dales, and a road to walk on that is very appealing. She eagerly starts to walk on it, but it begins to tilt. The earth is turning, and she is flying off into space. Variations of this dream continued for a number of years.

I suggested to Ms. P that her dream conveyed her deep-seated fears that, if she set off on her own trail (alone), "mother earth" would go off kilter. It was not only her mother who she believed knew best, but also former therapists and analysts who told her what to do. She said, "I sat at their feet." In further discussion of this dream, we both gave credence to how she, prereflectively, never felt nor had a concept that she owned her own life. Together, we recalled that earlier in her treatment she had discovered that she "lived in mother's consciousness of me." She then associated to an upcoming trip. Ms. P explained how she had had second thoughts about some travel arrangements and spoke her mind, albeit expecting her husband to be "exasperated." In fact, he welcomed her alterations. She gave some other examples, involving me as well as others, where she both knew what she wanted and was able to voice her preferences more forthrightly. It appeared to me that this was yet another indication that significant inner alterations had been occurring.

Ms. P reported in the next session, "I had an amazing dream about you and me, where you were putting nose inhalant in my nose. You left to get something else. When you came back, you seemed agitated. It worried and upset me. I said you seem angry and asked what's the matter? You didn't answer. I said, 'I'm terminating and that it's all right, we're friends.' You said, 'let's make one more appointment.' I saw you were thinking of me. We hugged. You said you were sorry I was so upset. We parted on a friendly basis."

I asked about her thoughts regarding termination. She said that it was curious, because she was neither thinking about nor feeling inclined to terminate. We talked about the dream in relation to the previous session, when she had observed, "I can talk about simpler matters now. Before, with you and other therapists, I wouldn't have brought up these smaller things. I only valued the big thing (and believed that you and my other analysts did too). The main thing in the dream was that you were putting in a great deal of energy to clean my nose, so I could get something across. I became worried that you were impatient with me."

We explored some of the possible meanings of my impatience. She said, "It's a strange thing, but I'm thinking of something with 'A' (a female analyst she had seen over 30 years before). A would scare me when she looked at me with what seemed to be impatience. It happened just a couple of times. I became frightened and wished I could have brought that up with her, but I didn't. I realized I was feeling very happy and carefree walking to her office. There was beauty all around me, and it was a warm afternoon. I felt I was fine. I didn't need her. But I got so frightened about having that feeling of independence and not needing her, I never told her about that experience. That was the kind of thing I'd habitually keep to myself.

I felt guilty. I was afraid she'd take it personally that I didn't feel like seeing her. I had to act as if it never happened. And there I was, over 40 years old!"

I asked Ms. P about my being angry in the dream, and she said, "It was your intensity. . . . It felt to me like a child's feelings when her mother's angry. I was enormously disturbed that you were mad at me." When I inquired about her associations to her nose, she said, "You wanted to make one of my senses operational, removing something that had been blocked, so I could breathe."

Ms. P returned to her association that she had not told therapist A how she felt. "I realized it was wrong to try so hard to fit in, so she'd still love me . . . like a very powerful child's fear. Like a feeling that the floor was dropping out, I'd come to an abyss. I am astonished that there never was a way to bring it up."

She elaborated on her feelings of insecurity, and I talked about her oft-repeated conflict that she couldn't have her life and her analysis too. I suggested that it was as if her analysis were not really hers. With astonishment, she said, "Until this *very minute*, I never gave the least thought to how nice it felt to be in a good mood and it's amazing I could not tell A."

Sanville (1997) has offered some ideas that have bearing on this dream. She notes, "The first recognition of mother is said to be through scent. The patient has come to know her mother better through discourse with her analyst and through her own writing." Further, Sanville looks at the possibility of reversals in the dream, namely, that it is the patient who is agitated and wants to enhance the analyst's ability to smell out when it's time to terminate.

Even though Ms. P was not consciously ready to broach such a loaded subject, it is now clear to me that this was a termination dream. But she had an accident before our next scheduled session, and we never met again. I imagine that, had we met, we would have continued to look at the dream and the termination theme. In the dream, the job was done and her senses had been cleared. We each could feel angry feelings and yet still be okay.

Ms. P's associations went to a former analyst of 30 years earlier and the significant experience she had withheld. Something that had been automatic was by the end of her analysis with me foreign and alien. I still wonder why I did not see right away that this was a dream about her readiness for termination. Was I unconsciously not able to let her go? Why was I so willing to go along with her denial? Might she have worked with the ending differently had I urged her more strongly to explore the termination implications of the dream?

After the patient's last dream, Ms. P's husband called to inform me about his wife's accident. She had tripped on a curb and broken her hip. During her recovery, I called her several times and we exchanged notes. A few months later, she sent me a note to tell me that she was walking with a cane and was in less pain, but did not know when she would be able to return. After not hearing from her for several more months, I called her and she said, "I am doing fine. I have recovered and am feeling fine. Samoan, I won't be coming back. I think it's a natural time to stop. It came to its natural conclusion. I have very good memories." She was quite definitive about not wanting to come in and talk about terminating. Thus, our 15+ years of analytic meetings came to an end. Apparently, she felt ready to try to walk on her own.

Some Additional Thoughts about the Treatment and the Nature of Our Intersubjectivity

Ms. P was a very pained woman, lonely and without direction. She felt socially isolated and dependent on her husband. Incrementally she came to initiate more social contacts and for the first time since junior high school began to feel that she had friends. It was Ms. P's introspective qualities, together with the depth of her anguish, that roused my interest and drew me to her and notably engaged me in our work.

At times, I fretted that Ms. P and I were simply telling stories and that we were both defensively staying in the past in a mutual-avoidance pact. It was as if we were just playing games and not acting like grownups facing life. After all, we were both getting older, and we were not facing such age-appropriate issues as aging and death.

What kind of an analysis was this? I had precious few unconscious interpretations to cite. Later on, some of Winnicott's (1971) views on interpretation appeared to me as if out of the fog. He had come to see the value in waiting until the patient could understand by herself: "If only we can wait. The patient arrives at understanding creatively and with immense joy" (pp. 86–87).

Likewise, I worried that I was aiding and abetting Ms. P to continue therapy in the service of avoiding termination. I also questioned whether I could go with her to the end. During such times of such doubt, I reminded myself that we did a fair amount of work on her fears of aging and death. In fact, we had many discussions around termination, as well as several abortive attempts.

As Modell (1997) tells us, "The act of seeking memory [is] to retranscribe the experience" (p. 32). Ms. P had an abiding drive to give voice to her earlier life experiences, embellishing them with pitch, volume, tone, and harmony. I believe her thrust to retranscribe was reparative (Sanville, 1991). This process was aptly described by Italo

Calvino (1986): "What he sought was always something lying ahead, and even if it was a matter of the past, it was a past that changed gradually as he advanced on his journey."

Buoyed by her initial dream and the changes that had occurred, I felt that I had experienced Ms. P's growth and development. Uncertainties not withstanding, the most enduring element of our intersubjectivity seems to have been our mutual interest in her narrative and the unfolding of her rich inner life. By and large, I found the sessions with Ms. P extremely interesting and often emotionally very moving. I was fond of her and was committed to our work, and admired her fine mind and native curiosity. I especially admired this elderly woman's ability to examine herself and to change and develop.

Ms. P's internal work was tantamount to the act of living. Spanning the years of this treatment there were countless oscillations between the repetitive and selfobject pole. At times, I was the new longed-for object; at other times, I was the powerful mother who needed to use her for my own narcissistic needs. In many ways, this woman's natural aptitude for self-exploration flourished in the playground of therapy, where new creations of meaning and identifications occurred. I accompanied her in her soul searching, and there was a reworking and coming into her own.

Although our backgrounds in time, place, and experience were so different, I could resonate with her experiences of her mother. I saw my own mother as powerful and was frightened of incurring her wrath. I have struggled with my own difficulties in assuming title to my self, and, further, I had a quality of grandmother-transference to Ms. P. There was something about her story telling, her elaborations of persons, settings, and events, that was reminiscent of my own grandmother and her tales. Freed of earlier experiences of impingement Ms. P and I could frolic for a time in this illusionary zone.

In the deepest sense, Ms. P's narrative included our relationship. There was a parallel and mutual identification, but not in the hierarchical sense of child and mother. Rather, the mutuality that was achieved pivoted around the fact that her liberation was my liberation. In a manner of speaking, her story is my story and many women's stories.

This woman, who had truly been her mother's daughter, with borrowed self-cohesion and difficulty experiencing herself as the center of her own initiative, struggled mightily to claim her own life. It is striking, given her character structure, that she both initiated therapy on her own and terminated therapy on her own. Ms. P was able to free herself from some of the most negative effects of her attachment to her mother. In addition, she was increasingly able to take ownership of her self and her therapy.

Through the treatment, Ms. P was able to loosen some of the old ties that had held her hostage and worked against her self-expansion. Her conflictual feeling of lack of entitlement and her grandiose sense of being came together with her inventive use of our work. She was able to tap some of her natural creative talents. She applied her aptitude for writing, her high intelligence, her exceptional memory, and her natural, introspective proclivities to her life narrative and thus was able to revive old memories and to shape and reshape them. Stolorow and Atwood (1996) describe their view of psychoanalytic cure as pivoting around "the patient's experiential repertoire becoming enlarged, enriched, more flexible and more complex" (p. 183). As things go, I believe the work we did helped Ms. P bring to pass such an expanded repertoire.

Ms. P's writing took on a life of its own, and she gained a heightened sense of self-worth. During what turned out to be the last year of her therapy, while preparing to take a trip, she talked about her "separation anxiety and fear of dying." She said, "My life work is not done . . . no one would know where my writing was kept."

I am reminded of some apt words by Barbara Grizzuti Harrison (1997):

> Don't live in the past, my brother says, get on with your life. How do I tell him that I am contained in my past (and my past is contained in me)? Can I explain to him that the past is not a place I revisit, but my present and future home? "If the past and the future exist," Augustine said, "where are they?" At this very moment, this instant—which is over the moment I call its name—I am incorporating the past (which included this moment) into the present; and the present has become part of my future—which is also meaningless, because it has already begun, and is therefore now: and the past and the future and the moment are one [p. 76].

References

Barish, S. & Vida, J. (1998), As far as possible: Discovering our limits and finding ourselves. *Amer. J. Psychoanal.*, 58:83–97.

Benjamin, J. (1988), *Bonds of Love*. New York: Pantheon Books.

——— (1995), *Like Subjects, Love Objects*. New Haven, CT: Yale University Press.

Brandchaft, B. (1994), An unpublished paper. Pathological accommodation, unpublished.

Calvino, I. (1986), *Invisible Cities*. New York: Harcourt Brace

Cohler, B & Freeman, M. (1993), Psychoanalysis and the developmental narrative. In: *The Course of Life*, Vol. 5, ed. G. Pollock & S. Greenspan. Madison, CT: International Universities Press, pp. 99–177.

Dupont, J., ed. (1988), *The Clinical Diary of Sándor Ferenczi*. Cambridge, MA: Harvard University Press.

Flax, J. (1990), *Thinking Fragments: Psychoanalysis, Feminism.*. Los Angeles: University of California Press.

Harrison, B. G. (1996), *An Accidental Autobiography.* Boston, MA: Marina Books.

Heilbrun, C. (1997), *The Last Gift of Time.* New York: Dial Press.

Kohut, H. (1971), *The Analysis of the Self.* New York: International Universities Press.

Modell, A. (1997), Interview. *Amer. Psychoanalyst,* 31:31–33.

Sanville, J. (1991), *The Playground of Psychoanalytic Therapy.* Hillsdale, NJ: The Analytic Press.

———— (1997), Discussant of "A Woman of Her Time" by S. Barish. Presented at NMCOP Clinical Conference, Seattle, WA.

Settlage, C. (1996), Transcending old age. *Internat. J. Psycho-Anal.,* 77:549–564.

Simburg, E. (1985), Psychoanalysis of the older patient. *J. Amer. Psychoanal. Assn.,* 33:117–132.

Spark, M. (1997), *Reality and Dreams.* Boston, MA: Houghton Mifflin.

Stolorow, R. & Atwood, G. (1992), *Contexts of Being.* Hillsdale, NJ: The Analytic Press.

———— & ———— (1996), The intersubjective perspective. *Psychoanal. Rev.,* 83:181–194.

———— & Brandchaft, B. (1994), *The Intersubjective Perspective.* Northvale, NJ: Aronson.

———— & ———— & Atwood, G. (1987), *Psychoanalytic Treatment.* Hillsdale, NJ: The Analytic Press.

Winnicott, D. (1965), *The Maturational Processes and the Facilitating Environment.* New York: International Universities Press.

———— (1971), *Playing and Reality.* New York: Basic Books.

Chapter 6

∽

Trauma, Transference, and Healing
A Case Presentation

Toni C. Thompson

The concept of trauma encompasses those disorganizing forces, internal and external, which interfere with stable ego functioning and render the ego helpless and vulnerable. Forced into a state of regression, the person resorts to more archaic means of self-protection in order to reestablish and maintain some level of personal intactness and control. In the case of the patient considered here, Miss W, a comingling of strain and shock trauma (Kris, 1956) had interfered with forward movement in her development, causing serious alterations and compromises in ego functioning and self-esteem regulation.

Strain trauma is a longstanding external noxious force that continuously stretches the defensive and adaptive capacities of the child, and shock trauma is a trauma caused by a single event, such as a seduction, that overwhelms the ego, flooding it with anxiety (Kris, 1956).

Trauma always initially involves interaction with the external environment and is thus associated with reality and the effects of reality on the person's development. One's affective reactions to the trauma and the meanings one ascribes to the traumatic interactions or events become an integral aspect of one's psychic reality. Psychic reality encompasses elements of actual reality, perception, fantasy, affect, and belief (Good, 1996).

The powerful tool that both patient and analyst have at their disposal for grappling with trauma, albeit each with differing tasks, is the medium of transference. Psychic reality fuels the transference. The compulsion to reenact aspects of the trauma, in defensive ways as well as literal ways, is very powerful. The defenses that a traumatized patient uses to help reestablish some necessary degree of control often serve adaptive purposes as well. When these defenses, including regression, are repeated in the transference, they need to be interpreted for both their defensive and their adaptive aims. When the defense of regression is employed, the "as if" quality of the transference may be affected. At these moments, the analyst's clarity about herself or himself is critical to the interpretative work and to aiding the patient's return to reality. Often, during regression, interventions other than those considered strictly interpretive are the only ones the patient can assimilate.

The importance of the transference in treating traumatized patients was highlighted by Loewald (1955). Noting the creative and adaptive aspects of transference work, he stressed their importance in organizing past traumatic events (which might have existed only as body memory) into secondary process. He proposed that the transference experience for the patient may be initially a passive reproduction. With help from the analyst and the analyst's belief in the patient's adaptive capacities, passivity can be transformed into active aims for the patient's mastery and ownership of his or her needs and wishes.

The patient, according to Viederman (1995) possesses the capacity to be an active participant in the discovery and understanding of the trauma. Through the transference as well as through dreams and memories, the patient can be helped to reconstruct the past.

The transference also provides a medium for the patient's growth. Along with the patient's capacity to integrate interpretations, the patient's self-righting tendency can provide the impetus for selective identifications with the analyst and, in some instances, the creation of identifications with the more benign aspects of the primary object (Sanville, 1991).

Miss W

Miss W, a high school graduate who was 34 years of age at the outset of treatment, sought treatment because of her social isolation and career disappointment. Prior therapies had not helped alleviate her concerns. She had few friends, kept mainly to herself, and seemed uninterested in men. Miss W never felt properly understood. She was easily hurt by, and disappointed in, others and withdrew from them. Preoccupied with thoughts about each of the individuals in her life who had emotionally injured her, she often constructed a fantasy wherein she was intensely connected to that person and assumed the bad qualities, real or imagined, that the person had attributed to her.

After a brief period of psychotherapy, during which her interactions with people continued to be painfully disappointing, Miss W entered a four-times-a-week psychoanalysis, which is currently in its seventh year. As the intrapsychic meanings of her interpersonal difficulties emerged in the transference, Miss W recalled a childhood trauma of sexual abuse inflicted on her by her mother, unpredictably and repeatedly over a period of one to two years.

The patient's rediscovery of this early trauma was an essential part of her treatment. The childhood shock trauma had occurred within the context of chronic emotional neglect (strain trauma). The effects of both traumas had become internalized and had colored and given distorted meaning to her current object relationships and had compromised her ability to regulate her impulses and her affects. For example, Miss W felt unable to cry. The effects of Miss W's traumatic experiences on her current anxieties and her capacity to form relationships became manifest in, and were dealt with through, the transference. The overall therapeutic work led to an understanding of the way in which the sexual abuse and the emotional neglect (strain trauma) she had experienced had become unconsciously organized into a pattern of defenses and internal object relations that had a regressive impact on her ego and self-esteem.

At the same time, certain of her defensive efforts contained seeds of progressive development that helped to serve adaptive purposes. One such seed, and a positive aspect of her inner life, was a detailed childhood conscious fantasy of a substitute mother, an adoptive mother who was an idealized good, loving, firm object. This fantasy had played an important developmental and adaptive transitional function in Miss W's childhood life. Once worked through in the treatment process, it served as a positive foundation for and eventuated in the creation of the analyst as a realistic, useful, and good object who could be trusted and with whom a therapeutic alliance could be formed.

Miss W was originally from Europe, where her parents continue to live. Both were high school teachers. The family had inherited money on her mother's side and lived in a very large home, but, according to Miss W, they behaved above their station. She has a brother nine years older than she, who now resides in South America. She has had little or no contact with him over the years.

Miss W felt unwanted and unloved by her parents. Her father was a distant presence whom she experienced as deadened and morose. He appeared emotionally alive only when fighting with his wife or arguing with his son. Her strongest memory of him was seeing him from the back as he entered his study and closed the door. The father of her childhood memories rarely, if ever, spoke with her and is still uninvolved with her.

It was her mother who raised the children. She also was experienced as self-absorbed. However, Miss W has remained in constant contact with her mother over the telephone. She mainly has taken the role of listener; she sees her role as that of mother's caretaker.

When Miss W was growing up, her mother worked part time. When she was at home, she compulsively cleaned the house and rarely talked to her daughter or responded to her approaches. Miss W felt alone. She would often overhear her mother talking to herself. This behavior frightened her and caused her to feel that she didn't really exist for her mother. She became preoccupied with what her mother was thinking. As an illustration of the loneliness of these times and the longing for a connection, Miss W remembers lying on the kitchen floor, next to the dryer, loving the rhythm of the machine's movements and the feel of its warmth against her body.

Despite her chronic anxiety, Miss W tried to have some life in school but found it painfully frustrating. She longed to play with other children but felt odd and awkward. Learning was sometimes difficult because of the interference of pleasurable adoption daydreams as well as her preoccupation with thoughts of her mother. Miss W persevered, though and, using her intelligence and love of reading, achieved good grades. She was an A student, but neither parent seemed to pay much attention to her accomplishment. She had to come right home after school, brought no friends with her, and alone with her mother, always silently wanted, but often was afraid of, interaction with her.

Miss W gave the impression of having felt emotionally abandoned, understimulated and yet trapped by her mother. When there was interaction, she felt invaded by her mother's controlling criticism. The emotional climate was bleak and dark, as Miss W rattled around the large house, forbidden to go out and play because "bad people could hurt her. "

When Miss W related her history or shared her memories in one or another session at the start of our work, she frequently seemed to be watching me in a cool, aloof manner, as if she were being careful not to give too much of herself away. Her language was often vague and elusive. Later in the treatment, she told me that, even though I had not said much to her during the initial phase of treatment, she had thought of me as a Nazi and that was good because it meant that I could handle her. Yet throughout the early period of the treatment, I sensed that Miss W was trying to reach out to me.

Miss W manifested certain ego strengths in spite of her childhood traumas. She was a very intelligent woman and, when not overwhelmed by infantile needs and conflicts, evidenced curiosity and a capacity to think and act appropriately. With the help of her therapy, these ego strengths aided her both in developing a therapeutic alliance and in understanding that her internal world was the center of her difficulties. Her perseverance in the work and her capacity to contain transferential regressive needs and wishes, without severe acting out, were most impressive. Her motivating need to love and be loved (object hunger) and her self-preservative needs facilitated her investment in our work throughout the treatment.

Miss W's need for a positive connection and her capacity for idealization seemed only partially diminished by her early disruptive experiences. Her adoptive-mother fantasy suggested to me that there might have been some positive early experiences, meager as they might have been, that she was drawing on. This fantasy, which did not seem to hamper Miss W's ability to function in reality, helped her to maintain ego integration. It served an anxiety regulating (preventing continuous panic) function and a self-esteem regulating function (preventing a decompensating depression). As she struggled with premature psychological separation it had helped her through a myriad of narcissistic disappointments and traumatic experiences, including her father's unapproachability, his failure to facilitate separation from her mother, and his unavailability as a clear oedipal presence.

Certain events that Miss W reported did suggest that there had been at least some positive experiences with her mother. For example, Miss W recalled her mother's occasional nostalgic references to other women's babies. She had also discovered her own baby clothes and toys neatly packed away. She mused that maybe, just maybe she had been her mother's good baby. She reported a fantasy of purchasing a baby bottle, taking it home and using it, and then bringing it to her session. At one of the sessions when Miss W brought this fantasy up, I interpreted that she believed that her "bad behaviors" (of her own invention) had disrupted a togetherness she once had had and longed for. I suggested that she satisfied this longing through her adoptive-mother fantasy and her tendency to use vague and global communication in our sessions, with its underlying wish that we could read each other's mind.

Throughout Miss W's life and during the early part of her treatment, she was unable to organize her feelings into words or to find the words to express what was going on inside of her. In the transference, she recreated, through somber, dark, often wordless moods, the silent and depressed family atmosphere in which she was raised. These moods, often accompanied by vague speech, reflected childlike behavior that served a defensive function and conveyed the belief that thoughts transformed into words would be ignored or harshly criticized. This regressive behavior also indicated the disruption of ego functioning that the strain trauma had had on her.

Although anxiety producing, Miss W's attempt to put thoughts and feelings into words, locate and organize memories, and find and rediscover fantasies began to lead her to greater self-expression and to discover the pleasure of speaking to me as a real person. This new-found ability to verbalize slowly reduced her reliance on projective identification (Klein, 1946) and furthered the process of ego expansion and integration. The gratification she derived from experiencing a sense of real power, based on the acquisition of new skills, enabled her to cope better with the frustration of not actualizing the adoptive-mother fantasy in the transference.

The adoptive-mother fantasy was expressed as wishes for closeness with me. Miss W spoke of her longing that she and I would stare up at the moon together and not have to speak about what we saw because we would both know what the other was thinking. It would be warm and close. This longing for an imaginary mother felt dangerous, though, in the present because she wanted to make it real and had to grapple with the pain and frustration of not being able to do so. She had felt this longing to be dangerous in her past as well, because it had become connected with a memory of walking into the kitchen and finding her mother playing with a big knife. She said that it looked as if her mother was cutting into the tips of her fingers, digging deeper and deeper. This memory fitted with Miss W's unconscious fantasy that her mother wanted to kill her because of her very existence and because of Miss W's longings for the fantasy adoptive mother.

This terrifying childhood belief that her mother would kill her and the corresponding, intensely conflictual wish to kill the much-needed mother constituted a powerful organizing unconscious fantasy (Arlow, 1969). This fantasy further influenced and was reorganized by the acute sexual trauma, which was reconstructed by us to have occurred sometime between her third and fifth year.

When the negative transference became manifest in the treatment, it sometimes lost its illusory quality. At such times, Miss W was compelled to relive and make real certain aspects of the abusive relationship with her mother. As emotionally difficult as this trans-ference was for both of us, it was imperative that the unconscious hatred my patient felt toward her mother, and the conflict surrounding it, be culled from her sullen-toned moods, be made specific, and be directed toward me if it was to find its original target and meaning. It was equally important that, within the negative transference, her hatred not remain in its projected form, with Miss W as its victim. Miss W painfully came to realize that she possessed profound hostility to her mother as a result of her own conflictual, frustrated desires. The degree of fear and guilt associated with her hostility was found to be due to, among other things, the omnipotence with which she had endowed her feelings and wishes and the overpowering intensity of the emotions she experienced. Under the sway of such strong feelings, she would become dizzy and feel the emotion as if it were physically moving through her body. In addition, she was overwhelmed with the fear of her capacity to do real harm to herself or me, and most important was the fear of the destruction of her loving self.

As we worked on Miss W's positive and negative transference fantasies, she was exquisitely sensitive to rejection and frequently turned interventions into criticisms. This state of affairs permeated the treatment off and on for some time. I initially interpreted this phenomenon from an adaptive standpoint. I spoke with her about her need to establish control over both of us and influence the pace of the treatment process in order to feel more powerful and worthwhile. Such adaptive-oriented interventions seemed to diminish the controlling superego influence on our work. Specific homosexual and sadistic features, which were unconscious and were being defended against by her concern about being criticized, were brought out and interpreted later in the treatment.

Clinical Process

A session from the third year of the analysis afforded an opportunity to see how powerful the patient's fantasy was about her mother's negative feelings toward her. In this hour, Miss W expressed anxiety about not being able to see me. She wasn't sure of my presence. She wasn't sure where I really was, or where she really was. She said this with a mixture of detachment mingled with a bit of anxiety. Then there was a long silence. I said to her that the feeling about us seemed to suggest her experience of her mother when Miss W did not know where her mother really was and where she herself was. They were both present and yet absent, lost in some twilight of daydreaming. She responded that it felt as if her words were coming out of her and she was disappearing, yet she was worried for my mental well-being. In the midst of this confusing regressive feeling-state, she suddenly reported that she couldn't breathe. She grew more anxious and asked what she should do. She abruptly sat up, breathed in deeply, and slowly turned to look at me. Feeling a little anxious myself and concerned for her, I asked her if she was all right and if she felt that she could continue? She calmed down and went on, describing that the feeling she had was one of drowning, of being held down, of having something heavy on her chest, and of time going on forever.

This led to a memory of a childhood boating accident, when she and her mother, while standing to change seats in a canoe, had capsized it. They were pulled from the lake by relatives who were canoeing close by. Following the incident, her mother would not look at her and did not offer solace. Miss W's screen memory of the incident was of going under the water, sensing light and darkness, experiencing terrible pressure, and having a feeling, which she recaptured on the couch, of being lost to her mother forever.

For many sessions following the memory of the boating accident, Miss W consciously cooperated and worked on the meaning it held for her. However, she appeared distant from me and cold in her manner, as she had been at the beginning of the treatment. This way of being was so subtle that I did not always recognize it in the moment.

Soon after relating the boating incident, during a session when I was jotting down some thoughts, Miss W exclaimed, in alarm and anger, "What are you doing to me?" She then became frightened that she had expressed anger in my presence and could only explain that the sound of the pen on the paper really upset her. I asked her to work on what had frightened her so, but she became guarded and silent and turned to reality events and conflicts with coworkers who she felt were wronging her. She also cancelled some sessions.

In the overall context of feeling wronged, Miss W began to play with the idea of telling me more of what was on her mind about my taking notes and the sound of the pen on paper that had previously upset her. There occurred a rapid oscillation between Miss W's passively experiencing me as if I were her mother, too invasive or too distant, and then her unconsciously and actively, in an identification with the aggressor (A. Freud, 1936), taking on her mother's role and placing me in the passive, often bewildered state she had experienced. It is difficult to describe the quickness in the switch and flow of associations and transference-countertransference feelings that transpired

I consciously tried to place myself in just the right place within her orbit, to stay engaged and to move the therapeutic work along. I did this by trying both to be quiet and to interpret her spoken content at a certain pace and rhythm. This use of regulated intervention is usually discussed under the technical concepts of tact and timing. I believe, however, that when a therapist has to be so careful about what she says and how she says it, she is usually responding to an unconscious communication from the patient. In Miss W's case, I believe that I was responding to her unconscious invitation to be aggressive and invasive with her. I had to be careful not to withhold my ideas and questions to counter her offering, but to interpret this invitation at the right moment.

During this period of the treatment Miss W was consciously acting as if she were being coerced to talk; at the same time, by withholding her associations, she unconsciously was trying to coerce me to reassure her, to promise her that I would not criticize her or make any interpretations or ask any questions. Yet my silence was also unacceptable to her. My interpretive efforts here were fruitless for something more powerful was going on, something beyond my wish to understand the material. The here-and-now action between us, organized on a preconscious level was the real work to which Miss W was drawing our attention. This enactment taught me the value of being able to move flexibly from content interventions to process interventions and to pay interpretive attention to the function of a piece of behavior or attitude.

My eventual refusal to perfectly locate myself within her prescribed orbit, as Miss W had done with her mother as a child, played itself out by my charging her for her missed hours. Once I realized the meaning of my behavior, I interpreted the totality of the action in terms of her projective identification (Porder, 1987). In essence, I said to her, over time, that I was meeting with her mother, that she had disconnected from her little-girl self because it made her feel weak and frightened, and that she wanted to put me in her childhood shoes. In addition, I said that she wanted me to know the depth of her tie to her mother, both its importance and how bad it made her feel and that she was doing all this out of a need to have some control over the bad, helpless feelings. My interpretive movements got her attention and moved her sufficiently out of the regressive transference so that she could reestablish reality contact and a therapeutic alliance. In this state of mind, Miss W expressed relief in the knowledge that I was strong and in control, in the best sense of the word, and, further, that I was me, a confident me, not her or her mother, and that she was safe and could trust me.

Using this growing sense of trust, the memory of sharing the experience of the boating incident, and the immediate trigger of my sitting behind her and taking notes, she revealed that her mother had repeatedly, and in secret from the rest of the family, sexually abused her. In a halting, sometimes whispering, sometimes fragmented narrative, Miss W related the memory of the abuse. She had been made to lie on her bed while her mother inspected her rectum. She thought that she was very little, which made her think that this abuse had begun before she had started the first grade. The rectal inspection had started out feeling good. Looking at her intently, her mother would gently wipe her anus with vaseline. Her mother's look and my patient's good feeling blended together. Her mother would then begin to poke and probe, sticking the vaseline and maybe other things way up inside. As Miss W began to squirm, her mother held her down by putting her arm across her chest and by covering her mouth with her other hand. Miss W had trouble breathing and felt tremendous pressure down there inside her body while watching her mother's excited or angry face, she wasn't sure. Pleasurable sensations turned into painful sensations and ultimately made it difficult and fearsome for her, even as an adult, to go to the bathroom.

Later in the analysis, Miss W revealed a masturbation fantasy in conjunction with her current bathroom difficulties. The fantasy involved her and a female nurse tending to a man with diarrhea. As he struggled not to let go, she became aroused, her orgasm connected with his release of explosive diarrhea.

Returning to her revelation of the abuse, Miss W related that, while her mother was hurting her, she felt that she both did not exist and keenly existed as she succeeded in having her mother's full, excited attention. She felt weak, as though she wanted to surrender to the mother, and at the same time she felt that she had to fight. She was afraid that her mother would go all the way up inside of her and she would explode. She didn't know where "down there" her mother had touched her. It felt like everywhere. As she spoke, we uncovered fantasies in which she believed that her mother had put something inside of her that had made her bad and contaminated her and was hurting her from the inside. This fantasy was linked to an unconscious but active refusal to take in and consider interpretations in the treatment. Consequently her spoken material remained superficial but under her control. She came to realize that she believed that if she took in my ideas she would be contaminated. In general Miss W felt like a no-good, dirty person. Sometimes she had conscious fantasies of smelling bad and saw this as the reason that people might not like her. She further realized that this self-experience contributed to her provoking a distance with others by becoming cool and some-what threatening, as she had seemed with me in the consultation period. Miss W felt searing shame in telling me all this, as if she were burning, and she wanted to disappear. She felt dirty and was fright-ened that she could forget herself, lose control, and wipe feces all over my wall.

A dream she had shared during the early period of the treatment flashed through my mind. The dream was about a room with two beige chairs (the color of my office chairs) placed face to face. As she walked into the room, beige powder fell out of her from somewhere "down there." At that time she was contemplating intensive treatment, and her thought was that something bad was bound to happen. I reminded her of the dream and stated that we could now understand her initial fear of treatment and the possibility of our uncovering the harm done to her "down there." We could also understand her terror about the abuse and anticipation of its repetition. We spoke too about her wish to talk about the trauma and have it understood as well as to repeat it under safe circumstances so that it might be dealt with.

A pattern of relating intensely, followed by distancing either through the use of identificatory defenses or by a defensive regression into a twilight state, followed this session. With the use of the latter defense, Miss W claimed not to remember anything of the previous hour and described a strange feeling that we had not spoken in ages, even though we had had a session the day before.

When Miss W was in these defensive postures, I felt—and interpreted to her—that either the material or I had been lost to her or evacuated by her, as she had felt lost from or evacuated by her mother. I went on, with a different emphasis, that she needed to lose these memories and fantasies in order to gain control over her feelings and inner and outer reality. With work on the defenses and enactments, Miss W gradually began to allow her anger to reside consciously within herself. She began to connect this anger to slowly emerging thoughts of being rejected and forgotten after being so intensely and inappropriately misused by her mother.

Now that Miss W felt safe in these treatment interactions, a very positive, consistent transference was established between us, with emerging fantasies of me being her mommy and she my little girl as we played putting on makeup together in front of a big mirror. This play-acting was a derivative of her childhood adoption fantasy, which created delight and pleasure. She wanted to linger in it and to make it real; she insisted that I make up dialogue as if I were really the mother with her as my child, something one might do in some forms of child treatment. As she once had used her childhood adoption fantasies to comfort herself, she now used the same defensive process, denial in fantasy, to ease the pain of her condition and to create a pathway to dissipate, or forestall experiencing, the rage and disillusionment that lay beneath the surface.

Her sense of safety in these transference experiences allowed Miss W to express wishes for closeness and attention beyond those contained in the idealized fantasy relationship. The demanding quality of these wishes increased. She had a dream of a tuna fish salad sandwich and said that it was her favorite food as a child and that she loved to take small bites out of it, let it melt and get mushy in her mouth, and savor it. In her hours with me she behaved in a like manner, taking snippets out of my interventions and mushing up what was said with a mix of affection and indifference as if I were quite irrelevant, except to fill her with ideas.

During this period of the work she also revealed that she had what she called sexual thoughts about me. We worked on her shame over the pleasure these thoughts brought to her. The content of the fantasies had the theme of her being a dominating woman while I was her captive, a plaything whom she tortured while I begged for mercy and relief. These fantasies aroused a countertransference response more in keeping with the aim of the fantasy rather than with the spoken conscious content. They seemed to convey her need to make me irrelevant as a separate sexual object. I seemed to exist in her experience at this time only as a target for her active and controlling sadistic wishes and not as a richly textured, separate oedipal object who is both desired and appreciated in its own right. Miss W confirmed my thinking by relating that what gave her shame was the pleasure in the meanness that she found within herself. This emotion gave her a feeling of aliveness, powerfulness, and definition. She explained that this sense of meanness was a feeling of powerful uniqueness within her. She was therefore not just a passive blob, a blob who only reacted to what had been done to her by her mother. Her fantasy, she said, told her about the strong wishes within herself and she liked this.

The fantasies that were more directly tied to sexual gratification also spoke to her preoedipal and pregenital needs and wishes. The nurse fantasy mentioned previously was retold by Miss W in the analysis. It remained unchanged in content and was her sole source of sexual gratification. This masturbation fantasy, although seemingly triangular and oedipal with anal coloration, really obscured gender differentiation. The primary emotional focus for Miss W was the nurse. In our analysis of it, we learned that the man with the explosive diarrhea symbolized for her the experience of the inside of her body when her mother abused her and when she could not achieve actual physical relief.

That this fantasy contained a disguised and defensive attempt to move to a positive oedipal position is not to be ruled out but has not been established thus far in the treatment. What seems more likely was that the establishment of a positive oedipal position was weakened and pulled regressively back to the fixations of the dyadic period of development. The absence of the father and brother in the treatment material could address symbolically Miss W's experience of their indifference to her as a girl child. It could further suggest the effect of their emotional absence on facilitating movement into clear gender differentiation and a positive oedipal position.

The childhood pattern of the mother-child relationship, a cumulative or strain trauma, now internalized, had negatively affected her ego's ability to regulate the conflicts around her aggressivity in an adaptive manner (Kernberg, 1990). An account of the following session illustrates her struggle.

The context for the session is Miss W's growing awareness of rage at her mother. Their telephone contact was increasing. This session occurred some time after I learned of the sexual abuse. In sessions prior to this one, Miss W had become gradually aware of some of her murderous wishes toward her mother and wanted me, at one point, literally to go through the fantasy of planning the murder of her mother. She concretely wanted my ideas on how to carry it out and in one session said in a demanding way, "So come on, give me an idea and you're going to help. So what are you doing just sitting there?" At such a moment she had the quality of a child patient who will not give the analyst the script for the drama and insists that the analyst make her independent moves. When I attempted to keep the work symbolic by stating, "This is a wish. This is a fantasy you're enacting," she became frustrated with me, which takes us to the following session.

Miss W: I feel that I've missed you. I feel that I could be hurt by someone, hit over the head, mugged, a vague feeling. I need to hear you talk, to hear your voice, to know you're here, not just your few sentences. I just imagined someone, like in a dream, coming after me, and I hide behind you. [pause] I'm wondering why I'm thinking this way. I saw this video over the weekend, a child was tied down, but I managed my feelings OK, on the surface. It was all right. I feel this undercurrent of anxiety. I need your voice for comfort, like a teddy or a "blankie" [laughs embarrassedly] Something inside isn't O.K. today. So, comfort me in a concrete way. Go ahead, I'm waiting.

Analyst: You're afraid the anger and the thoughts you have been having and talking about will hurt you and you want my reassurance and support.

Miss W: Yes, it makes me so needy. I want to try to stay with this anger. It's not easy; it's hard to believe that I could feel what I felt and think those thoughts. If I let myself get in touch with it, it's just going to be frustrating, not going to get rid of it, just have it in my mind. The feeling might be like a fire that can burn me. Once it starts, it's going to kill me, not her. [pause] It will hollow me out. I feel kind of stuck now. Last session, I remember how badly I felt. I wanted to put my head on your knee for comfort, because [pause] because I can't kill her, I can't get to her, I've never gotten to her. Your knee is like a refuge. It's fine to be there, stuck there, comforted, but not very helpful emotionally because then I'm not involved in what I'm doing. Over the weekend I thought about what we said, how I had started to feel. I got scared and made that picture of my head on your knee. What's next for me? To move away from your knee? That's not an option. To do that would bring back painful and intense feelings, so should I stay here? Short silence. It's premature, my thinking about that; it's where I am now. [silence] I feel very sad. That's where I am now. [silence] I feel very sad—that's where I am, sad and distraught.

Analyst: You ask whether you should stay near me. If it's all right to be there, I think to help yourself with that hollowed-out feeling, but you're also thinking of moving away, tell me more.

Miss W: In this feeling I couldn't walk away from you, I'm not interested in anything. I couldn't leave, overwhelmed with a feeling that I'd be all alone.

Analyst: How do you mean?

Miss W: [pause] I don't know exactly. In the image, if I walk away, the loss of physical contact, the feelings overwhelm me. I'm frightened and confused. I don't know what to do. I can't kill her. I don't know what to do with her. I can't protect myself; I can't kill her. Something bad will happen to me. I don't know what to do about it. I don't have any more ideas.

Analyst: You had an idea about being hurt, mugged, a kind of physical punishment for the feelings and fantasies you're having.

Miss W: To have these thoughts about my mother is a sin. [whispers], especially enjoying them. I think I enjoyed the fantasy when I was in it. I just muttered in my head. I wish you were dead. I have your knee now; I didn't have it when I was little. I don't know what I used. [pause] My fantasies, I used my fantasies. I learned that here. If I left your knee now, I'm afraid of being out of it, really out of it, like I was when I was a kid. You know I remember feeling fleeting anger at her. She never understood, always accusing me. It made me frustrated. It made me angry. I couldn't make her see me. I'd tell something that happened at school, but she'd be cleaning and not say anything, or she would say it wasn't so. I'd begin to doubt myself, wonder about what she was thinking. I couldn't express my anger. I was afraid; I was confused.

I remember something now. I was young. It was before I learned not to open my mouth. It was in that kitchen. I was in that kitchen with her. I was being angry. I used words. She grabbed me by my arms and slammed me up against the wall. "Don't you ever get angry

with me again," she said. I remember those angry eyes, the angry
mouth. Oh, this is bad. She's going to hurt me. I never did it again in
the same way. I'd get annoyed, but my feeling would disappear. I had
no security about it. I was very little. I was just being myself, unself-
conscious. The words just came out, bad thing to do, bad thing to do.
Scary, very bad, I don't know. That's not right what she did. I couldn't
defend myself. I can't defend myself. I don't ever remember wanting
to kill her. Maybe, under my breath, but I was on a different floor.
You don't think she heard me, do you? What I'm telling you now,
what's coming up now, was below the surface. I'm putting you in the
picture, preventing myself from feeling worse, I wish there had been
someone there to help me. [silence]

Now your knee doesn't feel good enough, not a real person to
protect me. I talked to her on the phone over the weekend. All she
talked about was herself and the house, some kind of repairs needed.
She went on and on. I couldn't tell her about me. I don't even know
what I wanted to say. She wants to have a party. She's cleaning like
crazy. She'll serve that dip. She says my father never speaks to her.
She was in that kitchen of hers. I've come to hate that room. I want to
wreck the whole house. It made her a slave. All she did was take care
of it, not me. I want to get her attention. I want to make her weep.
[silence] I feel frustrated, I feel depressed, I don't know how to express
it, I'm supposed to relive these emotions, but I feel helpless. You get
me out of this. I don't know how to do it, so do something. Help me
get out of this. I feel like a blob, no words, like I'm angry at everything,
but I don't know how to express it, channel it out of me. [pause]
Maybe I can't stand feeling sad, depressed, like when I was a kid. I
was angry for moments, I think it felt better. Now I'm rolling in it,
reliving it, frustrated, I feel stuck now.

Analyst: Perhaps you're angry at me that you're feeling depressed
and frustrated. Do you think it's because I didn't join you in the fantasy
about killing your mother the way you wanted me to and that hurt
you?

Miss W: No, I'm angry at myself. This is my fault, this mess I'm in,
I'm a hopeless case. Should I blame you? It's me, it's all me. [pause]
What you said so far doesn't help. I feel like I'm helpless and waiting
for you to say something that's going to make a difference. I don't
know what it is. [silence] You're not going to say a sentence that's
going to make a difference, are you? I'm going to stay frustrated.
You're not going to get me out of this frustration. I need you to say
something else. That wasn't it. My feeling isn't going to be taken
seriously. I have to be quiet, I'm going to be left alone with it. I don't
know what to do—you won't listen to me.

Analyst: Since I cannot read your mind and don't know what this sentence is, it feels like we're stuck together here in this frustration.

Miss W: You'll abandon me. It will get buried again; I'll have to cope with it. You don't know, you'll refuse to help me. What's the use? It's hopeless.

Analyst: I think it feels hopeless to you when you feel that all communication has broken down. You feel you can't reach me, and you feel I won't reach you, similar to how it felt between you and your mother.

Miss W: Yeah, she has the same attitude you do: go figure it out yourself. Instead of trying with me, she'd ignore me, or say one thing. She'd give up, that's it. You find a way to communicate with me. I feel now this is not my fault. There's more to put into words, I can't get to it, I'm all tied up with myself. Just never mind. You don't know how to help me, you're withholding. I am angry at you, and I don't know what to do, I'm just a blob.

Analyst: You know, I just thought that, even though you feel yourself to be a blob, you are doing something with me here. I feel rather tied up with my ideas, tied up in trying to reach you. Do you think that you might be trying to bring alive with me the fantasy you had recently, of tying up your mother, imagining her being so helpless and then killing her? You're bringing it alive now with all the sad, hopeless, rageful, and guilty feelings connected with it.

Miss W: Yes, [covers her face quickly] I feel foolish with this. I feel frightened, ashamed, as though my mother caught me trying to hurt her. I feel caught now.

Analyst: Yes, as if your mother were catching you in the privacy of your thoughts.

Miss W: Yes, like I muttered before, like I'm practicing a secret thought, I wish she was dead. But she can't be killed. No matter how angry I am at her, I can't get to her, I can't hurt her; I can't even talk to her. I have to kill her or walk away, and I can't do either. I'm glad you have patience. I feel your patience with me, but I don't have patience right now. You're the target for my anger. Where else can I go with it? If I leave it inside, I'll explode. When I talked to my mom on the phone I tried to talk to her about my new possible deal, but she just cut me off, gave me the silent treatment and went on about her party. My possible new deal is exciting to me, I could make a nice commission and my co-workers, particularly "P," will think well of me. It's very hard work; sometimes I think I won't be able to carry it off. I tried to do some work over the weekend, but I'm preoccupied with, oh, I don't know, her, I guess, my feeling, like she's in my mind all the time, criticizing me: I'm not working fast enough; I didn't talk to the customer confidently enough; I was wrong in my numbers. It's so depressing, so frustrating. When I heard about her party, I tried to talk about her guests. She rarely has guests. She corrected my thoughts about Mrs. S; they weren't her thoughts. But it's as if I didn't speak really. She just went right on, like I can't get into her strange kingdom, except [trails off] . . .

Analyst: You seem to move away from a thought.

Miss W: Yes, except when she used me. I feel afraid to say more. It's safer to be quiet; you say it.

Analyst: What I can say is, you're afraid you'll explode with feeling and kill me. These feelings are connected with your recent fantasies and the painful memories about being physically used by your mother.

Miss W: I feel so filled with hate I can't stand it; it's such a frightening feeling. It pushes at me, I'm afraid it will spill out, leave this room, and I'll get angry at work, scream and never stop. I'm embarrassed thinking of myself like this. I feel like a little girl again, like I want to run to you, put my head on your knee, crawl onto your lap. Be safe there and get away from these horrible feelings. When I think of her on the phone, smiling about herself, her house, her party—everything is her, I want to hurt her, pulverize her. Killing isn't good enough. I want to wreck that house; it was so bleak there. She wouldn't talk to me for days, I never knew why. The weekends felt like an enormous span of time, forever with nothing to do. I'd wake up and think, oh no, it's another day. No plans, no activity, I'd try to go back to sleep and stay in bed as long as possible. I'd go downstairs. No one was there. Where was everyone? Then I'd hear her off in the background, vacuuming. No one fed me. It was so lonely, like I didn't exist. She'd only speak to me about how such and such looked in the library, or something stupid like that. I could have been dressed in rags, she'd not notice. That's how it felt. I should have yelled at her then. What a wimp I was, but she scared me. I feel right now as if I want to express my anger. I almost want to be wild with it, but it's hard for me to be that angry. It's frightening. I dread this, but I feel I've just scratched the surface.

In a subsequent session Miss W exclaimed that she wanted "to do it," that everything inside of her wanted to kill her mother. Only a split second of her own mental weakness, and her mother would be dead. Miss W thought that this would feel so good, like a volcano releasing, and this action seemed like the only way to rid herself of the boiling rage, the hatred inside of her. Her literalness was alarming, and my countertransference reaction spoke to the level of her ego regression and her anxiety.

As she went further into this regressed state of mind, an utter bleakness came over the painful, memory-laden material and evoked an emotional atmosphere of deadness. I felt, uncomfortably, that I was losing contact with her. I believed that this was an enactment of her inner experience (externalized) of losing contact with the libidinal aspects of herself as well as the representation of the object. This was an actualization of the fantasy of being killed by and killing the mother. The adaptive need for self-regulation of these frightening feelings was diminishing under the onslaught of rage. Unlike in the prior sessions, Miss W was unable to find and use the metaphor of resting her head on my knee to calm herself and reduce the emotional distance her hate was creating.

Feeling that this regressive reliving had run its beneficial course, I interpreted in such a manner as to aid her in refinding the libidinal component within herself. I tried to diminish the power of the image of the murderous self. I shared with her the thought that she was under pressure (the volcano metaphor) to get through to her mother, to make her mother notice her, that there was contained within her wish to kill tremendous frustrated need and longing. Her hateful part wanted so much for her mother to care about her, and she actively longed for care, not just from her mother but also from me. She wanted me to stay in emotional contact with her and understand her hatred. My emotional effort toward her and my interpretive slant slowly brought about a transforming experience in the treatment.

In contrast to her dread of re-creating only the explosive and overstimulating frustrations in the transference, Miss W found a feeling of safety and relief in the reality of experiencing her sadness. She felt that she had found my knee again and could rest her head and as a consequence had regained her long-lost ability to cry. This adaptive use of her oral sexual longings was akin to a transitional soothing experience. She re-created the positive introject that supported and libidinized internally the picture of her longing self. This internal structure formed the basis for the derivative longings in the adoptive-mother fantasy of her childhood but was now more rooted in the real experiences of our relationship.

The disorganizing effect of the diffuse rage had been halted as Miss W was able to regain the boundary between past and present and reality and fantasy through her ability to use both the act of and the content of interpretations.

Summary

This case of childhood neglect and sexual abuse illustrates the psychological effects of trauma and how they came to be understood and worked through in the transference.

Because of the emotional deprivation she suffered through all phases of her development, Miss W had to regulate early narcissistic needs and did so through omnipotent fantasies that provided her with an illusion of control over the poorly differentiated object. She also used denial in fantasy (which did not impair her reality testing), in which she was the beloved child of idealized adoptive parents. This later defensive fantasy structure did not seem to have a family romance, oedipal meaning but, rather, followed from her splitting of the object world. She created in fantasy the good self and the idealized good object and the very early emotional nourishment that this illusion provided. Her prevalent use of projective identification, in and out of treatment, contributed to her omnipotent thinking and to a continuing experience of low-level anxiety and a weakening of reality testing. This defense posture contributed to her sense of isolation and distance from others, while at the same time she continued a private and intensely emotional overinvolvement with them. She came to learn that the people she chose to interact with (and fantasized intense but painful relationships with) unconsciously represented her mother.

The patient's ability to establish a solid foothold in the phallic oedipal position was weakened by the regressive pull of fixation points that had been established by the intense conflicts of the preoedipal period. Attempts at conflict solutions had contributed to a significant arrest in areas of her personality development and had prevented the negotiation of phallic oedipal conflicts from performing their transforming function on earlier established structures such as defense, self- and object constancy, and the content of her fantasy formations.

The shock trauma (the sexual abuse) contributed to a heightened, object-connected wish, in fantasy, to hurt and be hurt by the object for unconscious gratification and a feeling of safety. Finding or creating painful experiences gave Miss W a feeling of security in the familiarity of refinding her past and a means of coping with internal separation anxiety.

The therapeutic process of working through the emotion of hatred and its attendant fantasies contributed to the gradual shift in the internal balance of Miss W's hating and loving self-representations. The sense of herself as having been so singularly and globally dirty and bad shifted to include a more complex and nuanced inner picture. This more integrated self-representation now incorporated the once buried, thus almost atrophied, positive qualities of her self-image.

The more integrated, thus more realistic, image of herself allowed Miss W to tolerate her thoughts, wishes, and feelings and to experience them more firmly within her own boundaries. Miss W slowly became less burdened by persecutory ideas and the need for the resultant distancing maneuvers. This and other work done in the treatment led to her finding a job that provided satisfaction and allowed her, in time, to begin work toward a college degree. She also began to experience more positive interactions with other people. Her childhood longing for positive, safe connections and for companionship was finally being realized both in the real world and in her ability to use the therapeutic relationship for healing.

References

Arlow, J. (1969), Unconscious fantasy and disturbances of conscious experience. In: *Psychoanalysis*. Madison, CT: International Universities Press, 1991, pp. 151–175.

Freud, A. (1936), *The Ego and the Mechanisms of Defense*, Writing 2. New York: International Universities Press.

Good, M. (1996), Suggestion and veridicality in the reconstruction of sexual trauma, or can a bait of suggestion catch a carp of falsehood? *J. Amer. Psychoanal. Assn.*, 44:1899–1224.

Klein, M. (1946), Notes on some schizoid mechanisms. In: *The Writings of Melanie Klein, Vol. 3, Envy and Gratitude & Other Works*. London: Hogarth Press, pp. 1–24.

Kernberg, O. (1990), The psychopathology of hatred. In: *Rage, Power and Aggression*, ed. R. Glick & S. Roose. New Haven, CT: Yale University Press, pp. 61–79.

Kris, E. (1956), The recovery of childhood memories. *The Psychoanalytic Study of the Child*, 11:54–88. New York: International Universities Press.

Loewald, H. W. (1955), Hypnoid state, repression, abreaction and recollection. In: *Papers on Psychoanalysis*. New Haven, CT: Yale University Press, 1980, pp. 33–42.

Porder, M. (1987), Projective identification: an alternative hypothesis. *Psychoanal. Quart.*, 26:431–451.

Sanville, J. (1991), *The Playground of Psychoanalytic Therapy*. Hillsdale, NJ: The Analytic Press.

Viederman, M. (1995), The reconstruction of a repressed sexual molestation. *J. Amer. Psychoanal. Assn.*, 43:1169–1195.

Chapter 7

∞

The Unstoppered Heart
The Awakening of the Capacity to Love in a Person with a Schizoid Disorder of the Self

Karla R. Clark

Originally, this chapter was intended simply to tell the story of a woman who seemed made of stone: how she became at last a person able both to love and to be loved. As is so often the case, however, the ideas that seemed at first so simple and complete later came to be seen as quite complicated.

To begin with, a definition of love itself was elusive. Even within the psychoanalytic literature there is nothing that quite encompasses the complexity of the emotion. Often, for example, the word love is linked with the idea of mature sexuality, as though they are one and the same (see, for example, Kernberg, 1984). Although genital sexuality is a crucial part of some forms of love, I was searching for a more inclusive definition.

It seemed that trying to define love was like trying to describe the taste of chocolate or the smell of ground after rain.

I reformulated my question: what are some of the components of love that we can observe? From the psychoanalytic literature I was able to cull the following elements.

Two are the related qualities of *empathy* and *compassion* (Lewin, 1996). The more basic of the two is empathy (Kohut, 1977); the more emotionally complex, compassion (Lewin, 1996).

By way of illustration: I know a child who is 18 months old. The other night, while she was visiting with her grandparents, someone stepped on her grandfather's foot. He had recently broken that foot and someone stepping on it caused him a good deal of pain. The little girl, seeing him wince, immediately burst into tears and flung her arms around her own mother's legs. Everybody was at first surprised and a bit bewildered by her response. What had upset her? I think we were seeing a sort of protoempathic resonance with her grandfather's pain—her ability to use aspects of her own experience to identify with his. Having done so, however, being so young, she was overwhelmed and needed comfort herself.

By way of comparison, we—observing—felt both empathy and compassionate distress for both child and grandfather. We empathically felt her upset along with her, but we, being older, could do something more with it. We could stay outside of the experience far enough to have feelings of our own *about* what we were seeing. This response led, in turn, to our understanding how perhaps we might best offer comfort to each of them.

I am suggesting that there is an added, more mature and complex aspect to compassion. It involves four linked elements: the ability 1) to feel with another; 2) to stand outside the joined feeling in order to observe it; 3) to have feelings about what we experience from that vantage point; and 4) to translate all these elements into appropriate action.

Are empathy and compassion all that are necessary when we love? Of course not. We may (however reluctantly!) know that we are like someone we dislike intensely. Empathy and compassion must, when we love, also have a basically *positive* coloration.

But does this thinking also apply when the loved object is nature or football or music? It is easy to conceive of one's love of football or skiing or movies as something both of and not of the self—and to nurture one's passions with a simultaneous respect both for their relatedness to the self and their otherness. In this sense, we can extend our notion of love to include love of activities or things outside of ourselves.

Another ability besides the related abilities to feel empathy and compassion comes into play when one loves. That is, the ability *to feel passion*. Passion includes the ability both to acknowledge and to contain deep, primal feelings. By allowing these elemental forces to flow through us, we harness them and put their energy to use in our own service. Sexuality is, perhaps, the most important way that this aspect of love is expressed, but, as Freud (1905) so eloquently taught us, "sexual" passion is really a kind of life force: an element of all things we can be said to love.

A feeling of *spiritual connection* is also intimately associated with the ability to love. It is a feeling of being part of a larger universe that makes love expansive and generous, rather than turned inward and essentially self-referential (Bettelheim, 1982).

Are all people who can feel empathy and compassion for other people, or who are passionate about painting or furniture or baseball or who are sexually passionate or deeply religious, fully able to love? I think not. We all know people who can be deeply involved with others, with an artistic or intellectual endeavor, or with an animal or a cause, or who are sensual or devout, but who are unable to love. I cannot think of a single person, however, who can do *all* of these things whom I would call unable to love. When a person is able to love, he or she can do all these things and do them more or less at once, in layers.

But we must add one more element of love: that is, the capacity *to lose and to mourn the loss of that which one loves*, to understand that such loss is inevitable and that, in spite—or even perhaps because—of it one can love fully (Kernberg, 1984).

The capacity to understand the paradox that loving and losing are two faces of one coin and to commit oneself none the less, to people and to things and to the universe itself is another element of what I would define as the mature ability to love.

In the case discussion that follows, the patient, Ellen, gradually developed all these capacities. Before turning to the case, however, I would like to discuss briefly the therapy of the structure of the self and the associated theory of therapy that informed the treatment.

I treated Ellen using a theoretical synthesis based on Masterson's (1981, 1988) developmental, self and object relations approach with modifications that bring his theory into line with more recent developments in attachment theory. I have incorporated conclusions concerning the development of the self proposed by Stern (1985), Sanville, (1991), and Shore (1994).

In contrast to Masterson's, my underlying assumption is that each individual has a central self-structure that exists, in nascent form, from birth (Fairbairn, 1956; Stern, 1985; Sanville, 1991). This self is composed of genetically determined aspects of temperament, intelligence, and predilection (Fairbairn, 1956) which are both created and supported by adequately attuned caretakers (Shore, 1994).

In addition to a core, authentic self, all of us, as young children, have certain aspects of experience that are antithetical to authentic self development. These are experiences of painful misattunement by primary caretakers to aspects of the authentic self. These misattunements become encoded in the brain and also become part of the greater self-structure. (see Segal, 1974; Masterson, 1981; and Sanville, 1991 for related perspectives.) These painful misattunements are of two kinds. One is the person's experience that one has to pull oneself "off true" in order to be accepted by caretakers. The other sort includes one's experience that having a separate, individual self leads to alienation and abandonment by caretakers. Both kinds of experience induce the developing child to modify her more authentic self in ways that are contrary to her real nature. A bold child becomes quiet, for example, or a creative one dull or compliant in order to secure love, approval, or even basic safety. These adjustments become part of the person's inner life. They govern behavior long after the need for such accommodation has passed. Such accommodation can be thought of as the false, defensive self (Masterson, 1985).

Most people have some aspects of their personalities that are attributes of a false, defensive self. In healthy people, however, authentic aspects of the self form the basis of most of their interactions, while false-self aspects are weaker, more conscious, and therefore under better control.

According to Masterson, for people with disorders of the self, the opposite is true: false-self adaptations predominate (and may even be experienced by the person as "real") and more authentic aspects of the self are either hidden or may fail to develop. I wish to emphasize that a false-self adaptation is not necessarily destructive. It also serves to preserve and protect whatever there is of an authentic self. When the psychotherapeutic relationship goes well, what there already is of the real self can be remobilized. For example, schizoid people, like the patient I discuss shortly, believe that, if they become emotionally involved with others, they will be enslaved. Powerful feelings of shame, anxiety, rage, and helplessness are associated with this belief (Klein, 1995). At the same time, schizoid people believe that, if they attempt to express their own unique selves, they will be catastrophically ignored (Klein, 1995). Painful feelings of loneliness, emptiness, insatiable longing, frustration, and anxiety are associated with this belief.

Simply to survive, children who will become schizoid believe that their caretakers permit, even encourage, a passive, peripheral stance that is associated with feeling safe. This stance becomes the basis of a false defensive self that is remote, emotionally cut off, inexpressive, undemanding, or cold, superior, and aloof. This semidetached stance also precludes the expression of feelings, wants, and needs because these emotions are contrary to the "safety" to be found in the false defensive self. By the time those children reach adulthood, their self-protective stance has become habitual. They may even cease to think of it as an adaptation; rather, they honestly believe that aloofness is part of their basic nature.

Clearly, trying to treat such a person analytically presents unique difficulties. How can you treat a person effectively who cannot or will not tell you how he or she feels or what he or she needs or desires? One who cannot trust you to share in his or her fantasy life? One who feels, moreover, that he or she is a "good" person for being inexpressive and can be safe only be continuing to be unknowable? One who sees normal dependency as dangerous?

In some schizoid people the damage is so extensive that it is difficult or impossible to reverse. For many others, though, repair is possible. We can help such patients bring forward more authentic aspects of themselves and loosen the hold of the false, defensive self in two ways: 1) by helping them to become conscious of the false defensive self, of how and when and why it operates; 2) by creating an atmosphere in which safety may be found in expressivity (Sanville, 1991; Clark, 1996a). This experience provides patients with the opportunity to learn to identify and express authentic feelings about what they think and their honest thoughts about what they feel.

In choosing to be expressive in the presence of an other (the therapist) who is attuned to his or her authentic thinking and feeling—and whom he or she can now perceive to be so attuned—a patient opens the door to the expression and development of the more authentic aspects of the self that have been hidden, underdeveloped, or both.

The Patient: Ellen

Ellen is 54 years old, a relatively short woman, a bit plump, extremely carefully groomed (see also Clark, 1996b). When we first met, everything about her seemed stiff, self-conscious, manufactured.

In the early years of her analysis, almost all she thought about were her clothes. She appeared to have no interests aside from acquiring them. She told me, with pride, for example, that she (the wife of a prominent local businessman) had never read a newspaper in her entire life.

She had a curious effect on people: either she seemed to disappear or she annoyed or intimidated others. I was to learn that this effect was more or less intentional on her part. Her manner was designed to keep people, whom she greatly feared, at bay.

Needless to say, intent as she was on allowing nobody close, she felt no conscious empathy for others, nor did she allow anyone to feel empathy for her. This attitude was beautifully demonstrated by the way that she entered therapy. She did so without ever admitting a wish or need for help.

She consulted me when her husband told her that he had fallen in love with another woman. He complained that he was bored and fed up with her lack of affection and responsiveness. At that point, scared of impending divorce but not able to admit that she needed help in her own right, Ellen began therapy "to save her marriage."

She was angrily disengaged (if there can be such a thing) with me. To put it mildly, she came to sessions, but she did not put any investment into making anything happen once she got there. She was many things by turns—hostile, remote, haughty and aloof, anxiously placating. But, always, underneath it all, she was unrevealing. It was to be many years before she let down her guard and told me how desperately she longed for emotional connections with other people and how despairing she was of ever being able to achieve those connections.

How does such a tragically frozen, passive–aggressive condition come to be? In Ellen's case, there were probably some inborn tendencies toward introversion, shyness, and anxiety. In addition, her history provides us with ample opportunity to understand why it would have seemed to her like a wise strategy to develop a frozen, wooden, passive–aggressive façade. Briefly, Ellen was faced with the task of relating to parents whom she experienced as dangerous, unpredictable, and simultaneously controlling and indifferent.

As children often do when faced with painful and inconsistent treatment at the hands of caretakers to whom they must attach, she developed the theory that her father's abusive and controlling behavior and her mother's remote, cold unavailability were, somehow, the result of her badness. It never occurred to her that the source of the problem was in their own difficulties rather than in her behavior. As Fairbairn (1956) has taught us, almost all children, for the sake of attaching to caretakers, would prefer to think of themselves as bad persons in a good universe rather than good persons in a bad one, for the latter experience leads to dangerous feelings of emptiness, abandonment, and despair.

Ellen excluded from consciousness, and failed to incorporate, those experiences that might have helped her to correct her old beliefs. Contact with anybody seemed dangerous, yet she felt herself unable to survive without contact. She viewed herself as defective and unworthy, yet she longed for love and acceptance. She compromised by withdrawing emotionally from other people, hiding her emotions, wants, and needs, but staying in the vicinity of others by allowing superficial contact. Throughout her childhood her prevailing mood was one of sour discontent and a kind of inchoate hunger. She disliked herself.

A child with such a lonely, sad history sometimes, by way of compensation, develops a rich fantasy life full of passionate relations with others (Klein, 1995), but Ellen did not even do that. She was a poor student. She had no hobbies or creative interests, no talent for sports. Her lack of personal interests reinforced her emptiness and feelings of insatiability.

She met her husband, John, in high school. He admired her beauty and took her aloofness for sophistication. She treated him callously. A few months after graduation, without ever admitting any interest in him, she more or less deliberately became pregnant. She felt maliciously triumphant at enraging her father by forcing him to permit her to marry and leave home—but she had no feelings of love for John or, later, for their baby.

Ellen was utterly unprepared for pregnancy, labor, or motherhood, but she was unable to ask her parents or anybody else for help and advice. From the beginning, she was a frightened and inconsistent parent, both very controlling and neglectful. Her mothering worsened rather than improved with each of her successive children. Her relationship with John was strained and distant. She was cold, walled off, and empty. This was the Ellen who came into treatment.

Because she was so distant, it took me quite a long time to understand that I was dealing with a person who had a very distinct theory of attachment—how to maintain it and what would break it up. Attachment required that one person be a master and the other a slave (Klein, 1995). This was the way to connect, but this way of connecting also generated tremendous feelings of anxiety about engulfment and the loss of self.

The anxiety around what she saw as the cost of connection would become so intolerable that, to regulate it, Ellen would push away. She tried to free herself from all need for closeness, only to face another fear when she succeeded: that of unbearable isolation in an indifferent universe (Klein, 1995). This feeling of isolation generated intolerable levels of anxiety, despair, futility, painful, insatiable longing, and emptiness. Unable to bear these feelings, she was forced to try to reconnect with people—once again through the familiar channels of conflict and enslavement.

She regulated the feelings of anxiety, anger, and dissatisfaction, generated either by moves toward people or toward self-sufficiency, by "orbiting," that is, by allowing herself to be neither too close nor too far from others (Clark, 1996a). She did this by acting superior, aloof, and contemptuous of others. She did not, however, really believe in her superiority. While it offered protection, it did not offer real solace. She was left with underlying conscious feelings of self-hatred, little awareness of any emotions or specific desires, and a constant, chronic, diffuse feeling of dissatisfaction and hunger.

Orbiting defenses, which effect a compromise between a need for closeness and distance, are set into motion by the very act of wanting help and feelings of emotional connection with the therapist. The patient I *saw*, therefore, was the defiant, passive–aggressive, contact aversive false, defensive self. The patient I *saw* bit the hand that fed her. The authentic aspects of the person who had longings for real connection were hidden.

Briefly, the technique for uncovering the fears associated with being expressive of one's own feelings, wants, and needs involves the continuous interpretation of orbiting defenses as a way to maintain a feeling of safety and to soothe and regulate feelings of intense anxiety, rage, and emptiness (Klein, 1995; Clark, 1996a).

I interpreted the need for safety to Ellen in various ways until she began to identify and express her emotions and desires. When she could do so, she observed for the first time in her life that the problem was that she felt no love for or sympathy with her own emotional requirements. The problem, she concluded, was that she did not love herself. Paradoxically, admitting that she felt no love for herself was her first step in developing it.

True empathy with others begins only when one has it for oneself. This step was the hardest to accomplish, for any step toward developing self-love evoked tremendous feelings of loss and despair. As Ellen began to treat herself with more kindness and respect, she was forced to wonder, "Where were my *parents?*"

The painful fact that acknowledging kindness or care evoked feelings of deprivation and absence was also reflected in Ellen's relationship with me. On the one hand, Ellen found my empathy for her need for safety reassuring. It helped her to begin to accept and respect her own needs. On the other hand acknowledging her experience of being safe was highly threatening because it painfully reminded her of what her parents had not provided.

Consequently, we spent a lot of time discussing her fearful reactions to feeling safe. My attitude throughout was accepting of her distrust, while at the same time I empathically commented whenever I could on the logic of her stance in view of her childhood experiences. These discussions built self-acceptance. She started to look at herself with both more objectivity and concern.

Progress was not linear. She would typically follow a move toward more open self-reflection and freedom in self-expression by becoming hypervigilant to my responses to her and either detaching emotionally or returning to provocative behavior in order to keep me at bay.

Gradually, however, she became more reliably able both to look at herself in my presence and to turn to me for help.

She could now admit that her childhood experiences had affected her. She commented that it was difficult to think of emotionally separating from her parents because she felt that she had nothing positive from them to take with her. Her experiences with her parents were either negative in character or felt utterly empty to her.

The problem of how to leave when they have nothing to take with them is the stumbling block patients like Ellen experience when they start to separate emotionally (see Guntrip, 1969; Seinfeld, 1991; Clark, 1996b). Ellen was terrified in particular of feelings of void, and she would go to almost any lengths to stay away from them. Previously, she had stayed frozen to avoid feeling the void. Now she developed a newer (potentially healthier) way to avoid empty feelings: an idealization of me. She related to me as though I could provide her with all the maternal experience she had missed and thus fill the void without her having to feel it. She though of me as literally the good mother who could make her whole and well.

For a patient who had been so standoffish and unable to acknowledge a need for anybody, this idealization represented real progress. I knew that eventually she would have to face the limitations of the power that one adult has to reparent another. But it seemed important that Ellen experience the idealization first. I accepted her idealization without interpretation and tracked and interpreted her difficulties in identifying and expressing herself when, for any reason, I failed to meet her expectations (see Kohut, 1977, for a related perspective).

As we analyzed her reaction to my inevitable, unintentional failures in attunement, she began to experience her ambivalence toward me. She said that she craved my help and my existence as a role model, but she also feared being controlled or rejected by me. She revealed that her idealization had phony aspects as well. She thought that I required it or else I would punish her. As she expressed these thoughts without my retaliating, she began to relate to me in a more spontaneous and lively way.

In this mood she returned to the subject of her difficulties in accepting herself. "The problem is," she said, "I never feel satisfied with anything I do or have. The problem is that I do not love myself. I feel terribly inadequate. I am damaged. I try, God knows I try, but I am left kind of flat a lot. I can't feel what I want to feel. Like I'm bad. Really a bad person. When I get to the real me which I've been avoiding, all I feel is shame, and why would I want to feel THAT? I know where it comes from, but I just want it to go away. And I am even ashamed that I am affected by it, affected by the damage. I even feel shame for being angry."

As she discussed her sense of shame, it faded away. I was both amazed and moved as she began to take life and shape before my eyes. She developed an interest in movies and in reading. She began a new correspondence with a friend who lived (at a "safe" distance) in another state. With new spontaneity, she could now directly consider how she behaved with me. For example, she could now openly discuss either feeling superior to me or positioning herself worshipfully at my feet. I interpreted that positioning of herself as "one up or one down" had preserved a safe distance from me. I asked her if she had noticed what feelings started to come up before she adopted this "safe" position. Her answer to this question developed over many months as we repeatedly explored the emotional precipitants for her behavior.

"You know," she said, "I feel isolated and above instead of unique. I don't *want* my own uniqueness. I have this idea that there can be no connection if there is a difference between people. How do people connect though different? I, in my head, see it as a threat. I don't see it as beneficial. It's a threat. And because of that I feel a lot of resentment. I resent that people like you are different from me and that I am different from you. I really suffer."

This brought her back to a consideration of her parents' failure to acknowledge her uniqueness and thus to her feelings of defectiveness and void. "When I think about all of this and why I feel so threatened and lost and alone," she reflected, "I go back to my parents and I feel my damage. I feel *shackled*. And the whole time I am saying this I am thinking, if we are all the same then we are a bunch of frigging clones. But that's not what I want. I want to feel safe, and to think that different doesn't *not* feel safe. What I want is *that* kind of connection.

"I think," she continued, "what I mean is, will people love me? My parents didn't. They wanted me to be everything that I wasn't. I really believed that if I emptied myself, voided myself, I stood a better chance. You are the only person that has ever said to me that when I did that I was hard to be with. I always thought the opposite. This feels like an aftershock of the planets rearranging. I always thought people liked me because they could mold me. Nobody ever said they liked me because I was different. *Nobody*. I didn't know what to do with the person I really was."

As she and I kept exploring the same themes without my becoming bored or impatient with her, she grasped the concept that getting to know yourself or others is process, not product. It is an interplay of emotions and thoughts about them that eventually can lead to action, a form, in fact, of play.

Sanville (1991) has proposed that play is essential to recovery in psychoanalytic therapy; and indeed, as she suggests, the idea of play and process excited, revitalized, and liberated Ellen. "I always thought you became something and then you were there," she said. "But I don't think that's so. I think it is a process of becoming. I don't think it ever ends until you die."

Since self-discovery was process, to be playfully shared with another, not product (as she had always supposed), she could name parts of herself that she had previously disavowed because she was so ashamed of them. For example, she told me how much she resented and envied me. She disclosed her secret agenda—to defeat my efforts to help her and triumph over me. Thoughtfully, she reflected, "I think talking about resentment and envy has freed me. I don't feel good about those parts of myself, but they are there. It feels nasty. I don't want somebody to succeed because they are already better and now they are going to be *really* better." With new self-acceptance, she said, wryly, "Not very wonderful feelings, but they are there."

She started to express genuine interest in other people and in her relationships with them. My job at this point was to support her new ability to be interested in others and, simultaneously, in herself.

Masterson (1985) has discussed the need for "communicative matching" at this point in therapy, when the emerging real self needs encouragement and support. While I continued tracking her distance regulation when necessary, often I had the pleasure of joining in her explorations as a joyous and interested, playful companion. Sessions could be about just about anything, dream analysis, mourning of her own lost opportunities, discussion of books or movies or events that occurred with her growing group of friends, consideration of her feelings about her family, past and present. Some days we mostly simply laughed and joked.

The following interchange illustrates this process. It demonstrates how free she had become to introspect and share herself in an honest way. Notice, too, her interest in other people and her attempts to understand them as separate beings.

She said, "As this is taking place, I am seeing more and more how different John and I are. John's father has a bad heart valve and was over-radiated as well. John was up there and broke down crying. It lasted for all of three minutes. I was astounded. I watched him for any lingering traces."

"Was this, like, going superior?" I asked. "Because I notice you're talking about *him*, not your reactions to him, and also that you seem to think of yourself as an observer?"

"Well," she said, laughing, "I *do* think my way is better. You are right!" We laughed and joked about this together for a minute. Then she sobered. "I felt sad, actually. But I also felt assaulted because of the speed with which he cried and then stopped. It was too fast. I became frightened. How could it be so fast and then be gone? So I became virtuous. 'Here, let me show you how to run your life.' I say it kiddingly, but it's what I want to do."

When a patient has become self-accepting and playful in this way, the ability to make spontaneous genetic connections follows naturally. In this incident, Ellen paused and then burst into tears. "John was suddenly my mother. I *never* knew when she was going to lose it. *Never*. It came out of nowhere. It was never safe. It was totally unpredictable. I didn't realize how upsetting it was when my mother would do that. It's at the bottom of all that control of mine. 'I can't depend on you, mother,' but at the same time exercising all that control is like taking the key, locking myself up and throwing it away. My father was more predictable. My mother was—whoa!"

She linked her reaction to her mother to her reaction to her husband: "Exactly how I felt when John did that the other night." Then, weaving a consideration of her relationship with her mother together with an understanding of what effect that relationship had had on her, she returned to an exploration of the past. "It is so linked to spontaneity. I have always been terrified of it. What is spontaneity but unpredictability? It terrified me and my responses were terrifying. So spontaneity was terrifying. I think at those moments I knew I couldn't count on her. So I couldn't lose it, because she couldn't take care of me. I kept myself in this envelope. Sealed. Tight."

In this manner past and present separated out, and she experienced people in her present life as themselves rather than as representatives of past relationships and past pain. She saw herself as an actor rather than as a reactor and became much more spontaneous.

Her relations with her husband and children improved. She had long since faced the fact that she had been a poor mother and that the children had scars from her shortcomings, but now she faced the painful fact that she could not, through changing herself, cure them. She mourned but consoled herself with her warm and loving relations with her grandchildren. Astonished, I heard her delightedly describe her pleasure at the sheer fun of jumping with them on the (previously sacrosanct) white couch in her living room.

A crisis developed involving her youngest daughter, Joyce, and Joyce's child. Hoping to "get her on her feet," Ellen and John had supported them financially. It now became clear that their support was making things worse rather than better. Ellen, loving her grandchild and guilty for her early treatment of Joyce, realized that she nonetheless had to set limits. She hit on a humane yet realistic strategy:

she would tell Joyce that she would continue to support her for six more months; after that she would continue to pay for her grandchild's preschool, but Joyce had to do the rest.

In so doing, Ellen faced squarely the limitations of the reparative and protective powers of love. She understood that much of the damage she had done her children was beyond her ability to repair. She felt helpless, she felt guilty, and she grieved. To my mind, as Ellen felt the various feelings connected with this experience, she demonstrated many of the qualities of a loving person as I have defined them.

Ellen's work on family matters also reinforced the process of weaning her from me. By encouraging her interest in understanding her relationships with others and their effect on her, I was also indirectly encouraging her to step away from her previously almost exclusive preoccupation with our relationship and with me. My continued interest as she moved away weakened her belief that if she took her eyes off the caretaker to focus on herself she would have the door slammed in her face.

She openly expressed her feelings about this fantasy about the inevitability of rejection and traced its origins to her own childhood. Then she observed that it was possible to experience me as supportive in my own right since she finally could distinguish me from her early images of parents. For several months, contrasting past and present, she mourned the parents she had never had, the childhood she had missed.

It was time to talk about ending treatment. She set a termination date: "I feel like the pain I've been feeling all my life is surfacing and I'm stunned by the immensity. I am speechless. It is making an imprint on me. I am not used to allowing that. I'm used to chasing it away."

With tears streaming down her face, she continued. "This is strange for me. It's here. It's heavy. What I'm used to doing is chasing it away. It's really weird." As she faced loss squarely, the need for the false defensive self evaporated.

"Although I inhabit the same house, although I inhabit the same body, who is this person? It's really strange. I feel so unfamiliar with myself. I'm behaving differently, I'm responding differently. Part of me feels like I've come home. Part of me doesn't know the person responding this way."

Accepting herself, rather than holding on to a dream of transformation through my unconditional love, helped her invest even more in herself. In this context Ellen came to a new acceptance of her basic urges. She "discovered" her drives and allowed passion to enter her life. She openly discussed her sexuality in a detailed way. She was frightened by a sort of impersonal sexual urge that she expressed as a growled, "C'mere," not only toward me, but toward people passing on the street. She was relieved as she came to understand that such urges are normal. She surprised and delighted her husband by going home at noon one day and grabbing him for spontaneous, joyous sex.

At the same time she could face even more primitive urges. She spoke of wanting to devour me in order to have me with her always and of noticing similar urges toward her children and grandchildren.

Free access to primitive urges also can open the door to a higher self. At the beginning of this chapter, I made the point that the recovery of the capacity to love also includes the ability to feel connected in a spiritual way to humanity and human concerns. Ellen was a lapsed Baptist who had angrily abandoned the church as she became openly rebellious during therapy. Now she began an oriental garden, which she viewed as a spiritual place. She told me that she hoped to use this garden as an extension of her work with me when therapy ended.

She wondered somewhat apprehensively how leaving would be. Even in the face of her uneasiness, she held firm to her commitment to herself that she would stay emotionally present with me until the very end of therapy.

As termination day approached, she summarized: "I am between personalities. I am not who I used to be but I'm not who I am going to be either. I cannot say goodby to you in the old mode, but I don't know how in the new way.

"I feel lately that every session is goodby to something. A dream. A hope. An idea. Maybe that's why I go away so heavy."

"Do you know what I feel most strongly?" she asked. "The total lack of my mother. Her ways that I took on so as not to notice her absence. I don't really feel that I had anything to take from her, but I think I hold on in ways that I don't even realize. I feel like that's how my need for her manifests itself, and what's really hard is that I can't have my own personality and do that, so I have to let her go.

"I am furious with you. I feel stubborn. I know that I am circling the void, trying to tell myself that what I believed—that you could be my good mother and that I would never have to face the void—is not true. I believed it as hard as I could, and I feel stubborn. No! I am not going to give that up! I know that I have to, because if I don't I won't feel my own accomplishment, or anything else real about myself and my life. But I don't want to. Damn!"

Following this release of feelings, she felt hopeful and excited about ending, although sad at the prospect of leaving me. She spoke about how valuable our relationship had been to her, while she also experienced feelings of pleasure at the idea of going it on her own. It was in this mood that she ended therapy. In the years since, we have had occasional accidental meetings, and she has written to me from time to time. She tells me that all the progress she made has continued and that her sense of a loving self is stronger all of the time.

Discussion

It is undeniably true that the relationship I had with Ellen, which was warm, supportive, and affectionate, was fundamental to her improvement. This feature of our work together inevitably raises the question of whether love was indeed the basis of her growth. I think that the answer is a qualified no.

To explain this answer we must return to my original discussion of the definition of love. There is a distinction between the positive feelings that occur in a good therapeutic relationship (and that certainly form the basis of many a successful treatment) and love. For one thing, two people cannot really love one another in a deep way who share so little of real life. In fact, we deliberately foster this special sort of relationship through the position of analytic neutrality.

The very nature of analytic work requires constant monitoring and control of emotions on the part of the therapist so as to bring the patient's distortions (so fundamental to his or her difficulties) into bold relief. The analyst's neutral stance and the analysis of the resulting transference, while essential to therapy, precludes the development of the kind of complex amalgamation of elements and feelings between people that is characteristic of real love.

In fact, I propose that Ellen's recovery rested in large part on her own improved ability to make a distinction between our affectionate relationship and the real and passionate love she eventually felt for family, friends, and life itself. This distinction helped her to separate from me emotionally: to let her idealization of me attenuate in favor of ongoing, more truly satisfying relationships.

Ellen ended therapy in this spirit—healed and enthusiastic about life's possibilities. I am glad to see her go—and I shall miss her.

References

Bettelheim, B. (1982), *Freud and Man's Soul.* New York: Random House.

Clark, K. R. (1996a), The beginning phases of treatment of the schizoid disorder of the self: A developmental, self, and object relations perspective. In: *Fostering Healing and Growth,* ed. J. Edward & J. Sanville. Northvale, NJ: Aronson, pp. 125–151.

—— (1996b), The nowhere (wo)man. In: *Clinical Social Work Journal,* 24:153–166.

Fairbairn, W. R. D. (1956), *Psychoanalytic Studies of the Personality.* London: Routledge & Kegan Paul, 1990.

Freud, S. (1905), Three essays on the theory of sexuality. *Standard Edition,* 7:130–243. London: Hogarth Press, 1953.

Guntrip, Harry. (1969), *Schizoid Phenomena, Object Relations and the Self.* New York: International Universities Press.

Kernberg, O. (1984), *Object Relations Theory and Clinical Psychoanalysis.* Northvale, NJ: Aronson.

Klein, R. (1995), Intrapsychic structure. In: *Disorders of the Self,* ed. J. R. Masterson & R. Klein. New York: Brunner/Mazel.

Kohut, H. (1977), *The Restoration of the Self.* New York: International Universities Press.

Lewin, R. (1996), *Compassion.* Northvale, NJ: Aronson.

Masterson, J. (1981), *The Narcissistic and Borderline Disorders.* New York: Brunner/Mazel.

—— (1985), *The Real Self.* New York: Brunner/Mazel.

—— (1989), *The Search for the Real Self.* New York: Free Press.

Sanville, J. (1991), *The Playground of Psychoanalytic Therapy.* Hillsdale, NJ: The Analytic Press.

Segal, H. (1974), *Introduction to the Work of Melanie Klein,* 2nd ed. New York: Basic Books.

Seinfeld, J. (1991), *The Empty Core.* Northvale, NJ: Aronson.

Shore, A. N. (1994), *Affect Regulation and the Origin of the Self.* Hillsdale, NJ: Lawrence Erlbaum Associates.

Stern, D. (1985), *The Interpersonal World of the Infant.* New York: Basic Books.

Chapter 8

Vacation Breaks
Opportunities for Partings and Reunions

Cathy Siebold

*E*ach year as summer vacation nears, I begin asking patients about their thoughts and feelings regarding our break. One man said to me, "You know that movie 'What about Bob?' I feel like that guy." We explored his associations and the possibility that he might make bad decisions in relationships while I was away. This was only a tiny piece, however, of the imagery that his statement conveyed. The feelings that may be aroused in some patients and analysts in response to vacation breaks are complex and multilayered. Like Bob, who is humorously depicted as an extremely compulsive, phobic man, some patients may feel anxious about their analysts' departures and want to go with them. Others may be glad for the release from the pressures of analytic work, and some may feel sad about the break in intimacy. Alternatively, some analysts may be impatient to get away, and, as in the movie, they may be irritated by their patients' need to cling. Others may be relieved, and some may worry about their patients' ability to cope during lengthy breaks.

Despite the variety of potential responses to a vacation break, the literature has yet to capture fully the complexity of this topic. Current works (e.g., Barish, 1980; Sarnat, 1991) stress the patient's intrapsychic process related to separation and loss. Few articles have been written about the analyst's experience of a vacation break or the relational forces that are stimulated by this event. Moreover, psychoanalytic theory has yet to incorporate the significance of reunion, a finding of attachment researchers (Main, Kaplan, and Cassidy, 1985), to the analytic process. The paucity of articles discussing vacation breaks, like the absence of articles regarding loss, has been explained as an avoidance of the complex feelings of anger, guilt, and anxiety experienced by both patient and analyst (see Webb, 1983; Sable, 1992).

The analyst's avoidance of an array of feelings may partially explain the limited literature about breaks, but the evolution of psychoanalytic theory further explains why this avoidance has occurred. Increasingly, our understanding of psychoanalytic processes has been expanded from a one-person, intrapsychic emphasis to a two-person, relational emphasis. The analytic dyad is now described as bipersonal and bidirectional (Sanville, 1997). Historically, psychoanalytic theorists, believing that the development of psychic structure was primarily motivated by internal forces, have overemphasized the patient's intrapsychic experience. In this construction, structural change was an outcome of the analyst's ability to understand and interpret the patient's intrapsychic experience (Strachey, 1937; Greenson, 1967). Although relational perspectives have long been part of some psychoanalysts' thinking (e.g., Fairbairn, 1952; Winnicott, 1965), a growing body of empirical evidence by infant researchers (Bowlby, 1969; Mahler, 1971; Stern, 1985) has strengthened and deepened our appreciation of relational influences on the development of psychic structure and on the analytic process (see also Aron, 1996).

Research into developmental processes demonstrates that an infant neither exists in a state of primary narcissism nor constructs experience on the basis of internal need states alone (Sanville, 1987). We now understand that the infant's psychic development is affected by external as well as internal processes. As we acknowledge the significance of the mother–infant dyad on psychic structure, our understanding of the analytic process has also been amended. According to Sandler (1996), "We are nowadays particularly interested in the analyst-patient dyad, in analyst-patient and patient-analyst interaction, and here we undoubtedly make use of a two-person frame of reference, as well as an intrapsychic one" (p. 89). In this expanded construction of the analytic process, structural change is also a result of the analyst's actions (Gill, 1994) and the patient's experience of the analyst (Meissner, 1991).

The Literature: An Overview

Interruptions in treatment are described in the literature as important events in an analysis. Tarachow (1963), for example, asserted that real life events, such as vacations, are of great significance. Exclusive attention to vacation breaks, however, is unusual. It is more common for descriptions of vacation breaks to be included in articles that describe other aspects of treatment (e.g., Loewald, 1962; Firestein, 1978).

Emphasizing intrapsychic phenomena, some authors describe vacation breaks as opportunities for the emergence of infantile wishes, fantasies, and memories. In Jackel's (1966) description of one patient's response, he stated that, prior to his vacation, the patient expressed a wish to have a child. He interpreted this as the patient's wish to be both mother and child, because, "in such a fantasy, one can never be deserted and one is never alone" (p. 733). Peck (1961) observed that before breaks patients reported dreams more freely and with a sense of urgency. Firestein (1978) also notes an increased emergence of dream material that expresses conflicted wishes, longings for merger, and expressions of despair. Conflicts are more readily expressed because there is little opportunity for interpretation (Peck, 1961). Upon their return, analysts describe a deepening of the process, which Peck (1961) attributed to the relaxation of repression that allowed analytic work to continue during the break.

Along with facilitating the emergence of infantile need-states or unconscious fantasies, vacation breaks can tell us something about the transference and the patient's ability to cope with affects related to loss and mourning (Loewald, 1962). Patients who are experiencing a negative transference may threaten to leave or take an unscheduled break before the analyst does (Firestein, 1978). Repeated experiences of breaks during a lengthy treatment, however, help the patient to be able to tolerate his or her feelings at times of separation and loss.

The literature on vacation breaks has begun to reflect our increased appreciation of the importance of preoedipal strivings and the impact of the object on development. Partings are now viewed by some analysts (Barish, 1980; Sarnat, 1991) as opportunities to understand and rework the patient's early object experiences. Greater attention is being paid to the ways in which interruptions may arouse separation anxiety, with concomitant feelings of anger and annihilation (Blanck and Blanck, 1974) or serve as a source of narcissistic injury, requiring greater attention to selfobject transferences (Kohut, 1978).

Sanville (1982) criticizes the emphasis on loss and separation in the literature about interruptions because it neglects the positive aspects of this process. She notes a bias in the social work profession toward object relatedness. Sanville finds that a positive value is accorded to togetherness and a negative one to separateness. She believes, however, that partings are "felt as oscillations between connectedness and apartness" (p. 123) and should not always be viewed as resistances but as possible attempts at self-repair. Loewald (1962) also asserted that the patient's response to an interruption reflects the way that the absence of the object is experienced: as deprivation and mourning or as emancipation and mastery.

Barish (1980) observes that patients can have different responses prior to breaks and that these can be influenced by diagnostic factors.

For example, certain patients with narcissistic pathology may be distant in the sessions prior to a break, reversing the situation. It is as if they need to be the ones leaving rather than the ones left. Some neurotic patients may respond with compliance, focusing almost exclusively on the break without being able to integrate it into their life experiences. Other neurotic patients are better able to use their experiences of breaks to develop insight into past experiences of being left.

Analysts' countertransference experiences related to breaks are rarely described in the literature. Neutzel's (1991) is the only article devoted to the analyst's countertransference reactions when taking a summer break. He traces one patient's departure from treatment back to his summer vacation. For him, this was "a period of special counter-transference vulnerability" (p. 39) because at this same time he was ending his personal analysis. With hindsight, he recognized that his lack of attunement to the patient's fears of intimacy, as they were expressed through her dreams before and after his vacation break, resulted in her later abrupt termination of treatment. Speaking more generally on countertransference, Barish (1980) notes that analysts may have difficulty being attuned to their patients' feelings about being left because of their own feelings about being away.

Technical considerations are another facet of the discussion about vacation breaks. Many authors recommend giving adequate time to allow a thorough exploration of patients' anticipatory responses (Greenson, 1967; Sarnat, 1991). The most commonly discussed technical issue is deciding whether or not and when to use an interim analyst. Sarnat (1991) asserts that the decision to use an interim analyst is a collaborative process between patient and analyst. Optimally, the interim analyst is a transitional object who sustains the image of the absent analyst and encourages the patient's understanding of the experience of loss. The substitute analyst should not attempt to develop an active "real" relationship with the patient. Finally, authors note some difficulties associated with the use of interim analysts. For some patients, an interim analyst may seem like a distraction from the attachment (Sarnat, 1991), or use of an interim analyst may feel like a vote of no confidence in the patient's ability to manage during the break (Webb, 1983).

Expansions in Psychoanalytic Theory

Attachment Theory
Our heightened appreciation of the importance of relational factors in development and in analysis has broadened our perspective on vacation breaks. Of particular value are the insights derived from

attachment theory. First constructed by Bowlby (1969) and further elaborated by Ainsworth (1989) and Main et al. (1985), attachment theory holds that the need for attachment is innate and persists throughout the life span. Instead of conceiving of the object as a supplier of needs, attachment theorists state that the object is the need (Mackie, 1981). Because attachment needs are innate, threats of separation or loss "evoke behavior in order to make contact with an attachment figure, preserving or regaining feelings of security" (Sable, 1992, p. 274). Moreover, interactions between infants and objects are mutual, and failures in attachment are likely to lead to cognitive, affective, and social impairments.

According to attachment theory, the interplay between the infant and the maternal figure forms an internal working model of relationship that is dynamic and becomes increasingly complex during the first two years of life. Once established, working models are unconscious (Ainsworth, 1989), actively self-perpetuating, and resistant to change (Bowlby, 1984). The concept of an internal working model is the bridge concept linking attachment theory with other relational perspectives (Bacciagaluppi, 1994) because it supports the premise held by relational theorists (e.g., Fairbairn, 1952) that intrapsychic structure is a result of experiences with the object.

Two findings of attachment research that have treatment implications are that attachment is the core experience of personality formation (Schneider, 1991) and that the object's attunement is a determining factor in the infant's model of attachment (Ainsworth et al., 1978). A number of infant researchers (Mahler, 1971; Stern, 1985) have described the way that experiences with the object affect personality development. Attachment theorists have elaborated these findings by pinpointing reunion as a time of great psychic vulnerability and by describing the patterns of interaction between the child and maternal figure that shape psychic development (Main et al., 1985).

In his initial observations, Bowlby (1969) found that infants engage in attachment behaviors. Differences in attachment behaviors have been organized into four categories: secure, avoidant, ambivalent, and disorganized (Main et al., 1985). Building on these observed differences in attachment behavior, Ainsworth et al. (1978) studied toddlers' responses to their mothers' departures, absences, and returns. The researchers found that the toddlers' responses to partings were not predicative of developmental problems. A securely attached child was as likely as the others to protest and cry at the mother's departure. It was at reunion that attachment difficulties were observed. On mother's return, the securely attached toddler readily engaged with her. The ambivalent child might cry or become angry, whereas the avoidant child might ignore the mother's return even though he or she searched for the mother during her absence. The behavior observed at times of reunion was representative of the child's internal working model and was predictive of later psychopathology (Stroufe, Fox, and Pancake, 1983).

Studying the object's influence on development, Main and Weston (1982) found that the mother's attunement to the infant affected his or her attachment behavior and internal working model. Ambivalence or rejection by the mother resulted in the infant's becoming preoccupied with referencing his or her mother and being unable to engage in other age-appropriate activities. As the infant increased its referencing behavior, the mother's ambivalent or rejecting responses also intensified. The maternal figure's capacity for attunement also appeared to be more generalized than was previously thought (Bacciagaluppi, 1994). Those mothers who were unable to respond to their infants' needs in one area were unable to meet their infants' needs in other ways. Finally, different individuals influence attachment behaviors differently. Infants' patterns of attachment with their fathers are independent of their behaviors toward their mothers (Bacciagaluppi, 1994).

If variations in attachment behaviors that occur at times of reunion are predictive of psychopathology and if object attunement directly influences these behaviors, then times of reunion between patient and analyst offer potential opportunities to remember, repeat, and work through maladaptive patterns. It is my assertion that the experience of reunion can provide a facilitating environment for altering models of attachment as described by Main et al. (1985) and therefore provide opportunities for the new object experience necessary for structural change described by Loewald (1960).

The Intersubjective Perspective
Complementing the findings of attachment theorists regarding the impact of the object on the development of intrapsychic structure is our increasing acknowledgment of the intersubjective processes occurring in the analytic dyad. For the purpose of this chapter, the concept of intersubjectivity is being defined as the way that the analyst uses his or her memories, conflicts, and wishes as they emerge during the session to understand a patient's experience (Renik, 1993).

In a one-person psychology, the analyst is important not as an object but as an observer and interpreter of the patient's transference neurosis. Interpersonal aspects of the analytic dyad, characterized as the "real relationship" (Greenson, 1967), are acknowledged as present in the process, but change occurs through interpretation of the transference neurosis (Strachey, 1937; Greenson, 1967). Accepting a bipersonal or two-person process means that "the focus is on the ongoing role of both analyst and patient in shaping processes in each other" (Phillips, 1997, p. 16). Analysts are not detached scientific observers interpreting data about patients' dynamics. They are participants influenced by their subjective experiences of patients and their own histories.

Acknowledging that the analyst is a subjective participant rather than an objective observer, requires us to examine differently his or her contributions to the analytic process. Interpretation is not just collecting the associations and reactions of the patient, which are then formulated by the analyst into a verbal intervention that is "in the moment" (Strachey, 1937). Interpretation is also employing one's subjective experiences in the moment to understand the patient. We are not imparting some objective truth but, rather, using patients' communications and our subjective experiences of them to help us understand the interactions that are occurring.

Transference has been amended to include the patient's and the analyst's experiences of, and influence on, one another. Analysts are not neutral figures who become representatives for patients' early experiences, nor are they interchangeable. The style, character, and authenticity of the analyst are also being responded to by the patient. Moreover, patients exert pressures on the analyst that result in enactments of early object experiences (Renik, 1993). Analysts are also responding to their subjective experiences of patients. As Boesky (1990) points out, if the analyst does not become emotionally involved, the work cannot proceed. Allowing that there is mutuality in the patient–analyst experience blurs the distinction that has historically been made between transference and countertransference. If analysts are unable to be fully objective, and if their subjective processes and conflicts also emerge in response to their patients, then analysts too experience transference responses.

The activities of the analyst and their influence on the analytic process have also been reformulated. According to Gill (1994), everything that the analyst does, including being silent, is experienced by the patient as an action and is a part of the therapeutic action. The analyst's actions reflect his or her opinions, wishes, and needs. The patient is responding to the qualities of the analyst as well as to the transference experience. Taking a vacation break is an action, a need of the analyst, that will affect the patient's and the analyst's perceptions and experiences. Partings and reunions will inevitably arouse transference responses from analysts and patients.

Jan: A Case of Avoidant Attachment

Jan, a 43-year-old woman, described a childhood barren of love and filled with sadism, rejection, and abuse. Until adolescence, she spent most of her time sitting alone in her room trying to escape the hostility and criticism of her family. Jan's mother was excessively competitive, envious, and cruel toward her only daughter. Jan described her mother as physically abusive, and she experienced her mother's repeated inspections of her body as evidence that she was sexually perverse. Jan's father was rigid, moralistic, and absent. Jan felt that he did not want to know what was happening at home. When Jan was 16, her mother died and Jan's father became physically abusive toward her. She believed that he blamed her for his wife's death because her mother had frequently told him that Jan was killing her. At around age 17, she was hospitalized for the first time with depression. After this initial hospitalization, Jan's withdrawal, sexual acting out, substance abuse, and suicidal attempts escalated; and at age 20 she was hospitalized for approximately one year.

Although she had many different therapies, it was only during her last treatment, with a psychoanalytic therapist, that she began to believe that she could change. This treatment lasted about a year after which she moved and was recommended to me for an analysis. According to Jan, she left the previous treatment because she had to take a new job and relocate. I was struck, however, by the precipitous nature of the ending. She never told the therapist she was seeking employment; she impulsively took a job and two weeks later moved to another state. It seemed to me that her early disappointments in relationships may have been replicated in her last treatment and that this was a potential vulnerability in our work.

During the first month, we explored Jan's thoughts and feelings about analysis. We agreed to meet three times a week. Jan was a sophisticated patient; she had an intellectual understanding of free association, transference, and multiple sessions. Without much discussion, Jan chose to recline on the couch. As Gill (1994) has noted, the use of the couch can also be a resistance. It seemed to me that reclining was one way that Jan demonstrated her conflicts regarding intimacy. By lying on the couch, she could do the work of an analysis but could also avoid the demands of face-to-face interaction with me.

As Jan talked about herself, her difficulties with intimacy were further elaborated. As she commented about other figures in her life, she was easily aroused to anger. Simultaneously, Jan acknowledged that she was a difficult person. She also expressed sadness, commenting that she did not know how any human could survive without being touched. She claimed that because of an innate flaw she had been hated by both her parents, and she believed that her hostility would ultimately destroy anyone who came close to her. Listening to Jan, I was aware of the quandary that would be played out in our relationship: her wish and her fear. Jan wanted to be loved and to belong, but she believed that she was toxic, unlovable, and that ultimately everyone would turn on her as her parents had.

Jan's description of a childhood lacking in positive object experiences, coupled with her mother's death during Jan's adolescence, suggested to me that Jan's capacity to attach and to tolerate a positive object experience was significantly impaired. Altering her inner world and internalizing a new object experience would require that Jan mourn her past. This process necessitated that Jan experience the pain of remembering her parents' responses to her and of acknowledging the despair for the maternal experience that could never be. Attachment theorists (Mackie, 1981; Bowlby, 1984) assert that, for patients with disorders in attachment, analysts must first establish a secure base before regression or interpretive processes can be of benefit. I believed that attunement to Jan's experience of reunions as well as partings would be one way to establish this secure base. What follows is a description of the treatment during the first year.

In an analysis, the first and last weekly session provide opportunities to observe the patient's response to reunion and parting. After the first few months of treatment with Jan, a pattern began to emerge. Reunion was difficult, whereas at parting, Jan was able to say more of what she was feeling. During the first six months of treatment, in our first weekly session, Jan was silent and avoided interaction with me. When she did speak, she would become agitated and say things like, "I feel stupid coming and having nothing to say." These sessions were also dominated by her obsessive thinking or dissociation, Jan's characteristic defenses against experiencing her emotions. I frequently felt helpless waiting through her prolonged silences. When she spoke, I would respond carefully because my perception was that Jan was fearful of intrusion by me. My responses were to say, "Maybe you would like to be quiet," or "It's hard to trust that I am willing to listen to you."

In the early phases of treatment, she would assert that she wanted to keep life as it always had been—she would be alone but safe from abuse. She did not trust me because she was sure that I would change. Besides, she would angrily assert, she liked being alone. By the sixth month of treatment, however, Jan was able to speak of her sadness and anxiety at our weekend partings. She might begin a session by saying, "It's Thursday." At times she seemed to want only to recline quietly on the couch, experiencing my presence and her sadness at parting. She reported feeling more disorganized over the weekend and having memories of abuse that she then criticized herself for by saying, "It wasn't that big a deal.'

The feelings that Jan expressed at times of parting enabled me to understand better her behavior in our first weekly session. By being silent and avoidant, Jan was re-creating her experience as a child, sitting in her room, scared and alone. Jan's experience with me in these sessions was similar to the pressure that she had felt while she was waiting to see what her mother might do. She felt that I too might have sadistic intentions to hit her, laugh at her, or tell her she was mentally ill. As I was able to communicate to Jan that I understood the difficulty she felt in getting started, she was able to speak more openly about the pressure and threat she had experienced in starting our first weekly session. My absence over the weekend aroused sadomasochistic fantasies in Jan. These fantasies were so real to her that by the time of our Monday session she was confirmed in her belief that she had destroyed me or that I would destroy her. In her fantasy, she had hit me over the head or I had smiled as I allowed her to walk into my office while another patient was still sitting there.

In reunion, as I learned to be attuned to the meaning of Jan's avoidance, she was able to explore these fantasies and her fear that I disliked her. She suspected that I saw my "good patients" on Fridays and Saturdays but that I wanted to get a break from her. She experienced me as being like her mother, rejecting and comparing her with other, "nice" girls at school. Concomitantly, she was aware that her experience with me was different from her experience with her mother. At times, recognizing this difference aroused her desire for intimacy, but she quickly defended against it by criticizing herself for having "childish feelings." Jan also reported that she told me more about her inner thoughts and that she sometimes felt better. These positive statements were brief and quickly followed by her talking about her fear of losing me: if she gets better, I will kick her out.

The partings and reunions of our weekly sessions forecast some of the ways in which Jan would respond to longer breaks. Typically, vacation breaks from patients raise concerns in me about my impact. I am aware of feeling guilty that I have encouraged patients like Jan to depend on my consistent presence. This is my concern but frequently not the patient's most pressing issue. Nevertheless, these thoughts are part of who I am, as I listen to what the patient is trying to tell me. In Jan's case, her former therapy had ended soon after a two-week vacation. This knowledge added to my usual concerns about taking a break. We were in the fourth month of treatment, and I was only beginning to understand Jan's dynamics, one of which was her need for control and structure. The analytic frame, for example, was comforting to Jan. Being allowed to start sessions and my not answering personal questions were things that she liked about analytic work. They seemed to provide her with a sense of control. Change, however, provoked anxiety. Breaks were changes that aroused Jan's fears of loss of control and disorganization.

Announcing a vacation is an action taken by the analyst that influences the patient's communications. In the session following my announcement, Jan reported a dream in which she had killed a cat. As a child, Jan had tortured animals. In therapy, she had come to realize that cats represented her. By torturing them, she was turning passive into active, becoming like her mother in an attempt to protect herself from abuse. As she talked about her dream and her associations to her mother, I made a comment about her dream that was an attempt to explore her associations. She became furious with me and accused me of saying that she was a child abuser and that she could never talk to me again.

I felt confused and caught in an emotional storm. In my internal process, I tried to retrace what had been said, but I continued to feel confused about how we had arrived at this enactment. Finally, using my sense of confusion to frame my response, I said that I was not sure what had happened but that she was telling me a dream of hurting a cat and then somehow began to experience me as criticizing her. She responded by saying that she felt confused; I agreed that it was confusing and that we could talk more about it. This enactment, as I understand it, was Jan's way of re-creating with me the experience of being rejected and criticized by her parents. By experiencing me as her critic, Jan could become angry with me and avoid the sadness that she felt about my taking a break.

According to attachment theory, partings are times of protest and attempts to forestall the separation. As this enactment indicates, Jan expressed anger about my leaving, but, at times, she was also able to communicate her sadness. She recalled her last, "bitchy therapist" and the things that she had done wrong. She also acknowledged how important the other person had been. Once we were able to talk about this displaced sadness toward her "other therapist," Jan was able to say that she feared that I would leave her permanently.

Nearer to the break, Jan presented a memory of an event when her mother was nice to her, something she had never told anyone else. Although this was Jan's first acknowledgment that her mother might have been both good and bad, it was also a way to protest my leaving. Here were things that an analyst would want a patient to talk about! I recognized that this might be a way to protest my leaving. In response, I did not probe or clarify this information about her mother's behavior; instead I listened to what Jan was saying, but I also encouraged her to talk about her feelings about my taking a break.

During the last week before the break, Jan could talk of little else. She was angry that I was going away and anxious about what could happen to me. She said that it "isn't the right time of year for therapists to go on vacation." Jan also expressed concern that I would change my mind and not want to see her when I returned. Her fantasies were that she was too difficult, that people changed and disappointments were inevitable. After listening to her, I responded that I might disappoint her by going away but that I would be returning in a week and would be expecting to see her. Jan said, "But you might change your mind." I said firmly, "No. I won't." She asked how I knew and then answered her own question, saying, "You know your own mind."

In the first session after my return, Jan was on time and showed a glimmer of a smile as she entered the office. She lay in silence for about 15 minutes but finally began to speak of how bad she was and how she had many violent thoughts. On the basis of my understanding of Jan's avoidant model of attachment, instead of responding to these veiled allusions to her anger toward me, I spoke to her fears of rejection. I said, "I understand that it is hard to trust that I would want to listen to you." In the next few weeks, as I continued to encourage Jan to talk about her reaction to our reunion, her transference response began to change. She told me that if I didn't get angry with her, I would get sick. She was toxic, and I was an innocent who could be hurt. This was the first time Jan had suggested that she might hurt me as she believed she had hurt her mother. It was also the beginning of a shift from avoidant, angry interactions to more related ones. She was now beginning to talk about a pattern of angry interaction with me that was similar to her experience with her parents.

My anticipation of Jan's reaction to my second vacation was shaped by her responses to our previous partings. I expected her to assert that I wanted to kick her out and to express fears that something would happen to me. Two months before the break, I told Jan that I would be away for three weeks in August. There was little direct response to my announcement in this or the following session. Jan's communications instead focused on historical material and the weekend parting.

Attachment theory holds that pathological responses are more likely to occur on reunion, and this idea was borne out by Jan's activity in the first session the following week. She was unable to speak for 10 minutes, a common response in our first weekly session earlier in the treatment. She lay on the couch, shaking her foot and making agitated gestures. Finally, she said that she had nothing to talk about. Things were the same and she had been feeling very suicidal over the weekend. Ordinarilly, I would not introduce a topic for the session. In this session, however, I thought that Jan was feeling overwhelming distress about the planned vacation and in reunion was displaying the avoidance typical of her model of attachment. To demonstrate attunement to her feelings of loss and anger, I suggested that she seemed very upset and that I couldn't help but wonder if this had something to do with the announcement of my summer break. She responded by telling me, "It is irresponsible of you to go away for so long. I've never had a therapist who took such a long break."

In that session, Jan told me of her hopelessness about talking to me because everything was going to end soon. She had been "duped" by me, she said. Like everyone else, I couldn't be trusted. For her, the break would be a final ending. There was no future. To understand and be better attuned to Jan's experience, I found myself reflecting on memories of being left in my own childhood. As I thought about Jan's expressions of despair, I remembered a time when I was four and had gone with my parents to visit family in another state. My parents were going out for the evening and I protested. It didn't matter that it was only for the evening or that my cousin, whom I knew, would be with me. Fear was primary for me. I couldn't hear reassurances. For me, the evening might as well have been forever. I used this internal image to help frame my responses to Jan. I told her that my break was a long time and that it was hard for her to think about anything but that I was going away. My response helped Jan to reconnect with me and to associate to memories of her parents' vacations and her mother's death.

There also was a continuation of the shift in Jan's model of attachment; her avoidant behavior diminished. She was now able to talk about her feelings rather than act them out. For example, she talked about her wish to withdraw from me rather than abandoning the treatment as she had in the past. She said that she did not want to talk to me but that she found herself doing it anyway. "I'm a wimp," she said. Jan asserted that her inability to act on her anger by leaving me first was a repetition of her childhood experience. At that time, she retreated to her room and never spoke back to her mother. I replied by saying that perhaps this experience was similar and different too. It was similar because she felt helpless, but it was different because we were talking about it.

My taking this second and longer break aroused strong feelings in Jan. In the last month before my departure, Jan was consumed by thoughts and feelings about my leaving. Although she was having more difficulty functioning outside the session, Jan wanted to talk only about my vacation. During the last week before the break, Jan's pain and helplessness in reaction to my departure were palpable in our sessions. Jan kept saying, "Taking such a long break is unprecedented. Therapists don't really care, or they wouldn't go away like this." I acknowledged that I was hurting her and doing something that she could not control. Jan continued to protest my taking a break, but she was also able to talk about her way of relating to me. She spoke of her awareness that she was difficult to get along with and that she was always alone as a result. She asked if I wanted to stop seeing her. I answered that it was important for us to keep talking and trying to understand what made relationships so painful for her.

Jan's difficulty functioning outside the sessions aroused my concern for the sense of abandonment, annihilation, and disorganization that she might experience during my absence. When I spoke with her about the possibility of seeing another analyst in the interim, she refused. "What could another therapist do?" she asked. "It wouldn't be the same." We finally agreed that I would call her during the break, and we arranged a time for the call. Given the degree of difficulty she was having, I felt that she needed me to extend myself to her to help contain her anxiety in my absence. Because of her avoidant pattern of response, I knew that it was unlikely that she would contact me, even if she desperately wanted to. During the phone conversation that ensued, Jan was silent much of the time. When she did speak, it was to accuse me of not caring or of planning to terminate with her when I returned. My responses to her were that I understood that this was a long time for her to wait for my return and that I could hear that she was afraid that I would never be back.

On my return, Jan showed up on time but was silent for most of our first two sessions. She stated that she had nothing to say, that everything had changed, and that I probably thought her response was childish. At this point in the treatment, I was aware that she had yearned for me during my absence and so I replied that it seemed she was very hurt by my leaving. She responded, "Don't say that. I hate when you talk like that." She went on, however, to talk about how difficult it was for her during my vacation but she knew that I didn't care about this. This deepening in Jan's ability to experience her desire for connection was quickly negated by her. She became upset, saying that these were immature feelings and only a child should feel this way. Again, Jan was attempting to defend against her pain about the past and her fear of intimacy by avoidance. In response, I said that it sounded as if she were telling me her feelings but that she thought that she wasn't supposed to have such feelings. These interactions facilitated the process of altering Jan's model of attachment because they encouraged her to talk with me rather than to avoid her experience.

A week later, I spoke with Jan about changing one of her appointment times. I explained that because of my teaching obligations I needed to make a change and offered her a time on that same evening. In this instance, I decided to tell Jan something about my request. We were just coming together after a lengthy break and, in reunion, Jan's insecure attachment responses were intensified. One way for the analyst to provide a secure base, according to Mackie (1981), is by being real, genuine, and authentic. By explaining my reasons to Jan, I was attempting to be real with her rather than leaving her to take in the information and interpret it on her own.

Her reaction to my announcement was powerful. She accused me of lying. She said that she had kept saying that everything would be different and that I had denied this but now everything was changing. She also said that when I told her times she wasn't given any choice. I did not engage in explaining that I had offered to discuss the time change, nor did I try to qualify that the changes she had been asking about before vacation, and what was happening now, were different. Instead, I acknowledged that I changed times and went on vacations and that she did not have a say in these decisions. The change in my schedule gave Jan another opportunity to express her feelings rather than be avoidant. It also fulfilled her fear that something would change. Jan's thinking was at times magical, and it was a relief to have something happen, particularly since it was not as bad as she anticipated.

At the same time, my response to her had not changed. I continued to be benign and receptive to her communications. She expressed her complaints and tearfully told me that it was hard for her to adjust to change and that I probably thought that was silly. She then associated to memories of childhood when she was alone and fearful of what could happen. At the end of this session, she commented that no one had ever explained things to her the way that I did.

As the analysis continues, Jan has begun to experience a more secure attachment that allows her to express her disappointments with me, but she is also quick to hold herself responsible for these disappointments. Concomitantly, as she experiences something different from me, she has begun to question her belief that she was the bad child. Moreover, she has begun to mourn her mother's death, her emotionally absent father, and her inability to have been a different child. Her torment as she speaks is poignant. As her model of attachment with me has become more secure, she can also momentarily tolerate the soothing tone of my voice. As one might suspect, she also becomes anxious because taking in a new object experience means letting go of early object representations.

Old identifications are not easily relinquished, and, when the process begins to occur in treatment, the patient may experience a sense of disorganization and depersonalization (Sandler, 1992). The more Jan mourns her past, the more difficulty she experiences at work and the more she retreats from any interaction other than her analysis. Her connection to me continues to intensify, but her fear of losing me continues as well. In the comings and goings that are part of the weekly rhythm of any analysis, we continue to address her wish for and her fear of attachment.

Conclusion

In a one-person psychology, the analyst is perceived as an objective observer rather than a participant in the process and his or her actions, such as going on vacation, are explored only in relation to what they tell us about the patient's intrapsychic world. In a two-person psychology, there is greater appreciation for the relational influences affecting the therapeutic action. Moreover, in a two-person psychology, the analyst is a subjective participant who influences, and is influenced by, the patient. This expansion in theory has led us to explore in greater detail the interactive forces that are inevitable when an analyst introduces his or her needs into the process. Treatment breaks are one example of a need of the analyst that affects the therapeutic action. This chapter has described some of the ways that relational forces can influence the patient–analyst dyad at times of partings and reunions.

References

Ainsworth, M. D. S. (1989), Attachments beyond infancy. *Amer. Psych.*, 44:709–716.
────── Blehar, M. C., Waters, E. & Wall, S. (1978), *Patterns of Attachment*. Hillsdale, NJ: Lawrence Erlbaum Associates.
Aron, L. (1996), *A Meeting of Minds*. Hillsdale, NJ: The Analytic Press.
Bacciagaluppi, M. (1994), The relevance of attachment research to psychoanalysis and analytic social psychology. *J. Amer. Acad. Psychoanal.*, 22:465–479.
Barish, S. (1980), On interruptions in treatment. *Clin. Soc. Wk. J.*, 8:3–15.
Blanck, G. & Blanck, R. (1974), *Ego Psychology*. New York: Columbia University Press.
Boesky, D. (1990), The psychoanalytic process and its components. *Psychoanal. Quart.*, 59:550–584.
Bowlby, J. (1969), *Attachment and Loss*. New York: Basic Books.
────── (1984), Psychoanalysis as a natural science. *Psychoanal. Psychology*, 1:7–21.
Fairbairn, W. R. D. (1952), *An Object Relations Theory of the Personality*. New York: Basic Books.

Firestein, S. (1978), *Termination in Psychoanalysis* . New York: International Universities Press.

Gill, M. (1994), *Psychoanalysis in Transition*. Hillsdale, NJ: The Analytic Press.

Greenson, R. (1967), *The Technique and Practice of Psychoanalysis*. New York: International Universities Press.

Jackel, M. M. (1966), Interruptions during treatment and the wish for a child. *J. Amer. Psychoanal. Assn.*, 14:730–735.

Kohut, H. (1978), *The Restoration of Self*. New York: International Universities Press.

Loewald, H. (1960), On the therapeutic action of psychoanalysis. *Internat. J. Psycho-Anal. Assn.*, 41:16–33.

——— (1962). Internalization, separation, mourning, and the superego. *Psychoanal. Quart.*, 31:483–504

Mackie, A. J. (1981), Attachment theory: Its relevance to the therapeutic alliance *Brit. J. Med. Psych.*, 54:203–212.

Mahler, M. (1971), A study of the separation-individuation process and its possible application to borderline phenomena in the psychoanalytic situation. *The Psychoanalytic Study of the Child*, 26:403–424. New York: Quadrangle Books.

Main, M., Kaplan, K. & Cassidy, J. (1985), Security in infancy, childhood and adulthood: A move to the level of representation. In: *Growing Points of Attachment Theory and Research: Monographs of the Society for Research in Child Development*, ed. I. Bretherton & E. Waters, 50(209):66–104.

——— & Weston, D. (1982), Avoidance of the attachment figure in infancy: Descriptions and interpretations. In: *The Place of Attachment in Human Behavior*, ed. C. M. Parkes & J. Stevenson-Hinde. New York: Basic Books, pp. 31–59.

Meissner, W. W. (1991), Empathy in the therapeutic alliance. *Psychoanal. Inq.*, 16:39–47.

Neutzel, E. J. (1991), Analytic interruptions. *Bull. Menninger Clin.*, 55:38–47.

Peck, J. (1961), Dreams and interruptions in treatment. *Psychoanal. Quart.*, 30:209–220.

Phillips, D. (1997), Subjectivity, analytic theory, and the analytic relationship. *Clin. Soc. Wk. J.*, 25:11–18.

Renik, O. (1993). Analytic interaction: Conceptualizing technique in light of the analyst's irreducible subjectivity. *Psychoanal. Quart.*, 62:553–571.

Sable, P. (1992), Attachment theory: Applications to clinical practice with adults. *Clin, Soc. Wk. J.*, 20:271–283.

Sandler, J. (1992), Reflections on developments in the theory of psychoanalytic technique. *Internat. J. Psycho-Anal.*, 73:189–198.

——— (1996), Comments on the psychodynamics of interaction. *Psychoanal. Inq.*, 16:88–95.

Sanville, J. (1982), Partings and impartings: Toward a nonmedical approach to interruptions and terminations. *Clin. Soc. Wk. J.*, 10:123–131.

——— (1987), Theories, therapies, therapists: Their transformations. *Smith Col. Studies in Soc. Wk.*, 58:75–91.

——— (1997), Philosophical considerations in psychoanalysis. *Clin. Soc. Wk. J.*, 25:19–26.

Sarnat, J. (1991), When a therapist goes on leave: Toward a rationale for clinical management of the interim. *Psychother.*, 28:650–59.

Schneider, E. L. (1991), Attachment theory and research: Review of the literature. *Clin. Soc. Wk. J.*, 19:251–266.

Stern, D. (1985), *The Interpersonal World of the Infant*. New York: Basic Books.

Strachey, J. (1937), The nature of the therapeutic action of psychoanalysis. *Internat. J. Psycho-Anal.*, 15:127–159.

Stroufe, L. A., Fox, N. E. & Pancake, V. R. (1983), Attachment and dependency: A developmental perspective. *Child Devel.*, 54:1615–1624.

Tarachow, A. (1963), *An Introduction to Psychotherapy.* New York: International Universities Press.

Webb, N. B. (1983), Vacation-separations: Therapeutic implications and clinical management. *Clin. Soc. Wk. J.*, 11:126–138.

Winnicott, D. W. (1965), *The Maturational Processes and the Facilitating Environment.* New York: International Universities Press.

Chapter 9

∞

A Case of a Stalemate Reversed
A Second Chance

Monica J. Rawn

_T_he reader may recall Kohut's (1979) case of Mr. Z, the patient
he reputedly first treated unsuccessfully in a traditional
Freudian analysis and then, later, successfully by using a self
psychology approach. This chapter presents a variation. I analyzed
the same patient twice, although the second time we were a different
analytic couple.

Soon after I had completed my analytic training, Beth, a young
mother of a toddler, sought my help. She had recently relocated from
Canada after her husband, a surgeon, obtained a hospital staff position. Alhough she loved him, Beth dreaded her husband's sexual
demands, which she resentfully submitted to and, in spite of herself,
experienced orgasm. She worried about her marriage and suffered
depression intermittently.

Beth looked like an attractive Barbie doll. She wore a masked smile
and comported herself in a self-contained manner. She had graduated
with honors from college and graduate school and had performed
well in her nursing career, which she gave up after the birth of her
daughter. Beth enjoyed enduring friendships and various interests
and had a stable family life.

As a concession to her husband, Beth initially limited her commitment in the first treatment to a twice weekly psychotherapy. She
presented herself as a compassionate and empathic person who
suffered at the hands of others and sacrificed herself to their needs.
She aimed to please everyone and eventually succeeded in pleasing
me. She was engaging, expressive, charming, and witty, virtually never
missed a session, and paid her bills promptly. She was a "good patient."

Beth's childhood experiences were her dominant concern in the
first treatment. She was the oldest and only girl of four children. She

slept in her parents' bedroom until she was five, when she was replaced by her baby brother. Beth was three when she was briefly hospitalized for an infection her mother had allegedly neglected. This screen memory became elaborated as a core organizer of Beth's tenacious reproach and secret desire for revenge against her caretakers. As a child she had been privy to her parents' quarrels and her father's rebuke of his wife for withholding sex. In a conspiratorial bond, he turned to Beth as confidante and advisor. She believed that if her mother would agree to sex, as Beth would have done, they could all live happily; and she so advised her mother.

Beth's love for her physician father was ambivalent. He was affectionate and caring but eager to placate his wife; he raged against Beth when she displeased her mother. He chased after her and hit her on the head as she took flight to lock herself in the safety of the bathroom. There she calmed and numbed herself, gazing into the mirror, soothingly telling herself that everything would be all right; she was a good girl. She saw in the mirror a reflection of a "beautiful good/bad girl" whom she admired. This mirror image was woven into a valued but secret dimension of her self-representation. This "other Beth" sought liberation and found it in secret defiance. The father who drove her to the mirror was a tyrant whom Beth held in secret rage and contempt. She could not reconcile him with the beloved father who sought her in his need.

Like her father, Beth felt love-starved by her mother, a beautiful woman, communicative but distant, withholding, and lacking in the motherly adoration that Beth yearned for. In later years, Beth felt valued by her mother for her beauty and good counsel. Beth came to believe that she surpassed her mother, a school principal, and that she could better mother herself. She viewed her mother as powerful in possessing the key to her father's love and to her own secret longing, but also as weak for having chosen a flawed man and for failing to protect her from him.

Beth handled sibling rivalry by psychically obliterating the competition. She carved out an indispensable place with her parents by lending them her wisdom. Self-sufficiency, self-containment, being all-knowing were essential components of her self-esteem and Beth's insurance for securing her place. They were formidable elements of her transference resistance.

The First Treatment

Beth approached the early phase of the first treatment with inordinate caution. She was puzzled and felt deprived by my explorative stance.

She had expected "nourishing" advice and directives. Beth associated her longing for my words with longing for more than words from a mother who starved her emotionally. She expressed feeling starved for love and "feedback," which reminded her of her own distaste for feeding her family.

After treating her for a year and a half, I thought that increased frequency and use of the couch would facilitate Beth's deeper immersion in the treatment. This was the traditional psychoanalytic prescription, and I believed it to be the treatment of choice for Beth, whom I considered a psychoneurotic patient with narcissistic features. With a mix of reticence, curiosity, and compliance, she agreed to my recommendation. Initially Beth lay still and silent in stubborn fright. She struggled against her growing dependence on me and resented my authority and requisites of treatment. I was a critical judge, she feared, who would injure her with insights and expose her flaws. "Everybody seeks my advice, but here I have to force myself to be the patient and seek yours," she said.

This phase yielded to the next. Having come to a reluctant but gradual appreciation of my interest in understanding her, she appeared a most cooperative patient and anticipated her sessions with an abundance of thoughts. The pattern of basic themes, perspectives, and affects unfolded. Beth grew adept at the symbolic language of metaphor, simile, and analogy, with dreams and associations, fantasies and memories. She brought insights, was reflective, introspective, and, it seemed to me, involved in the process.

Beth revealed a childhood masturbatory fantasy that had brought her to climax: "A bad man is doing bad things to me." She told me this in the context of describing an upsetting row with her husband. An improved version of her father, he was nevertheless Dr. Jekyll and Mr. Hyde. He was kind but demeaning of her attempts to become independent of him. She was intimidated by his temper when he felt sexually deprived by her. After their quarrel the night before she consented to sex to appease him and, as usual, begrudgingly climaxed. I noted that she had described her "bad man" fantasy while telling me of this experience. Beth elaborated that the fantasy, like reality, permitted her sexual pleasure while sparing her the responsibility for having it. She was chagrined to be repeating her parents' battles but acknowledged that she was now the desired partner her mother had been, not the excluded witness of the past. Still, she was resolute that sex with her husband "reduces me to a servicing machine."

Beth's revelation of the "bad man" masturbatory fantasy in the context of her marital discord followed a session in which I had initiated a discussion about raising her fee. Her response had been

conciliatory. Characteristically, she rejected my transference interpretation that I, too, was the bad man of her dream who wanted to
use her for my needs. Beth handled her negative feelings toward me
by diluting and displacing them (this time onto her husband), offering
protective excuses and rationalizations, perceiving things from my
perspective, and absorbing blame for her discontent. She warded off
anticipated attacks from me by complying, hoping to give me no cause
to criticize her. In retrospect I understood the measure to which Beth
appeared to align herself with a potentially dangerous analyst who
required submission and compliance.

Beth had attempted a way out of her sexual dilemma. Early in her
marriage she met an older, married man, a teacher her mother had
introduced her to. She was excited by the flirtation that developed,
her passion fueled by his adoration. Illicit sex with him made her the
powerful conqueror—the "bad, beautiful girl of the mirror." It
assuaged her fear of being overwhelmed by her husband's sexual
power. Compartmentalized, the two men complemented her good/
bad, impotent/powerful, passive/active selves. Guilt free about
betraying her husband, she insisted, "It has nothing to do with him.
It's separate."

Slave and master, polarized selves, was an internalized conflict with
which she struggled in raising her daughter. Beth felt enslaved by
this toddler, another master who tyrannized her with demands she
alternately submitted to and battled. In identification with her withholding mother, she attended her daughter resentfully. She expiated
her guilt by indulging her (as she wished to be indulged) and, in so
doing, identified with the good mother she had craved.

Beth had a repetitive bathroom dream: "I need to relieve myself
but I can't find a clean and private toilet." She reflected on the bathroom haven of childhood and on her treatment, where she sought
relief of her inner mess but not by way of exposing it to me. She felt
impinged on and caught up in the mess others created; she felt at the
mercy of satisfying their needs while ignored for her own.

Another dimension to the transference emerged. I became her ally
whom Beth defended when her husband derided the treatment and
insisted she terminate it. The transference took on a triadic coloration
with Beth situated in the middle of two powerful figures, each vying
for control over her. I observed that she used her husband to contain
and articulate her negative transference to avoid responsibility for
her own ambivalence. She likewise used her treatment with me in
conspiratorial alliance to defy him. Beth recognized these echoes of
her past.

In time, Beth appeared to evolve into a person of deeper substance,
willing to consider multiple perspectives to understand her life. I was

lulled into a comfortable compassion for her. My assessment of her and the complementary reaction that it evoked in me was an unconscious collusion, which had an impact on the treatment and resultant stalemate. Imperceptibly, as in Ingmar Bergmann's *Personna,* a film in which nurse and patient begin to resemble one another, Beth began to sound like me, and I began to think like her, to find her self-portrait too convincing.

This first treatment glanced at Beth's grandiosity. It emerged in her fantasy that she was her parents' keeper. Her narcissistic traits were revealed in her wish to remain Peter Pan, the precocious child entitled to get what she had in childhood been deprived of, relieved of expectation of servicing others. Fractured splits of her self (good/bad beautiful) and her objects (weak/strong), with their attendant affects, were explored. Oedipal and preoedipal derivatives in their multilayered condensation were factored into my diagnostic assessment. As Beth's development seemed increasingly to progress, I assessed her as healthier than she later proved to be. My initial diagnostic assessment remained unaltered. I viewed her as suffering the centrality and derivatives of an oedipal conflict yet to be resolved. I found evidence to support this diagnosis. This perception made the prospect of analyzing her less daunting and more promising.

The treatment was terminated after three years by mutual agreement. Beth claimed to have gained relief from sexual inhibitions with her husband in her newfound pleasure in intimacy. She no longer diluted it with an extramarital relationship. As she empathized more deeply with her family's needs, she said she enjoyed her power in meeting them. She gave the impression that she was developing a growing ability to separate past and present, husband from father, and mother from herself, so that she no longer needed to seek vengeance on her current family for the crimes of her first. She wanted to be a woman, not a girl. Wistfully, she said that her interests apart from her day-to-day family involvement sadly lacked "passion," but she could take this thought no further. The therapy, in spite of Beth's claims of its success, came to lack direction or purpose. It became stuck in her intractable satisfaction. Around this time Beth became pregnant, and we both felt this might be a propitious time for her to turn to the dyad within. It was understood that at some time in the future she would return to understand better her general sense of constriction. This first treatment enabled her to do that.

The Second Treatment
Beth returned many years later. She had left therapy content with her life but dimly aware that a nebulous "something" was unfinished, and she now felt ready to finish it. She felt that "some key would

unlock the door to the unfinished something," and I was to be or provide the key. As before, she bemoaned the lack of passion to commit herself to anything beyond the prescribed duties of homemaking and motherhood (she now had four children). This constituted her presenting problem. Beth looked the same despite the passage of time. During her leave of me, she had had cosmetic surgeries. She later confided that she had withheld her plans for surgery from me for fear I would disapprove and discourage her. This was but one of the lies of omission that Beth apprised me of. Since last I saw her, she had come into great wealth, acquired and controlled by her now prominent husband. Beauty and buying power had become arsenals in her attempt to fill the nagging "lack of something" she suffered, but the rewards of acquisition were short lived and required constant renewal.

The sexual problem for which Beth had initially sought help, and that, upon termination, she had claimed remedied, was as problematic as before. Had she regressed? Had symptom relief been a transference cure? Had she lied about its resolution? That she would lie to me was a new consideration. Beth continued to experience sex as a humiliating but necessary submission to her husband, for which she received tangible compensations. She felt like a whore and tested his love for her by withholding sex. "Does he want me for me or for sex?" She wondered. She donned jewelry during sex to feel power in beauty. She was contemptuous of her husband's need of her, as she was self-contemptuous of her dependency on him.

She sought power and worth in another extramarital affair with a man she considered her inferior. Beth assuaged her guilt by imagining a benefit to all. Gaining power in his adoration, she could infuse him with the strength of her sexual favors and intellectual prowess. Then she could be a more powerful lover to her husband. I was the audience to her "sexploits," and this was part of her excitement. She scheduled her trysts either just before or just after her sessions with me. I conjectured that this was a transference version of her mother as backdrop to her last affair. I had understood that as a quintessential oedipal drama and primal scene reversal. It seemed to me that as a wife, Beth felt compelled to repeat her mother's life of submitting to or rebelling against dutiful sex. In an extramarital affair, she was the woman her father would have wanted. Subsequently I considered a graver, more insidious drama, which I will later expand on.

Though Beth looked the same as in the past, I now saw her as a very different patient. Beth brought bountiful and interesting material to explore; she continued to be reflective and insightful. Nonetheless, nothing changed. I began to understand why. What had earlier impressed me as her developing psychological mindedness led me to overestimate her level of object relatedness. I gradually discerned that it was the acquisition of insight, not its application, that she sought. She acquired insights addictively as she did her possessions, but she used them in lieu of genuine attachments and affects to remain a detached observer.

Disconnectedness from herself and others was most apparent in Beth's relationships with her children. She perceived and responded to them as various parts of herself. She viewed her eldest daughter as a genius whom she indulged in exchange for alliance against Beth's husband. When the school nurse correctly suspected the child was diabetic, Beth delayed seeking medical consultation. She could not bear confirmation that her daughter was defective. She could not follow through on a recommendation from the school that she seek treatment for a son who was a discipline problem. He was her designated "beautiful/bad self of the mirror," who sought the freedom denied her. She was out of touch with the child's suffering and signal for help, much as her mother had been impervious to Beth's. Beth unduly delayed another child's toilet training. She indulged his "babyness" in an attempt to fulfill her own frustrated dependency yearnings, which she could neither acknowledge nor gratify. Identifying with her own greedy acquisitiveness, she was dismissive about her child's being caught shoplifting.

Beth deluded herself that her children were improved, normal versions of herself, but her idealized picture of "lovely family" defied reality. Interacting with them made her anxious. Giving to them depleted her; she sought replenishment in material supplies. In the absence of something that felt genuine to give, Beth gave a performance—her version of how she imagined I would talk to my child. She was relieved when I noted, "What you show me is your idea about the right way to talk to your children, but it doesn't feel alive to you." She agreed. Feeling guilty, Beth ignored, denied, avoided, or minimized what she had painfully come to know. I felt the strain of trying to infuse her with relatedness in the absence of her own. Eventually, Beth allowed us to see that underneath her veneer of loving mother was a deprived angry envious child. The neediness of her children repulsed her: "Why can't they be their own mother like I was? How can I be a mother and give to my children what my mother didn't give to me? Why should I?"

A synopsis of a session illustrates Beth's identification with her offspring as a deprived, abandoned victim of a detached mother; her attempt to turn passive suffering into an active infliction of it; and her use of me—to subject me to witness and contain her conflict. The issue Beth avoided discussing was her recently disclosed secret arrangement to send her six-year-old child to Canada to spend the summer with relatives, whom he had not seen since he was two. Beth registered her own mood: "Not terrible, but not good. I've felt in the past I could handle things. I'd like to feel that way now." I asked her what she was having trouble handling now. "Nothing really that I can't handle." Sounding nonchalant, she said she looked for the relief of school ending. I commented that relief seemed the only pleasure in sight. "True," she said. She listed chores she had to tend to. I said, "Perhaps thinking about concrete things you must do is helpful in allaying your anxiety. It reassures you that you are competent to deal with what you have to and spares you worry about intangibles that you're unsure about handling. I'm thinking of Charlie, whom we spoke about last time." Responding airily, she said, "I can't say I worry about him. I'm feeling different, not helpless about him. I work hard to give him what he's asking for." She enumerated what she had bought for the child. "When school ends I'll be able to run some errands for him." I remarked that it sounded as though she were thinking about Charlie as another task she must tend to. She agreed.

I became conscious of my worry about this child, soon to be sent away to strangers for a prolonged time—a child who could not yet sleep alone through the night. I felt alone in my worry. I wondered if Beth had unconsciously split off her affects for me to contain lest they overwhelm her. I commented that I had heard her say *she* was feeling different these days, not helpless, but I inquired whether Charlie was likewise feeling different, less frightened at night. Beth responded defensively: "Charlie has sleep disturbances, but we talk about it. If I had time, I'd probably get help for him." I said, "I haven't heard how it *feels* to *you* not to be able to do what you think you should do for Charlie." "Well," she said, "I'll do more for him next semester—pack his lunch, take him shopping—he needs socks."

Then there was a crack in her armor, a tremor in her voice. "I just can't get to everything," she said. I no longer felt the designated worrier—Beth was anxious. I said, "You seem to feel that helping Charlie is up to you alone. Both of you are in the same boat, feeling anxious, and perhaps you think of yourself as too fragile to do the job. No one answers the call for help—for Charlie or for you." She reverted to her complacent posturing. "I'm used to managing." I said, "By not feeling connected, not letting yourself know you're worried." "Yes, I know I'm worried, but I don't want to be overwhelmed. I hope Charlie won't be homesick in Canada. My cousins have animals, a lake. He doesn't have trouble making friends.

It's a nurturing place, not like the camp I was sent to for the summer when I was seven."

Beth had not mentioned this experience before. She described how lonesome she had been, scared that something would happen to her family in her absence. Would they ever come to claim her? Was this a banishment forever? Now she was repeating that nightmare by inflicting it onto her son. She was made conscious of the probable impact on Charlie. Beth circumvented her guilt with defensive dismissiveness. I commented that perhaps in describing her own abandonment to camp Beth was also conveying a feeling that I was ignoring her needs by examining Charlie's. She came alive. "Well, yes. I hear criticism," she answered, becoming teary. "I have the image of being whipped." I ventured, "The risk is that you feel blamed if we talk about things, but you blame yourself all the time. You don't let yourself hear my concern for you, and you don't let yourself hear your concern about your son. Nevertheless, you do convey your worry in what you tell me about Charlie. And you give me an idea of what you might have felt when you were a little girl left alone to face your worries about being sent for so long so far from home." "I have an image of balancing plates up in the air on a stick," she said. "My kids are the plates–up there, twirling about, but not falling. So I'm not worried." "Sounds like a pretty precarious situation to me," I said. With nervous recognition, she chuckled at her metaphor of balancing china and elaborated on what she feared was her breakable tottering self. I wondered if, by my making her aware of her worries, she felt I was shattering her. She said, "Worry is a luxury I can't afford." I said, "But you do worry; it's just that you don't connect it with the ideas you're telling me." "I guess," she said, "it's like the self-soothing mirror: I'm okay, you're okay." I added, "You're okay, Charlie's okay." Beth sent Charlie to Canada.

In the illusion that she could be her own therapist, Beth covertly defied being the designated patient. Her burden, she insisted, was to fix others by getting herself fixed. "But what in me needs to be fixed?" she asked. Her hidden agenda was to normalize herself by contrasting herself to others who were irrational, corrupt, and out of control. She had to be sane while they had the luxury of acting up and out. I became aware that my assignment was to validate her views and efforts to cure her family and friends. In a rare outburst, her rage broke through and frightened her. "Last night I got so angry I kicked the wall and broke a mirror. I acted just like the maniac my father was," she said. I commented on how much effort she needed to spend controlling herself by controlling others, all the while maintaining her cool in the midst of the chaos around her for fear she'd become part of it.

Lacking conviction that she was a patient, the best Beth could do was masquerade as one, preserving the façade of an alliance with me. Issues were displaced onto the past and away from the immediacy of our exploration or her expressed need of me. Beth announced that she no longer used marijuana but that her husband did on occasion. I had not been aware that she used it. I addressed this issue: "You must have thought this would be a problem with us so you needed to dispose of it before bringing it to me. You want to feel understood by me, connected, real—but it feels too risky to expose yourself." To get my help, she felt compelled to appear in harmony with me while arming herself against our discoveries with secrets and lies. Beth said, " If you tell me what you think I can get into that mode of thought." Lying, omissions, and deception were her means of maintaining compartmentalization, autonomy, and the status quo to ward off anticipation of my criticism or intrusion. Analytic exploration was antithetical to her need for coverup.

The gradual illumination of Beth's narcissistic character and unfolding nuances of the transference uncovered her fragmented self, a mosaic of vacillating bits and pieces that seemed as if there were many Beths. A troubling symptom emerged—anorexia. She condemned eating as greedy self-indulgence and felt stronger for defying it by starving. Beth wished she could have the pleasure of food, but the telltale flesh would expose her pleasure. She felt that therapy, like food and sex, should be forbidden her. Food and therapy were permissible if she were sick, but in sickness she would be imperfect and unlovable. On the other hand, sickness would entitle her to the care she craved from her family and me. She relished eating in restaurants where she was served *her* choice by strangers, no strings attached. In food as in sex she preferred the safer love of strangers. While it demeaned her to ask for help, Beth used her body to show her need.

Consistent with the nature of her fantasies and relationships, sadomasochism was the prominent feature of Beth's anorexia. Saying no to food was the ultimate defiance of her mother, who could feed food but left her starved; a therapist who offered food for thought ("like a hit on the head") but not the thoughts she wanted. To eat, have sex, be a patient were commands that she perform like the mindless Barbie. She identified with the deprivation she experienced and reversed it on herself, her family, and me. She used her skinny body to obtain the secret joy of victory in thwarting and worrying us. She found pleasure and power in flaunting her sick imperfection before those for whom she had to fake perfection. We had denied her right to be real, to feel depression, unhappiness, anger, neediness, all that she had felt compelled to hide behind a smile. We sought reassurance about ourselves in her façade of normality but now she withheld it. "I'm feeling miserable, but I feel grateful to feel alive and real," she would say. Her palpable suffering was mixed with the unmistakable pleasure of revenge. "My mother asked why I can't ask her for help. Helping someone makes you feel good. I won't give her that pleasure." Nor did she wish to give it to me. Validating my treatment would diminish her. "We need to find a way that you can feel good about using my help to take better care of yourself," I said. How she regulated food made her powerful or weak, victim or victimizer. To eat or not to eat was a question without easy solution. The position she took left her starved and angry, convinced that she could depend on herself alone, not on people who were supposed to help her.

I was increasingly alarmed as Beth enjoyed her skeletal appearance. The impact of projective identifications I experienced countertrans-ferentially made this stage of treatment particularly stressful. Used as container for her worry and "badness," I worried about Beth's physical health and the efficacy of my treatment. Was I inflicting on her some derivative of my own sadism? Was I gratifying her quest for sadism? I felt guilty in response to her nonverbal, guilt-provoking demands. Like her, I was self-reproachful and accused myself of not "feeding" her properly. I felt helpless in the face of her fragility and became aware of being oversolicitous and inhibited in using my aggression in the service of interpretation, doubtless a reaction formation to my anger at her for inflicting on me this disquiet. My rescue fantasy— that her life depended on me and she would not let me help her unless I did something tangible for her—was a countertransference response to her demand that I *show*, not just *talk* concern. Distancing herself and unable to experience my concern for her, she told me, "You're just a detached voice I hear in the distance."

Beth's anorexia evolved during her trial return to nursing. Emula-tion of me as a professional woman had been part of her motivation to resume part-time work, but success fell short of her expectations. In the face of her resentment of taking care of needy people, her work as a nurse was destined to fail. If she could not be the best healer, then she would distinguish herself by being the worst patient. We talked about her competition with me, her need to program herself for failure, her wish to undo my success to join her in defeat.

Concerned about Beth's anorexia, I referred her to a psychiatrist for antidepressive medication. My reluctant admission of need for help mirrored Beth's. The psychiatrist provided potential for further transference splitting. "You're just talk. The psychiatrist gives me concrete stuff," she said, wondering which of us she could discard. "Do I need medication or therapy? Am I sick or self-indulgent?" Her questions sought an answer to the basic one, "Who am I?"

Beth's façade of normality was an attempt to defend against her fear of fragmentation, manifest in her shifting identifications and attendant affects. To be valued as special, she said, "I have to be not me. I have to give up my own view to keep peace. I don't know what my own view is." Splits in her representational views was her attempt to keep boundaries intact and affects appropriate to the needs of the moment. I told her, "It's a struggle for you to know what's real. Different parts of you feel different ways. Sometimes this keeps us from knowing what you're up against." In the absence of her own self, she borrowed one. Imitating me, Beth created a caricature, a distant voice that did not feel or get involved.

The complexity of Beth's sexual conflict was elaborated. I had understood it in terms of oedipal taboos and triangulation. Altercations with her husband left Beth feeling demolished, "like a shell without thought or words." What she wanted from me was a prophylactic—to tell her how to manage sex, not how to enjoy it, as she had attempted to manage her mother's frigidity. She was in an insoluble bind. Her orgasms diminished her by acknowledging her husband's power to pleasure her. Fantasies of merging with her husband in sex threatened her boundaries yet provided a powerful phallus to identify with. Beth felt like an empty child who was expected to be properly asexual but, at the same time, to be the sexual woman her husband wanted her to be. At best, she could only pretend to be that woman. Her power lay in controlling him, extracting from him compensatory accoutrements for the sacrifice of her "true self." This was her "pact with the devil." The forbidden pleasure of sex was forced on her, not her claim or responsibility. She lived with an adversary, the bad man of her childhood sexual fantasy. I was the bad mother who witnessed and neglected her in her affliction.

My summer vacation was imminent. Beth decided to preempt it by taking hers first. She announced this uncharacteristic maneuver nonchalantly with a breezy, saccharine dismissal of me, which I commented on. Beth said that, although she sounded as if "I'm blowing you off," she was giving me the break from her she imagined I needed. Eyes tearing, she said she knew she was a tough patient. Seconds later she said, "I have another bizarre thought. You need to get away from me because you're too attached to me." That night, after sex with her husband, she dreamt that he molested and castrated a male child. She fantasized that he could slash her too. She reproached me with, "You're going to leave me with my guts hanging out." Feeling like an endangered, depleted child with "no stuff inside," Beth had a restitutional bisexual fantasy: "A woman makes love to me, adores me. I passionately suck her breasts, and they fill me with stuff to have inside so I can then have something to give to a man." Unconsciously, her husband, the provider of "stuff," was the conflictual, preoedipal mother she yearned for, but he was aggressivized, sexualized, and taboo. What constituted her deep disappointment with me became more clear to us both. The hidden agenda, the "do something, give me something" demand, was not that I fill her with the stuff of understanding but, rather, that I be the woman who would fill her with love and adoration, restore her wounded narcissism, confirm her perfection in order to transform her into a woman for the man. This was the key she had sought in me. The triadic fantasy was a composite of preoedipal, oedipal, homosexual, and heterosexual yearnings.

Uncovering this fantasy together revealed Beth's secret agenda in all her relationships—to submit in order to be fulfilled and transformed. Deprived of this fulfillment, she substituted revenge. This central fantasy posed a profound resistance to honest exploration and change. I said, "We've been giving each other the wrong thing. To get the love you want from me, you've been giving me compliance, which is not what I want. I've been giving you alternative ways to consider things, which is not what you want because it feels like a demand that you sacrifice your true self." She was in genuine agreement. We arrived at a turning point in this stalemate.

Discussion

I have attempted to describe a treatment stalemate set in reverse. The nature of the stalemate was my mistaking the patient's presentation of a false self for a therapeutic alliance. I first treated Beth while still under the influence of what was then au courant—the centrality of the Oedipus complex, the narrow definitions of transference and countertransference, and the narrow definition of psychoanalysis. My altered assessment of the patient was enriched by contemporary theories I found compatible with my own, particularly those which addressed earlier, more primitive issues. In the second treatment, which followed years later, I was listening with a more seasoned ear and a readiness to make use of myself as an analytic instrument. It became apparent that the entrenched stalemate was a derivative of the patient's dynamics and of compromise solutions and was an integral part of the transference–countertransference configuration. I had been treating a pseudoneurotic in a pseudoanalysis.

Apart from the vogue of the times in the initial treatment, what could explain my underestimation of Beth's pathology? A diagnosis of psychoneurosis was supported by Beth's presentation of ego strengths, enduring relationships, capacity for introspection, and stability of lifestyle. She met the criteria for analyzability. Martin Stein (1981), describing patients like Beth, whose masked pathology is not easily uncovered, writes:

> These are "good patients" who are cooperative, interesting and very adept at analytic process. They demonstrate very little evidence of severe pathology, their conflicts appear to be centered about the resolution of the oedipal phase . . . transference neurosis is very highly developed, taking on distinctly oedipal forms: it is powerfully defended by these patients, who demonstrate the characteristics of brilliant, charming and precocious children . . . [p. 873].

Beth's presentation was synchronous with the kind of patient I had been trained to treat psychoanalytically. In that context, I interpreted the triadic elements of her relationships, and, by extension, the transference, to be primarily oedipal derivatives. I viewed her defenses—repeating, reversal, undoing, and revenge (typical psychoneurotic mechanisms)—to further substantiate my analytic myth, the countertransferential response to her personal myth. Loewald (1986) ascribed this kind of diagnosing upward in part to the limits of how analysts were trained to treat developmentally advanced (oedipal) patients who met the selection criteria of psychoanalytic training institutes. Patient selectivity of this kind hampered inexperienced analysts in identifying and understanding the countertransference evocations of the more primitive narcissistic transferences.

Freud (1912) narrowly viewed transference as resistance when it was negative or took an eroticized detour from the positive transference. Transference resistance, thus defined, required analytic investigation. The "friendly or affectionate" aspects of the positive transference, on the other hand, were considered the "unobjectionable . . . vehicle to success . . ." (p. 105). Until relatively recently, countertransference, considered narrowly, was presumed to be an impediment to treatment. Countertransference was identified as such when it was negative, either in overt dislike of the patient or in more subtle derivatives of aggression or erotization. Positive countertransference, ego syntonic with the analytic ego ideal of compassionate doctor and archetypical maternal caretaker was less subject to the rigors of analytic scrutiny. Positive feelings toward the patient were as acceptable as the unobjectionable positive transference and left to lie under the mistaken guise of a working alliance. Beth's "friendly and affectionate" feelings masked compliance, which I mistook for a working alliance.

A component of resistance to countertransference examination at that time was the emphasis on the patient's dynamics isolated from my response. Transference and countertransference were not then viewed as intertwined facets of the analytic process. Early in the second treatment, as Beth's session was about to begin, I became aware of my reverie thought: "I can get a break. It's time to see Beth." Having had a difficult session with a volatile patient, I anticipated my session with Beth for a measure of relief. This thought had probably occurred to me before but had gone unnoticed. Reflecting on it, I realized that I had responded to Beth with unquestioned comfort. Influenced by the thinking of "Contemporary Kleinians," I pursued new avenues of introspection. How does the patient make me feel? What part of the patient am I containing and reacting to? Of what use does she wish to make of me? My assessment was recast by Schafer's (1992) focus on the patient's self-narrative, potentially becoming a shared version in the countertransference atmosphere of empathy, projective identification, and enactment. Countertransference consideration was no longer relegated by the mainstream analytic community to narcissistic indulgence that detracted from the primary focus on the patient. Rather, awareness of the intersection of transference and countertransference gained credibility as a tool to inform and vitalize the treatment.

In Beth's first treatment I had succumbed to her coercion to leave her self-presentation intact. I dismissed my positive countertransference as unobjectionable until I became conscious (in the second treatment) of my association of relief with Beth. It alerted me to my core countertransference response to Beth's central fantasy—submission for transformation. In this enactment I had yielded to Beth's demand for approbation, reparation, and unchallenged acceptance of her *Weltansicht*. Grossman (1982) maintains that the patient's representation of the self is a much invested fantasy that one is likewise invested in narrating: "Self-description may serve many interpersonal functions, such as appeal, reproach, revelation, gift. . . . By no means the least important is the invitation to appreciate and approve the style, wisdom and self-knowledge" (p. 930). The patient seeks the analyst's support to maintain his representation and fears that interpretive endeavors will undermine it. Beth shaped the dialogue to please, impress, lull, and control me, to secure protection from me. We could thus make this analytic journey a smooth voyage destined to stand still. In the first therapeutic effort,

I was informed by a close reading of the content of our sessions, that is, the analytic conversation, its latent underpinnings as decoded by context, contiguity, sequential links, metaphors, allegories, and inferences. This listening process is well described by Langs (1978) and Arlow (1979). But consideration of the mutual impact of the dialogue and motivations influencing it offered yet another level of insight.

The greater emphasis on genetic interpretations and reconstruction during my training was based on the belief that looking through the rear view mirror of the past would bring curative insights. Lifting repression of past traumas to make the unconscious conscious and thereby redress a patient's fixations and regressions was the therapeutic aim. That effort was reflected in Beth's first treatment. This approach was recast by the object relations school just beginning its ascending influence in my training institute. It altered the focus of treatment from lifting the patient's repression of causative historical "truths" to that of uncovering the patient's representational world and the psychic meanings he attributes to life experiences. Emphasis on repression was redirected to the vicissitudes of splitting, in which polarized parts of the self exist side by side or are projected and contained elsewhere to avoid painful affects. The expanded aim of therapy was to integrate these parts to promote cohesion. Patients described in the literature by Kernberg (1975), Kohut (1979), and others were understood to suffer pathological narcissistic and character disorders, in contrast to the transference neurosis of primary concern during my early training. Mahler, Pine, and Bergman (1975) extended our understanding of preoedipal development.

This altered focus on narcissistic and borderline pathology eclipsed our preoccupation with treatment of transference neurosis. A broader spectrum of defenses associated with these disorders was illuminated. The forceful impact of projective identification on the analyst revised our conceptualization of transference, countertransference, and resistance. Freudian analysts were becoming conversant with the contributions of the interpersonal school, which expounded the centrality of the relational aspect of therapy. The *mutuality* of impact on each in the analytic partnership was now grist for the analytic mill. Psychoanalytic technique was modified to accommodate the widening scope of patients and theoretical perspectives. My second treatment of Beth focused pointedly on narcissistic and preoedipal vicissitudes in revised views of resistance, transference, and countertransference through the changing psychoanalytic lens.

Beth's first treatment was defensively organized around her presented history. Transference configurations narrowly embellished her narrative. This narrowed focus served as a counterresistance to her defensive displacement onto the past in order to deflect the present. My interpretations reflected greater emphasis on genetic material and reconstructive efforts, the "then-and-there." Beth considered them plausible and placidly added them to her collection of insights. Kris (1956), describing a failed first analysis of a patient, faulted the treatment for failing to "penetrate the autobiographical screen . . . the patient's life continued under the spell of the personal myth . . ." (p. 656). In this case, Beth had a tenacious stake in preserving her one cohesive version of her autobiographical self. This self protected the syndrome of aggrandizement, victimization, and entitlement. It warded off the link between guilt and aggression. Informed in the second treatment by my countertransferential oversolicitation, I was able to enlighten myself and my patient about the missing links to her aggression, penance, and adaptive endeavors to forestall retribution. Earlier, I alluded to my view of Beth's triadic sexual affairs as oedipal derivatives, a defensive reversal of primal scene and oedipal wounds. Her history gave credence to my surmise. I later conceptualized and addressed these more broadly as metaphor rather than as literal historical event. The second treatment was conducted with greater *emphasis* on the "here-and-now" immediacy of transference and countertransference. Joseph (1985) broadly defined these as operative in the "total situation":

> Everything of importance in the patient's psychic organization . . . will be lived out in some way in the transference . . . how our patients communicate their problems to us is frequently beyond their words, and can often only be gauged by means of the countertransference [p. 167].

Focusing more broadly in the later treatment on Beth's use of me as witness and audience to her acting out of sexual fantasies expanded the interpretive field.

Reflecting on the patchwork self Beth presented, the levels of her deceptions, I was reminded of similar patients described as false self, "as if" personalities, and impostors. Greenacre (1958) describes the dynamic of the patient's reliance on an audience for confirmation of reality in the context of an illusory self, of needing others to believe in what is the unbelievable: "It is from the confirming reaction of his audience that the impostor gets a 'realistic' sense of self, a value greater than anything he can otherwise achieve" (p. 100). To paraphrase Descartes: "I'm seen, therefore I am—what I present myself to be."

There is a powerful countertransference pressure on the analyst to believe. Beth's affairs impressed me as theater staged to repair and reconstitute herself in her feelings of unreality and depersonalization. In drama she could experience intense excitement, which validated her sense of being. Beth poignantly described her lack of feeling a genuine connection to those she was required to be closest to. Weeping, she told me, "I want that feeling of connection. When I don't feel it, I imagine how you would feel in the situation and that's how I act." We began to understand that her extramarital affairs were sham relationships that felt more real to her when she could concretize her experiences by talking about them to me. Beth observed that her "beautiful good/bad girl in the mirror," her more powerful and admired self, was the self that was revitalized in these affairs. A semblance of flesh was given that self in the show-and-tell to me of this girl of the mirror.

Beth's imitation of me, perhaps a rudimentary step toward internalization, served a confluence of functions. As an identificatory function, it served to keep me close. It was also a defensive measure designed to destroy her need of an object by *becoming* the object. Historic precedence was her fantasized supersession over parents she psychically destroyed and replaced with herself. Beth's defense against her need for and envy of me was to defeat and destroy me. Discarding people felt freeing but left her a hollow orphan. She had a deep sense that what she was and what she had were someone else's property. Uncovering and working through the disappointment that motivated her desperate measures to secure a genuine self was the formidable task of the second treatment.

Beth concealed the unacceptable by creating a false self, which she invested with self-idealization, deception, and fractured perception. She was made ephemeral by the fragmentation of her internal representations, identifications, object relations, superego, and ego ideal dicta. Distorted communication undermined Beth's belief in her own authenticity, in her words and mine. She was a mere mirror image and I was but a detached voice. Communication that was so compromised challenged her capacity for working through to change.

The adaptive function of the false self is to protect the true self's core (Winnicott, 1954). The false self becomes its own self-caretaker: "That which proceeds from the true self feels real (later good) whatever its nature, however aggressive; that which happens in the individual as a reaction to environmental impingement feels unreal, futile (later bad), however sensually satisfactory" (p. 292). The false self feels life as false.

Bromberg (1994) accounts differently for the phenomenon of oscillating selves. What I have understood as a mechanism of splitting, as vicissitudes of the false self or "as if" disorder, or as the more conscious presentation of the imposter, he describes as altering states of dissociation, with their attendant perceptions, memories, moods, and sense of self, supported by multiple narratives. Bromberg holds that along the continuum of normalcy to pathology lies the potential for existence of multiple selves. From this vantage, one has multiple "true selves." These selves are preserved by dissociation, which serves repression of trauma and the fear of self-fragmentation. Linguistic links become accessible by way of the patient's enactments in the relational context of analysis. Bromberg describes the proscribed analytic aims: "Psychological integration . . . does not lead to a single 'real you' or 'true self.' . . . it is the ability to stand in the spaces between realities without losing any of them . . . the capacity to feel like one self while being many.' " (p. 534).

Conclusion

I have outlined the multifaceted layers and nature of a stalemated treatment that I had an opportunity to reverse. The patient affords a panoply of psychoanalytic paradigms with which to contemplate her. I have attempted to portray the gradual illumination of the defensive measures used by my patient in her desperate attempt to maintain cohesion and the integrity of her hidden selves. Anorexia was the symptom of a negative therapeutic reaction that served a core unconscious fantasy. The skinny body was evidence of her preoedipal mother's failure and her expression of reproach toward her. To use my help was to give up this bittersweet revenge. Finally, I tried to illustrate the unfolding transference–countertransference configurations in their various levels of determination as they illuminated this twisting analytic journey. We were, both of us, changed at journey's end. Beth learned to hear her many voices. I learned how many ways they could be heard.

References

Arlow, J. (1979), Metaphor and the psychoanalytic situation. *Psychoanal. Quart.*, 68:363–385.

Bromberg, P. (1994), "Speak that I may see you": Some reflections on dissociation, reality, and psychoanalytic listening. *Psychoanal. Dial.*, 4:517–547.

Freud, S. (1912), The dynamics of transference. *Standard Edition*, 12:97–108. London: Hogarth Press, 1958.

Greenacre, P. (1958), The impostor. In: *Emotional Growth, Vol. 1.* New York: International Universities Press. 1971, pp. 93–112.

Grossman, W. (1982), The self as fantasy: Fantasy as theory. *J. Amer. Psychoanal. Assn.*, 30:919–938.

Joseph, B. (1985), Transference: The total situation. In: *Psychic Equilibrium and Psychic Change*, ed. M. Feldman & E. B. Spillius. London: Tavistock/Routledge, pp.156–167.

Kernberg, O. (1975), *Borderline Conditions and Pathological Narcissism*. New York: Aronson.

Kohut, H. (1979), The two analyses of Mr. Z. *Internat. J. Psycho-Anal.*, 60:3–28.

Kris, E. (1956), The personal myth. *J. Amer. Psychoanal. Assn.*, 4:653–681.

Langs, R. (1978), *The Listening Process*. New York: Aronson.

Loewald, H. (1986), Transference–countertransference. *J. Amer. Psychoanal. Assn.*, 34:275–287.

Mahler, M., Pine, F. & Bergman, A. (1975), *The Psychological Birth of the Human Infant*. New York: Basic Books.

Schafer, R. (1992), *Retelling a Life*. New York: Basic Books.

Stein, M. (1981), The unobjectionable part of the transference. *J. Amer. Psychoanal. Assn.*, 29:869–892.

Winnicott, D. (1954), Metapsychological and clinical aspects of regression within the psycho-analytical set-up. In: *Collected Papers*. New York: Basic Books, 1958, pp. 278–294.

Chapter 10

∞

The Patient, The Analyst, The Termination Phase
Transference and Countertransference Considerations

Ellen G. Ruderman

For patient and analyst alike, termination is often the most intense, painful, and tumultuous phase of analytic treatment. The termination phase can reactivate, or it can activate, for the first time, memories of intrusion and loss from the patient's earliest developmental phases. For both patient and analyst, vulnerabilities, resistances, reactivations of early traumas, and separation and abandonment phenomena become integral to this part of the psychoanalytic journey. In addition, symptoms that had significantly waned or disappeared as the analysis progressed often reappear during the ending phase of treatment.

In the termination phase, analysts must continually examine their own countertransference and inner experience. In addition, because of the intensity of the termination experience, patients should be allowed to set their own pace and, if their circumstances and needs require it, should even be allowed meaningful contact with the analyst during the aftermath.

Using a 10-year psychoanalysis as illustration, this chapter considers the many dimensions of termination: transference and countertransference; contemporary psychoanalytic approaches; posttermination considerations; and comparisons of natural and artificial (forced) terminations.

Theoretical Perspectives on the Termination Experience

My own psychoanalytic thinking vis-à-vis termination has changed dramatically over the years. I was trained to believe that future resolution of the transference neurosis necessitated and depended on 1) the analyst's remaining incognito; and 2) the analyst's main-tenance of neutrality. I had complied with this belief in my analytic practice.

My early social work education and training emphasized relation-ship, the use of self, and starting where the patient is. As the years went by, the influence of this training became clearer. It was blended with and supported by more contemporary relational and intersub-jective frameworks in psychoanalysis. That change was apparent in the 10-year analytic experience with my patient Louis.

Essentially, my approach to termination is now more in keeping with contemporary infant research and explorations of the preoedipal phase. The contributions of infant research and those works focusing on early infant attachment and loss are crucial to any discussion on termination and were most helpful to me in my analytic work with Louis and other patients. Perhaps the most notable of these are the works of Mahler, Pine and Bergman (1975); Bowlby (1960, 1988); Ainsworth (1989); Main and Solomon (1990); Tustin (1990); Beebe and Lachman (1992); and Hamilton (1994).

In addition, since analysis involves two people, the subjective states of both patient and analyst must be considered during this phase of treatment. This conviction has guided my thinking in practice and has enriched and enlivened the termination experience.

The literature on termination and the termination phase contains surprisingly few studies or articles of self-report describing analysts' inner processes as they move through the termination phase with their patients. Analysts tend to write "about" the termination process as if they were not "in" it. This lack of self-report indicates a need for more in-depth interviews and research exploring and addressing the feelings and fantasies of analysts in this crucial phase of psycho-analysis. The dearth of analysts' self-reports may suggest that the feelings associated with termination are sometimes so difficult for the analyst to contemplate that encountering one's vulnerabilities prompts the same kind of denial and avoidance that patients experience when they are heading toward termination.

A few works are notable, however, for their refreshing illumination of the termination phase. Sanville (1982) speaks of lifelong "partings and impartings" and encourages a "nonauthoritarian" approach to termination. Further, advocating an "open door policy," she feels it is always the patient's right to define discontinuance. Also, the work of Shane and Shane (1994) on ongoing developmental issues and understanding mourning and the failure to mourn expanded my thinking during the analysis with Louis and during the termination phase in general. Hamilton's (1994) work, in which she discusses

Fairbairn's concept of the "moral defence" and emphasizes the intense fear and anxiety commonly associated with the release of the "bad internal object" has also been illuminating. As repression, through the moral defense, lifts or loosens, the patient experiences loss and terror of traumatic proportions. As Fairbairn (1943) pointed out, the child prefers a tie to a bad object to no object at all. This edification was particularly relevant to an understanding of Louis's identification with his masochistic mother and his subsequent relinquishing of this identification to the more benign internalization of the analyst's superego. Siebold's (1992) work on the experience of forced terminations from the therapist's point of view, and anticipatory grief prior to the termination phase, was also useful.

Although my focus is always on the patient, my analytic perspectives have shifted to include focusing on the analyst's feelings about termination. As a faculty-supervisor at a major medical training center, I realized that trainees of all disciplines had considerable difficulty and little guidance in dealing with endings. Their avoidance and denial of this phase of treatment and its meaning to their patients and to themselves were reflected in their enormous discomfort with it, often leading to short-lived or forced terminations or no termination phase at all.

For the termination experience to be truly reparative, patients must be allowed to develop in their own fashion, move at their own pace, and end when they are ready. As the description of Louis's analysis demonstrates, the timing of termination unfolds through the patient's feelings, fantasies, statements, and dreams. We cannot specify either a "golden timing" for the termination, or a "correct" number of years for a treatment. Lindon's (1994) wider reflections on provisions in psychoanalytic work and the need to consider the patient's early deprivations have been most helpful in this regard. Many patients who have experienced the early and severe intrusion of abandonment and loss may feel the need and actually do return to the analysis for what one of my past patients described as "that bench back there where I know you will be sitting and I can always come should the need arise."

Countertransference: Resonant Empathy as a Tool for Healing

As used here, countertransference reflects the analyst as a total person: one's age and stage of life development; one's life experience in multiple roles; and one's experience of acute life crises, separations, and losses. It is the sum total of what one feels toward the patient and within oneself in the context of the analytic treatment process (Ruderman, 1983).

In my view, countertransference is an instrument by which analysts can feed back empathic feelings and images to their patients, thus helping them clarify their feelings and the inaccessible residue of important early experiences. Properly managed, such countertransference can contribute to patients' healing. It can also prompt deeper integration of experiences evoked in the analysts, helping them, too, to heal, and promoting reciprocal growth and repair (Ruderman, 1983, 1986, 1992a, b).

This view of countertransference is derived from the assumption of such theorists as Sullivan (1953), Greenberg and Mitchell (1983), Mitchell (1993), and Stolorow and Atwood (1992) that the analytic situation is a relational, interactional, and intersubjective process in which the past and present of both participants fuse into a unique emotional position involving both of them.

Searles (1979)and Racker (1968) agree that analysts can promote their own growth through attentiveness to countertransference. Casement (1991) alludes to countertransference as a way to enhance the treatment process through "resonant empathy" between analyst and patient. At the same time, he notes, the countertransference can offer the analyst new opportunities to resolve old conflicts.

These contemporary views of countertransference draw much of their inspiration from the influences of such contributors to psychoanalysis as Ferenczi (1927) and Balint and Balint (1939). Wolstein (1997) reflects that Ferenczi, in his 1932 clinical diary, notes that his work with R.N. produced the first analysis of countertransference in vivo, "and so, . . . extended and redefined the therapeutic boundaries of psychoanalytic knowledge, irreversibly" (p. 509).

Insights into adult experiences as well as their own analyses can further analysts' understanding of certain patients during termination. A particular example of this was my recovery of a "lost piece," which had occurred in my analytic practice with another patient a few years earlier and reawakened a memory of a still earlier experience in my first analysis. I had been working for five years with Jeanette, a 52-year-old, self-devaluing woman who suddenly announced that she wanted to end treatment. While startled by her announcement, I did little to explore her feelings or examine her resistance to continuing her analysis. Instead, I noticed that I made a number of soothing comments, supported her wish to leave, and sympathized that her pressed finances necessitated reducing a number of valued activities.

Following the session, I felt extremely uncomfortable, realizing that something of grave importance was missing! Driving to a meeting later in the day, I let the inner flow of feelings take over. A memory as startling as my patient's announcement emerged. I recalled that many years earlier, as a patient terminating a course of analytic treatment, I had felt unfinished and confused with my psychoanalyst. In a later psychoanalysis, I recognized that my first analyst had relinquished the connection with me prematurely. Indeed, her soothing comments had made it more difficult to express my pain, grief, and frightened and angry feelings about the separation.

My recollections of that unsatisfactory termination gave me a sense of Jeanette's anger and grief. When I named these feelings with her in the next session, she was able to talk about how frightened she felt that I might leave her and to recognize that she was attempting to abandon me before I abandoned her. As her feelings toward me had intensified, she had felt anxious and afraid that I might pull away from her, as everyone else in her life had. By working through our respective "unfinished good-byes," we were able to continue treatment and move to a different and deeper level of work.

My analytic work with Louis demonstrates that analysts who explore their countertransference, while being attentive to the patient's transference manifestations and feelings, may attain an even deeper understanding of their patients. This is especially so in the termination phase of the analysis, when analysts as well as their patients often experience grief and mourning in saying good-bye.

The 10-Year Psychoanalysis of Louis

It is hard to imagine that the carefree, handsome, debonair man of 41 who recently terminated his analysis could be the same person who came to me almost 10 years ago. Louis was facing major crises in his life: his wife was about to leave him because of his inability to relate to her, and his self-destructive behavior threatened his job.

The first session was memorable. He walked like an automaton. He did everything "correctly." He showed no signs of animation, vitality, or spirit. He spoke brilliantly, articulately, dotting each "i" and crossing each "t," but made no eye contact with me the entire session. When he said, in a voice resembling Hal the Computer from the film *2001*, "I do not know how to feel, I want to know how to feel, I am afraid to feel," his wish to repair, his desire for release, and the pain he carried within him daily were glaringly evident.

Shortly before the session ended, I softly spoke to him of his pain. He slowly shook his head and said, "I am afraid. Everything which is precious to me I have lost, and this, I think, will be precious." With that, he put out his hand, indicating he wished to shake mine. I was so affected by his wish to connect that my eyes welled with tears. Our journey had just begun, and he was already signaling his fear of the end.

Developmental Milestones in Early Childhood

Louis started his treatment with me at two times per week, but within six months he had requested an additional session. He continued coming three times a week for a year, when he again requested an additional session. As each phase of treatment reassured him of my constancy, understanding, and "thereness," he felt an increasing sense of safety and trust. After another year, he was motivated to ask for more and bring his sessions to a full five times per week, signaling a new dynamic in his life. Up to this point, needs, wants, and "more" had always been forbidden words to him.

Louis was the oldest of three children born to poverty-stricken, Italian-Catholic parents in a lower class section of New York City. When Louis was eight months old, his father, owing to the family's desperate economic circumstances, left for a job in Alaska. His mother, frightened and alone, clung to Louis as her only link to the world. She doted on him; he was "her precious Louie!" But when he was two years old and his father returned, Louis lost his doting mother and was "replaced" by two more siblings. To protect against his smoldering rage over these successive impingements, he became "good Louie, Mommy's helper," always longing to return to the soothing comfort of his "special place" with his mother.

Louis spent his early childhood learning how to survive in a violent world of fist fights. His early Catholicism was rigid, "almost fanatical." He wished to be a priest, unconsciously hoping that arduously self-imposing his Catholicism would act as an external control over his feelings and actions. His was a relentlessly punitive superego, condemning, judging, and exacting punishment for the most natural and human of feelings: most important, anger, need, and sexual feelings.

The internally introjected superego parent of his early life was his mother, a highly critical, repressed woman who was masochistic and depressed. She was locked into an optionless world by her traditional values, which rigidified her female role into servitude, deference, and acquiescence to his father. Louis and his siblings became the object of her displaced rage toward her husband, who left her for long periods to attend to his work. The burdensome task of raising three children in near poverty led her to behaviors that could be characterized as "sadistic" and "abusive."

Louis, made a parent by his fifth year, became the resentful caretaker of his siblings and of his mother. She was an orphan and was prone to unpredictable fits of depression that left her first son suffering deep feelings of abandonment. Years later in his analysis he would speak of "pain and darkness," recalling and reliving "voids," "chasms," and "holes inside which can't be filled." When he was eight years old he ceased to function altogether. This episode was a classic posttraumatic stress reaction to the enormous adult expectations imposed on him. For over a year, this brilliant, articulate child was unable to read, write, or do homework. Some sensitive family friends intervened and enjoined his parents to reduce their stringent expectations of him and to begin to treat him as the eight-year-old child he was.

The family's economic condition changed when Louis was ten years old. His father, a talented draftsman, acquired a prominent position in a respectable West Virginia architectural firm. The family moved from the slums of New York to a spacious home in a middle-class suburb.

By this time, however, Louis's mother was locked into her repressed role of servitude and had become an alcoholic. During his adolescence, Louis often returned home from school to find her drunk and curled up on the floor. He would then have to put his mother to bed and prepare dinner for his siblings. He could not complain, as he and his siblings kept his father unaware of her condition.

Although harsh repression and censorship of feelings prevailed in the family (his father would banish his children from the table if they dared to question him or oppose him), both parents were intelligent and had ambitions for their children. Today, Louis is a pediatrician, his brother, Antony, is an engineer and the head of a major computer firm, and his sister, Katherine, is a successful writer.

Core Conflicts

The external picture of Louis was exemplary. He was an exemplary, A⁺ student, an exemplary doctor, an exemplary son, but not the least bit exemplary in what he gave himself. Because of his intense unconscious conflicts, he would act out inappropriately. His provocations threatened other colleagues in more powerful positions and endangered his chances for advancement. He frequently used the phrase "shoot yourself in the foot" to describe these situations, which usually involved his flirtation with falling over the edge of the precipice by doing, forgetting, or saying something that might lead to disastrous consequences in his personal or professional life. As each episode was analyzed, a persistent pattern emerged of self-punishment and identification with his mother's masochism. Unable to enjoy the fruits of his success, either in a relationship or in his profession, he would try to undo it.

As the analysis began, Louis immediately set out to be my "special child." He alternately saw me in the transference as the powerful and dominating mother, who could, at a moment's notice, turn him out into the cold (as his mother had sometimes done literally in the freezing cold of winter); or as the all-giving, soothing, nurturing mother who would hold him close to her breast and sing Italian melodies to him.

As the treatment progressed, it became evident that Louis found repugnant his intense feelings, needs, and emotions. Inexplicable and unpredictable separations and abandonments had led to intense conflicts related to intimacy and relationship. He suffered feelings of isolation and loneliness, was fearful and distrusting of relying on others, and yet desperately needed them. In addition, Louis felt personally and sexually insufficient and defective, always searching for the defect within himself that had caused his mother to reject him.

Reflecting his unresolved issues with his father, his competitive conflicts with males took the form of avoiding relationships with male friends and "shooting himself in the foot" with other male doctors. The emergence in the transference of intense rage toward me (mother) for leaving him to be with my husband (father) enabled Louis and me to return to the highly charged period in his life when he felt that his father had won the ultimate victory. Louis's dreams at this juncture were replete with penises large and small. In one dream, he stated the following: "There is a fire; I have set it. You are trying to help me to put it out. It threatens to disturb the garden, which is filled with huge cucumbers. I want to crush them and decide to pull them out. You say, 'Why don't you concentrate on growing your own!' We laugh and together we replant the garden."

During the middle phase of Louis's treatment, we explored a set of symptoms that I had labeled the "letting feelings out the backdoor phenomena." (These repetitive behaviors suddenly reemerged during the termination phase.) From the onset of treatment to almost his fifth year in analysis, Louis had two distinctive ways of nonverbally manifesting anger and anxiety: by farting (which he did a great deal) and by emitting a high-pitched, ear-piercing laugh—his "contralto scream."

In session after session, Louis used these enactments to show me his negative feelings or fears. A typical session took place when my three-week vacation was a month away. While Louis had known about it for two months, he had not acknowledged my impending vacation in any way. One morning, Louis entered very quietly and made no eye contact with me. He looked around the room (again, no eye contact), settled onto the couch, turned his head away from me, emitted a loud fart, immediately said, "Excuse me!" and fell silent again.

Despite my obvious discomfort and impulse to focus on this as a display of hostility, something told me to do otherwise. My inner association at that moment focused on a scene from an Ingmar Bergman movie wherein the heroine for the first time is able to experience disappointment and to say, "I want!" This association prompted me to say to Louis, "I'm feeling that you wish to tell me something that you want, something that is upsetting to you, but whatever it may be, you feel uncertain about it, or, maybe it even feels dangerous to you." He pondered, then said, "Like what?"

"I don't know," I responded. "I'm not certain, but whenever you express yourself in that way, I see it as a backdoor approach as if part of you wishes to express frontally what another part feels must be kept hidden."

In past sessions, his farting had been a prelude to the desire to protest, complain, or express disappointment (none of which he was allowed to do as a youngster). Suddenly, he emitted a shrill, piercing sound. It was difficult to tell whether he was laughing or screaming. Whatever it was, as always, it was startling and I realized I was scared. I wondered if he was too. I asked him, "Are you frightened?" His silence increased. Then, almost in a whisper, he said, "I do not want you to go away. I feel too alone. I need to know I can contact you if I need to."

First, I told him how positive it was that he could express these feelings to me and that I found them completely understandable. Second (keeping in mind the traumatic instances of his early childhood when he was left in charge of younger siblings with no adults to turn to and felt, in his words, "dangerously thrown out into space"), I told him that, when the time came for my vacation, he and I together would decide on scheduled times to speak by telephone.

That seemed to reassure him. That feeling of safety, as well as the safety to express his feelings without fear of rebuke, allowed Louis to reveal to me early memories that had never been brought to the analysis. He was then ready to address for reworking further significant pieces of his early confrontations with abandonment. As many of the early sources of repression of his feelings came to light, Louis's symptoms of farting, shrieking, and lack of affect began to diminish. His farting and the "contralto scream" reappeared in the termination phase, followed by our exploration of his transference yearnings. Only then were we able to fathom the true extent of his early terrors and how often he had had to bury his primitive urges and anxieties.

As his analysis progressed, Louis became increasingly able to relax his scrupulousness, overconscientiousness, and perfectionism. He was able to move beyond his restricted expression of affection and became more decisive and more confident of his decisions. His excessive devotion to work and productivity gave way to increased involvement in relationships at home and with friends.

Louis was now able to explore his own very distancing, hostile, and hurtful behavior toward others (most evidently his wife) and tentatively began to examine his sexual feelings and behavior. His sexual interactions had been like his speech: fast, sharp, and accurate, but unfeeling. Now, however, he became aware of feelings of tenderness which were new to his experience. A decided shift in his marital relationship began to occur. His feelings changed from animosity and distance toward his wife to attempting to be more sensitive to her feelings and more encouraging of her aims and desires. Their sexual relationship, according to Louis, changed "from night to day," and his penis was now "an affectionate conveyor" instead of an aggressive tool.

He engaged in meaningful work on his feelings about and identifications with his father. Although he was a cold, austere man, Louis's father had given up a highly successful position so he could spend more time with his family. Louis's choice to give up a prestigious position on the medical staff of his hospital reflected this positive identification.

The working through of his core conflicts led to a monumental shift in his life: he moved from the scathingly punitive and repressive Catholicism of his youth to a more accepting, tolerant, nonjudgmental version of his religion. No longer was the angry god inside, demanding retribution, but a god who resided in all human beings, who were entitled to their feelings and needs.

Revisiting Separation and Abandonment Anxieties
Despite all his advances, the intensity of Louis's anxiety concerning separation and abandonment was manifested again during the eighth year of analysis, when he and I experienced a minitermination. At that time, after much internal deliberation, I found it necessary to reduce the treatment to four times a week for personal reasons. My decision reawakened early intense feelings and affects in Louis. Dreams, fantasies, and associations led to the uncovering and revivification of the early experiences of losing his mother when his father returned from working in Alaska.

Louis raged at me. He accused me of giving *his* "precious alone moments" to other patients and "turning away" from him to outside people. He recounted a dream in which I was at a spa with James

Garner, and when Garner and I saw Louis we ran off to the beach together, laughing. A flurry of his further associations, feelings, and remonstrations occurred in the sessions. He would repeatedly punch the pillows of my couch, while screaming "bitch," "cunt," and the like. These sessions reawakened memories of searing rejections by women in his life and brought to the fore long-standing feelings of painful and helpless rage at mother, wife, and analyst. His feelings of despair and rage toward me continued for over a year. While I would sit calmly and listen, I felt drained at the end of each of these sessions. My thoughts ranged from images of the two-year-old thrashing and stamping his foot to getting in touch with feelings of grief over the passing of a member of my own family. Throughout, I felt empathic with his rage and reflected from time to time that, in addition to the rage, he was now in touch with the full extent of his pain and grief.

At last, he had a dream in which he and I were at Nepenthe (a Bohemian restaurant overlooking the idyllic northern California coastline) chatting over a cup of capuccino, heralding the beginnings of "peacetime." Nepenthe symbolized his awareness of a new inner calmness and serenity and a desire to go on to create and to venture onto other pathways. (I later discovered that Nepenthe was the name of the beautiful hideaway in Big Sur that Orson Welles had bestowed as a gift upon Rita Hayworth.) The meaningfulness of having been able, for the first time in his life, to pour out his disappointment, pain, and rage to another human being was the crucial turning point of Louis's treatment.

Loss of the Old Object

As we moved beyond the middle phase, the softening of Louis's scathingly critical superego and the internalizing of my, more benign superego through the transference were reflected in many ways. He was relinquishing the "bad object," which had been the core of his identification and had accompanied him throughout his development. By finding a new life-affirming object in the analysis, he was now free to find a more authentic self.

One particularly important dream heralded his feelings of "liberation" from the internal constrictions he experienced and his lifelong internalizations of the "punitive, finger-wagging mother" of his childhood. Louis experienced considerable relief from this dream, as it brought the recognition of the very deep and meaningful change going on within him. The dream is as follows: "I am running down a New England road. The police are after me and they are waving beer cans at me. You are running beside them frantically waving a piece of parchment paper. The paper is the Declaration of Independence, and afterwards all of us—me, you, and the police—read it, and then we all go to Fanueil Hall where we will celebrate."

This dream reflected Louis's enduring fears that he, like his mother, would become an alcoholic. The dream also revealed his overpolicing of his sexual desires and fantasies. During his adolescence, the family had spent a month in Boston on holiday. Faneuil Hall was the scene, during this holiday, of one of his first dates with a girl when he was 14 years old. He vividly recalled his internal sexual awakenings; and, while his body throbbed, his mind reverberated with enjoinders that his sexual feelings were impure. In association to the dream, he realized that in his subsequent fantasies the sexual wishes were also needful wishes for closeness, holding, and touching. His fantasies shifted from perpetual recalling of "rejecting and humiliating women" to the sensitive family friends who "softened" his mother, and to me, who became a new kind of love, both mother and friend.

He once had said about his internalizing his mother's punitive superego, "When I stop carrying her wherever I go, I will begin to come alive." In his eighth year of treatment, he began to let go of her. When he did so, he was able to cry, laugh out loud, hug and kiss, enjoy his sexual life, and relish warm, intimate moments with his wife.

Termination: Preparation

Nine years after he began treatment, Louis announced that he would be terminating the analysis. He was feeling better as a person, was less aggressive sexually, and had more self-esteem. When he accepted a job offer in another state, his termination date became more definite.

During the termination phase of analysis, most patients struggle with making the analyst real, and this was also true of Louis. In the first and middle phases of the analysis, I had been not only the tyrannical, withholding mother, capable of incalculable retaliations for his "sins," but also the high priestess hearing his confessions daily and having the power to give absolution. As the analysis deepened, I became in the transference the all-giving, tender, softer mother, who provided a safe and trusting holding environment. Atonement was no longer necessary, because feelings, needs and wants were simply what they were.

As the termination phase progressed, Louis went from crying for the "good mother" he was leaving to the realization that he had created me out of his own needs. Whereas he had long seen me as his "mother surrogate," he now saw me as his "special and unique friend."

Louis began to sit up in sessions, instead of resuming his position on the couch. In his view, this change represented his readiness to see me as I was. Also, his fears and anxieties had increased as he faced with more clarity the reality of his leaving, and he found it soothing to see my face.

In the fifth year of his analysis Louis had wept over his lost childhood and the lack of an empathic and attuned human being to understand, accept, and guide him. As the time for termination loomed, he began to weep again, this time for the loss of the "newly found good mother" and because of his terror of going out once again to the "terribly cold outside." In a session four months prior to termination, he was bereft; he was lying on the couch, his head in his hands, and he was weeping. "This is driving me crazy," he said. "I will miss you . . . While I want to leave, at the same time I yearn for you to come with me . . . It is like falling into an abyss . . . I am crazy with grief . . . I have a strange sensation of my body feeling cold . . . like ice."

His words triggered thoughts and images for me. First, I imagined a pond; it was winter, and a child, while skating, had broken through the ice. I recalled Louis telling me, in an earlier session, how much he had hated being thrust outside, alone, into the treacherous New York winter where his mother often sent him when she was having a "blue time."

I asked him, "Do you think something is trying to break through but is afraid of hitting an icy bottom?" This question evoked a memory of himself as a six-year-old. He had complained to his mother that the meal she had served him was not enough and that he was still hungry. In response, she had peremptorily ushered him outside, into the freezing cold.

Floods of feelings followed in the session. He told of how he was forced, throughout his early childhood, to comply with the parental demand, mainly his mother's, that he "put on a happy face." Anger, protest, pain, sadness, and disappointment were forbidden feelings. We could now understand that farting and the shrill, laughing scream reflected an earlier time in his development when the only way he could find relief for his feelings was to go out the back door of his house where he would scream and cry. Once, when his mother came upon him in this way, he turned the screams and cries into a shrill laugh, feigning laughter at something he had seen outside, so as to not risk her disapproval or punishment.

The meaning of these symptoms became clearer during the termination phase. Throughout his life he had longed for someone to "hear him," to "see" his pain, and to lift him from the "abyss" of his loneliness. Now, having found that person, he was overwhelmed with grief that he was leaving her behind.

The theme of "desertion of the analyst" was pursued further in a dream he brought to the treatment soon after. "Everything was blue— the sky, the room, and you were there, too, also dressed in blue. You assured me, however, that you had dresses of other colors too. We were both crying, but you said, 'It's time now to leave; don't fret. You go by plane, I'll stay.' With that, you opened the door and pointed to the airport. I wanted to leave you something to keep for me, so I gave you my Dartmouth/UCLA banner. You assured me I could always come back and get it if I wanted it, as you would safely keep it for me."

The multiple meanings of this dream became evident and were worked through over many sessions of the termination phase. First, Louis got in touch with his enormous guilt over having abandoned his mother, leaving her to the emotionally and financially poverty-stricken surroundings of his childhood. She was depressed, and he, who had been her "caregiver," was now the one leaving her. He realized, with some pain, that he had always felt responsible not only for her becoming an alcoholic, but for her several suicidal attempts some years after his departure. Through this dream, Louis also connected with his strong wish that she had been a healthier mother, one who could have given him permission to leave and, indeed, encouraged him to have a future of his own, without guilt or shame. That is what he perceived me as doing in the dream. He realized that I had become his wished-for "healthier mother." He saw me as successful, balancing my needs with his needs. I was not acting as the "proverbial doormat," which was how he had seen his mother react to his father's treatment of her.

And, finally, he realized that I was not angry or retaliative toward him for leaving me or for his feelings of anguish and frustration that I would not accompany him, although he consciously knew that this was not possible. He recalled earlier sessions in which we dealt with the integration of his love and his rage toward me. I had said to him, "I am a woman of many colors. You may have many kinds of feelings toward me. You can be enraged with me, yet still appreciate all we have been through together." This was very meaningful to him and was brought forth in his dream. He also realized that termination was reactivating his terrors of "losing something precious" and that he needed to deal with how he would cope in its aftermath.

Aftermath

In the last 10 years, considerable literature has been devoted to the question of whether full resolution of the transference and the trans-ference neurosis exists. Bergmann (1988) expounds on this subject, validating my own point of view and that of many colleagues that full resolution of the transference is a myth.

In my view, the discovery, reworking, and integration of self, analyst, and the analysis continue long after the analysis is concluded, perhaps for a lifetime, without the analyst needing to be present. As time goes on, the analyst undergoes a significant transformation in the internal representations of the patient. These representations will change as the patient continues to grow and develop in the analysis and outside of it.

Since Louis's anguish became palpable following his announcement of his wish to terminate the analysis, it was my feeling that he needed special provision for the aftermath of termination. I saw this as consistent with his developmental dynamics and losses he had suffered.

As Louis's leaving involved settling in another state and reestablishing his practice, I felt it was important that he be able to contact me when and if he needed to. In response to his terrors of "falling through icy waters" and his near-panic of "starting this new development all alone," I made it clear that I was staying in place, could be contacted when needed, and was there as a resource for him.

In past terminations with former analytic patients, my hesitation to offer this condition (although I certainly felt the need for it strongly even then), was due to my concern that I would intrude on my patients' fields. Such an offer, I felt, might hamper their further working-through of the termination, or their decision to continue treatment with another person. In my view, these *are* important considerations that the analyst must keep in mind. I also still subscribe to the belief that the year or two following the termination are extremely important to the analysand's and the analyst's free flow of feelings and integration of the analysis. Nevertheless, I am convinced that what takes primacy is recognition of the uniqueness of each person's human condition in relation to his or her development.

For Louis, as well as for many other patients, a year without contact would have been much too long. Consequently, we arranged to speak by phone when he felt the need, and we arranged for a return visit six months after the termination. This was his choice, which accorded with his needs and tolerances. Louis did his own "weaning" in his own time; the termination phase unfolded at his pace. We agreed that should he need to return, the door would be open.

In a letter written to me soon after his termination, Louis ended by saying: "I thank you for that session you labeled, "Preparation." My sadness, my preoccupation and grief at times seem to overwhelm me, but had we not talked, I think I would have assumed a loss of my sanity, a failure in grounding. This way, when those intense feelings hit me with the impact of my Hiroshima Dream, which neither of us will ever forget, I was, while in misery and pain, immediately aware of what was happening. You were in my head, I saw you, I heard you, and I knew I would come through it."

(The Hiroshima Dream was a repetitive dream occurring throughout his childhood and adolescence. He presented it twice in the beginning of his analysis. While the dream "disappeared" during most of the analysis, it reappeared during the termination phase. Its chief significance echoed and reflected the statement he had made at the beginning of his analysis: "Everything precious to me is taken away," a statement that referred to the loss of his mother, the many actual, unwanted physical moves in his life, and now, during the termination, the loss of the analyst. With regard to his real mother, it was the loss of a beautiful and rational person to the ravages of an alcoholism that rendered her (in his words) "crazy" and "out of control.")

Conclusion

In our decade-long journey, Louis and I touched each other's inner world and together traveled down many surprising and unexpected roads. The journey was challenging, anguishing, and poignant but, in the end, mutually growth producing and reparative for both of us.

From each patient we learn in depth not only about another human soul but also about our own deeper selves. We do not learn to the same degree from every patient, but each imparts something to us. While Louis often stated that he was "reborn and rejuvenated" through me, I also was enlivened by him. One of the challenges Louis presented me in the analysis was that he was a deeply religious and spiritual man whereas I was a consummate agnostic; I had a great deal to learn from Louis about spirituality. Further, as he became able to expose his vulnerabilities, I was able increasingly to become aware of my own. Indeed, Louis's devotion to his analysis and his determined wish to know himself and make better choices in his life have my deepest respect.

I have focused here on countertransference issues, in particular, as they relate to the termination phase of Louis's analysis. My aim, however, has been to emphasize that the termination phase offers to both the patient and the analyst the richest potential for reworking early issues of attachment, loss, grief and mourning. It is only through this mutuality of experience that both can experience new beginnings.

References

Ainsworth, M. D. (1989), Attachments beyond infancy. *Amer. Psycholog.*, 4:709–716.

Balint, A. & Balint, M. (1939), On transference and countertransference. *Internat. J. Psycho-Anal.*, 20:223–230.

Beebe, B. & Lachmann, F. (1992), The contribution of mother-infant mutual influence to the origins of self and object representations. In: *Relational Perspectives in Psychoanalysis*, ed. N. J. Skolnick & S. C. Warshaw. Hillsdale, NJ: The Analytic Press, pp. 43–61.

Bergmann, M. S. (1988), On the fate of the intrapsychic image of the psychoanalyst after termination of the analysis. *The Psychoanalytic Study of the Child*, 43:137–153. New Haven, CT: Yale University Press.

Bowlby, J. (1960), Grief and mourning in infancy and early childhood. *The Psychoanalytic Study of the Child*, 15:9–52. New York: International Universities Press.

———— (1988), *Secure Base*. New York: Basic Books.

Casement, P. (1991), *Learning from the Patient*. New York: Guilford Press.

Fairbairn, W. R. D. (1943), The repression and the return of bad objects (with special reference to the "War neurosis") In: *Psychoanalytic Studies of the Personality*. London: Tavistock, 1952, pp. 59–81.

Ferenczi, S. (1927), The problems of the termination of the analysis. In: *Final Contributions to Psycho-Analysis*. New York: Basic Books, 1955, pp. 77–86

Greenberg, J. & Mitchell, S. (1983), *Object Relations in Psychoanalytic Theory*. Cambridge, MA: Harvard University Press.

Hamilton, V. (1994), Resistance to the release of the bad object in the psychotherapy of a refugee. In: *Fairbairn and the Origins of Object Relations*, ed. J. Grotstein & D. Rinsley. New York: Guilford Press, pp. 244–259.

Lindon, J. A. (1994), Gratification and provision in psychoanalysis: Should we get rid of the rule of abstinence? *Psychoanal. Dial.*, 4:549–582.

Mahler, M. S., Pine, F.,& Bergman, A. (1975), *The Psychological Birth of the Human Infant*. New York: Basic Books.

Main, M. & Solomon, L. (1990), Procedures for identifying infants as disorganized-disoriented during the Ainsworth strange situation. In: *Attachment in Pre-School Years, Theory, research and intervention*, ed. M. Greenberg, D. Cicchetti, & E. M. Cummings. Chicago: University of Chicago Press, pp. 121–160.

Mitchell, S. (1993), *Hope and Dread in Psychoanalysis*. New York: Basic Books.

Racker, H. (1968), *Transference and Countertransference*. New York: International Universities Press.

Ruderman, E. (1983), Gender-Related Themes of Women Psychotherapists in Their Treatment of Women Patients: The Creative and Reparative Use of Countertransference as a Mutual Growth Experience. Unpublished doctoral dissertation. California Institute for Clinical Social Work.

———— (1986), Creative and reparative uses of countertransference by women psychotherapists treating women patients: A clinical research study. In: *The Psychology of Today's Woman: New Psychoanalytic Visions*, ed. T. Bernay & D. Cantor. Hillsdale, NJ: The Analytic Press.

———— (1992a), Countertransference, parallel process and gender-related themes in supervision: Overcoming treatment impasses. Presented to Committee on Psychoanalysis in Clinical Social Work, Los Angeles, CA, October.

———— (1992b) Countertransference: A vehicle for reciprocal growth and repair in women psychotherapists treating women patients. *Clin. Soc. Work J.*, 20:1.

Sanville, J. (1982), Partings and impartings, toward a non-medical approach to interruptions and terminations. *Clin. Soc. Work J.*, 10:123–132.

Searles, H. (1979), *Countertransference and Related Subjects*. New York: International Universities Press.

Shane, E. & Shane, M. (1994), Object loss and selfobject loss: A consideration of self-psychology's contribution to understanding mourning and the failure to mourn. *The Annual of Psychoanalysis,* 18:115–132. Hillsdale, NJ: The Analytic Press.

Siebold, C.(1992), Forced termination. *Smith College Studies in Social Work,* 63:325–341.

Stolorow, R. & Atwood, G. (1992), *Contexts of Being.* Hillsdale, NJ: The Analytic Press.

Sullivan, H. S. (1953), *The Interpersonal Theory of Psychiatry.* New York: Norton.

Tustin, F. (1990), *The Protective Shell in Children and Adults,* London: Karnac Books.

Wolstein, B. (1997), Analysis of transference and countertransference. *Psychoanal. Inq.,* 17:506–509.

∞

Coda

The Editors

The foregoing chapters represent, in large measure, variations on several basic themes from early social work education. All the case studies hold in common time-honored concepts put forth by past social work leaders, such as begin where the client is, view self-determination as both the means and the goal of therapy, take a flexible, responsive, nonauthoritarian stance, and respect the uniqueness of each individual. The contributors marry their earlier social work experiences to an analytic approach that seeks to adapt technique to the particular needs of each analysand. Whether in the foreground or the background, the relationship is regarded as an important component in their analytic work, as it has long been in social work practice.

The writers' social agency and clinic experiences have accustomed them to working with a highly diverse group of patients of all ages, races, cultures, and economic groups, as well as varying family constellations. They know what it is to try to involve individuals who are frequently defined as hard to reach or multiproblem, and they have long served the most troubled members of society. They are no strangers to the effect of deprivation, neglect, trauma, poverty, prejudice, and the many other vicissitudes of life that all too many people experience. They are therefore well prepared to meet the widening group of today's analysands, some of whom the reader has met in this book. Their common attitudes could be viewed as springing from their social work education and practice.

The recitals are presented in the unique and sometimes contrasting voices of the psychoanalysts who tell them. They perforce differ in tone and timbre and range from the dramatic to the lyric. The treatments reflect the analysts' differences and illuminate the uniqueness of both analyst and analysand and the usefulness of both the fit and the misfit between them. They present as well the numerous perspectives on which they draw. These represent to varying degrees the change in paradigms that has taken place in American analysis over the past 15 years.

Some of the contributors have moved to a two-person psychology, primarily focused on the intersubjective nature of the exchanges between patient and therapist and with a major emphasis on the importance of the here-and-now treatment relationship. Others focus on the analysand's character, history, fantasies, and conflicts predating the analysis and regard interpretation of the past in the present as one of the essentials of the analytic work. They think of uncovering as a central task, albeit in the context of a positive therapeutic alliance. Some of the writers appear to draw on both old paradigms and new. They oscillate between a one-person and a two-person psychology, between viewing the experience of the therapeutic relationship as more mutative at one moment and the understanding and interpretation of that experience as more efficacious at another.

In the following commentaries on each of the chapters, we highlight some of the ways in which these clinicians are combining what they have derived from social work with their analytic training and experience.

The writing duo of Kerri and Peter Malawista presents the case of a histrionic man, who is standing on the other side of an apparently unbridgeable cultural gulf. In this case, finding where the client is begins with the analyst being confronted by the analysand's attacks against her as a caricature-like symbol of her culture. The patient is soon alternating these assaults with a dramatic transference phenomenon of pseudoepileptic seizures. The analyst meets the two-fold confrontation by patiently waiting and listening. Only then, having located her patient, can she offer her interpretive comments in the form of observations about the transference. These originate in part from the uncomfortable feelings stirred up in the analyst. Thus the slow rhythm of the beginning phase of the analysis is established: an andante tempo grounding the emergence of mutual understanding and respect.

The dramatic beginning of this cross-cultural relationship involves careful attention to the cultural context of this analysand's life and the unique interpretations he has given to it internally (Applegate and Bonovitz, 1995). In the course of the analysis, we see the analyst move back and forth cognitively between her own sociocultural surround and that of her analysand in a way that enhances her empathy (Saari, 1986).

Jean Sanville, who has a deep interest in the impact of culture on analytic understanding, suggests that analytic theory now seems to be evolving as a bio-psycho-social theory similar to that of social work. She observes that, at the conjoint meetings of the House of Delegates and the Executive Council of the IPA in Buenos Aires in 1997, it was extensively discussed and seriously proposed that analytic training needs a fourth leg—education about the interplay of the psyche and the sociocultural surround.

Another feature of the Malawistas' analytic approach used here is pliability, as shown by Ms. Malawista's accommodation to her analysand's work schedule. She offers him two two-hour sessions rather than the traditional four single hours per week. She follows the social work tradition of flexibility in finding ways to meet with her client. Many social work sessions have been held in clients' homes, in places other than offices, at odd and varying hours, sometimes with a friend brought to the office or toddlers playing on the floor. Some psychoanalysts might not have anticipated that treatment could be done under such circumstances, though there are now accounts of mothers who bring their babies to sessions (Loewald, 1982). There has also been at least one report of an analysis conducted in part on the telephone when circumstances made it impossible for the analysand to continue coming to the office (Zalusky, 1998).

Analysts have rightfully valued the maintenance of an analytic frame. Social workers uphold the idea that the frame must be capable of modulation but remain intact. They tend to feel that among the reasons for the current crisis in psychoanalysis has been its inflexibility and inability to adapt to real changes in society. When the analyst arranges to see her analysand for twice-weekly sessions of two hours each, she is respecting and adapting to the fact that people travel frequently in their work in this modern world; and if we do not arrange our schedules accordingly, these pateints cannot be analyzed. There is scant research evidence that four single sessions per week are more efficacious than three sessions or any other variation. Perhaps social workers, as well as those from other disciplines who are being welcomed into the larger analytic community, are bringing a greater degree of flexibility to analysis for the benefit of our wider range of analysands.

Gail Steger presents an analysand who initially experiences primitive and self-destructive states of mind, a patient for whom analysis may not have been previously available. This analyst was able to find within herself enough hope, strength, and suppleness to engage her patient and endure the lengthy span of their mutual process.

Although the analyst does not name the social work concept that guides her clinical acumen, it is implied in her first "action interpretation" of holding herself available 24 hours a day; she understands and joins her client "where she is." She understands her client's strong motivation to change and underscores their mutual hope that together they can accomplish that goal. For Steger, the relationship and insight are not in competition. They join forces to move the treatment along at the patient's pace. Social workers have long realized the value of the positive relationship for actuating change in their clients. With social workers' introduction to psychoanalytic concepts, they have come to understand that the state of the relationship can be understood and verbalized by both partners to help create deeper transmutation in each of them. Steger, in this analysis, reflects her use and timing of interpretation to effect insight within the context of the relationship, always following her analysand's lead. She tends to value a mode of interpretation that involves first giving back to the patient what the latter has communicated and then engaging in dialogue out of which interpretations are made (Winnicott, 1968).

Steger translates the outer unity and diversity of a group into unity and differentiation inside the patient. She uses Matte Blanco's theory to explicate her becoming one with her analysand; but always underneath the treatment is the quest to locate the client and join her "where she is." Thus the analyst applauds as Beth creates and re-creates herself, playing variations on the themes of helpless, hopeless self in transition to becoming self-helping, and finally able to help another.

This is an example of the influence of social work education and experience for reading new and sometimes exotic analytic scores. Although the theories used and their combinations are different from those of the other chapters, the blending of her social work background with that of psychoanalysis comes through clearly in the approach of this author.

Laurie Hollman integrates the idea of play with a contemporary drive/conflict model of analysis. She draws on certain of Jean Sanville's contributions while offering her own particular conceptions. Her understanding is informed by structural theory, in which drive, conflict, defense, and unconscious fantasy are in the forefront. Interpretation is an important constituent of this therapeutic process, an effort in which both partners are engaged. One gets the sense of a positive and effective working alliance, with the relationship appearing to serve mainly as a context for their work rather than being in the foreground. Particular to Hollman's approach is the way in which she utilizes the link between the intrapsychic and the interactive to facilitate the emergence and discovery of transference.

In her careful focus on the surface of the patient's associations, she stays close to the latter's ideas, thus rendering safe the analytic space. Her moment-to-moment attention to the nuances of sequence, figures of speech, contiguity, and context all lead to an increasingly deeper understanding of what is going on in the patient's mind and constitute a form of empathic communication. These concepts come from both psychoanalysis and social work and seem written in the same key.

A subjective attunement to the other is implicit. For example, Hollman's affective response to her analysand's disheveled appearance alerts her to the potential significance of the patient's verbalization of her house-body metaphor, the exploration of which leads to fruitful understandings. The use of this enactment illustrates the dyadic context in which insight develops. This process makes use of and fosters a relationship between the two partners. Considering interpretation and insight in terms of the therapeutic relationship brings to mind a comment Friedman (1983) once made which highlights our musical metaphor. Insight, Friedman proposes, is the score that the patient learns while practicing on a well-tuned therapist (p. 348). Finally, Hollman's efforts to strengthen her patient's observing ego and foster her ability for self-reflection within the spirit of collaboration are in the social work tradition of drawing on and increasing a person's capacity for self-determination, for promoting what Sanville has referred to as self-as-agent.

Samoan Barish presents her analysis of a woman in her 70s, who not too many years ago would have been considered beyond the age to be analyzed. A long history of a number of seemingly unsuccessful prior treatments might also have discouraged another analyst from beginning with her anew. However, Barish engages with her and stays the course, sustained by a fuller appreciation today that growth can continue throughout the life span, as well as by the opportunity she found in this treatment for her own self-expansion. Like Mary Richmond (1920), Barish sees treatment as a reciprocal process in which the clinician as well as the patient can grow.

This is an analysis in which the promotion of self-determination is central. Today social workers are apt to talk of this as empowerment, encompassing not only the personal but the political. While using different terms, many psychoanalysts, particularly since Stern (1985), have recognized the importance of the reclamation of a sense of self and consider its achievement an important goal of treatment. One of the means by which Sanville (1991) has brought social work and psychoanalysis together is in her emphasis on the importance in all treatments to restoring and strengthening this sense of agency. It is clear in Barish's case study that both she and her analysand deeply valued the latter's growing capacities to take the initiative and claim her own life.

In her analytic approach, Barish has the advantage of a number of analytic theories, including the contributions of Sándor Ferenczi, who has been experiencing something of a rebirth in this country. According to Sanville (1966) Ferenczi had a major influence on American social work, though that influence has not always been acknowledged. She reminds us that Ferenczi accompanied Freud to America and that the Clark Lectures, through which many social workers became acquainted with Freud, were in part derived from his daily conversations with his colleague and friend. Ferenczi's thinking and experience was, in fact, close to that of many social workers at the time. He treated a similar population: people who because of their severe pathologies were deemed in those days unanalyzable. Ferenczi concluded that the relationship represented the major ameliorating factor in their treatment and recommended that, in some instances with certain patients, an analyst might be called on to serve as a real object. Barish's efforts show her to be in accord with Ferenczi. For example, she at times responded to her analysand's urgings to get her to tell her what to do by directly offering her impressions of a given situation.

At other times, she encouraged the patient to work with her in gaining an understanding of the meanings of such requests. It is striking to read how Barish uses the romantic Ferenczi of the classical period to harmonize with Richmond (1920), thereby creating a postmodern tale of a woman of her time.

In her treatment of a mentally and sexually abused woman, Toni Thompson plays a role, albeit as a psychoanalyst, that social workers have played in this country since the 19th century. Providing services for abused, as well as neglected and dependent, children has traditionally been the responsibility of social agencies. While Helfer and Kemper (1987), Shengold (1989), and others from varying disciplines have significantly raised the awareness of the enormity and complexity of child abuse and promoted the involvement of the medical and other professions in serving this population, it is mainly social workers who serve on the front line of practice.

How much familiarity with abuse Thompson may have derived from her own earlier social work experiences she does not say. In her analytic approach, however, her efforts to begin where her patient is are evident, as is her therapeutic use of herself and her ability to view the patient from an adaptive perspective.

This was a challenging analysis, particularly at those times when the patient sought to engage her analyst in a fantasy of killing her mother and when she was directing her rage at Thompson, as if the analyst were the bad mother of the past. In this highly charged atmosphere, she remained with the patient, using her own responses to enhance her understanding of what was being enacted. Thompson, realizing that it was essential for the patient to direct her unconscious hatred and rage toward her, allowed the transference to unfold, so that in time the patient could understand for whom her anger was originally meant and why she was so rageful. Thompson carefully assessed the point at which the regressive reliving was extending beyond its usefulness and offered an interpretation that enabled the patient to connect again with the loving parts of herself.

In this analysis, transference provided the vehicle for the reconstruction of the traumatic events of the patient's past, the patient's responses to what had occurred and the sometimes distorted meanings she had ascribed to her abusive experiences. Simultaneously, the transference provided a relationship that served as a catalyst for growth. While it was Freud who taught social workers the transferential significance of their interactions with their patients, social workers have, from their early history, appreciated the growth-promoting role of the relationship, both real and transferential.

Karla Clark draws on Masterson's developmental, self, and object relations approach in her analysis of a woman whom she considers to be suffering from a schizoid disorder. She modifies this approach to accord with recent developments in attachment theory. She has also drawn from several other theorists including Jean Sanville. Clark's use of theory like that of social workers over the years reflects a facility for borrowing from a variety of perspectives and then integrating, and at times modifying, the theories they borrow. It has been clear to social workers that no single explanatory theory can encompass the wide range of personalities, situations, and needs of the diverse populations they serve. While trying to avoid eclecticism, the field as a whole has favored openness to new and different ideas and a flexibility in using them. At best, social workers have sought to draw from theories selectively in the light of their clinical experience and to hold to them lightly. Thus Clark, while obviously much influenced by Masterson's understandings, selects some aspects of his offerings and yet is free to differ with him, as she does with regard to his ideas about the formation of the self.

In this chapter it is clear that a therapeutic relationship involves an exchange between analyst and analysand that must be especially fitted to each of them. Clark's analysand found an empathic connection simultaneously reassuring and disturbing. She addressed this phenomenon through consistent interpretation of the patient's orbiting defenses and the fears and needs that had given rise to them. Her interpretative efforts appear to have met the patient's feared conflicts around both connection and distance. Insofar as interpretations convey an empathic understanding of the patient, they can foster connection. At the same time, the analyst's dependence on the patient's words to understand and the analyst's own use of words in the interpretative exchange affirm their separateness.

Clark seems to draw on her social work background to provide support for her analysand's adaptive capacities, something well tuned to current analytic concepts. In conveying to the patient that her distrust of others had been a logical stance in view of her childhood experiences, Clark affirms that some of what is so troubling to the patient represents an effort that she once made to deal with adverse developmental circumstances. Implicit in this acknowledgment is the idea that the patient has strengths, the affirmation of which lead to an increase in the patient's self regard. Highlighting the patient's capacities may also help to promote feelings of hope, which are so important to sustain both patient and analyst.

Cathy Siebold uses mainly attachment theory in understanding and responding to her analysand's reactions to the separations and reunions occurring around vacation breaks. She also draws from intersubjective and other relational theories. Her approach, though different in very important respects, may remind some social workers of the functional school during the 30s (Taft, 1937) in which social workers of this persuasion paid close attention to their clients' responses and to negotiation of such experiences as fee payments or arrangements around time, experiences that inevitably occur in treatments of all kinds. Analysts have, of course, also recognized the therapeutic potential of addressing their analysands' responses to similar events, although as Siebold points out, vacation separations have so far received less attention in the literature than have other partings.

Like many of the other analysands in this book, Siebold's patient is a seriously troubled young woman for whom, in years past, analysis was unlikely to have been regarded as the treatment of choice. She is a patient with whom social workers are very familiar: a woman who tried to commit suicide, has been hospitalized, has a history of drug abuse, and has been involved in several previous outpatient treatments. Siebold appears to be less focused on diagnoses as criteria for analyzability than clinicians were likely to be in the past. In the last several years analysts of all disciplines have been increasingly analyzing persons suffering from the more severe pathologies and in the literature describe these analyses as efficacious. Although we know of little research that has so far been reported on the outcome of these analyses with adult patients, the value of analysis in the treatment of seriously troubled children has been demonstrated in studies done by Fonagy and Target (1996).

Siebold's attunement to this difficult analysand reflects her effort to relate to the patient where she is, drawing on her ability to use her own personal experiences and inner responses. Out of this affective resonance, Siebold is able to convey her recognition of what the patient is experiencing without attempting to defuse her feelings. For example, when her analysand becomes enraged around a change of appointment, Siebold does not explain that she had prepared her for this previously. Instead she acknowledges that she had changed times and gone on vacations and that the patient had no say in these changes. Like therapists of all disciplines, Siebold knows that some pain cannot be eased by empathic understanding. What she as an analyst can and does offer is her ability to tolerate her analysand's pain and rage and to help the patient alter those maladaptive efforts, to which she originally resorted in an attempt to deal with her suffering. At the point in the analysis that Siebold describes, it is the patient's avoidant pattern that she seeks to modify so that the patient may become able to express her feelings in words and take in experiences with a new object. Siebold reminds us that the latter is often a hard and painful process, for it means letting go of earlier object connections, which though negative have been vital to the person.

Presenting her "Case of a Stalemate Reversed," Monica Rawn provides a rare learning opportunity by demonstrating openness and courage. She examines herself as a youthful analyst in the first analysis and as a mature explorer and collaborator in the second.

The first analysis describes a young analysand who allows only her false selves to be seen, who wants to please the analyst. This seems to be parallel with a young, unseasoned social work analyst who wants to please her institute, using the prevailing theory of that day, which featured the centrality of the Oedipus, structural theory, ego psychology and a narrow view of transference and countertransference. She mistook the transference–countertransference relationship for a therapeutic alliance. This presumption led the couple to a stalemate.

After many years, the analysand, searching for self-integration, returned to analysis, giving them both the opportunity for a second chance. As the field had grown more open, so had the analyst matured and was now an independently thoughtful analyst. She had a much wider scope of analytic theories from which to choose. She now was able to use herself as an analytic tuning fork, resonating to her patient's revealing transferences in ways that her newer emphasis on a range of object relations theories made possible: seeing, feeling, and interpreting the parallels between her analysand's views of her mother and of her analyst; seeing, feeling, and interpreting the immediacy of their interchange in the moment.

Now having become an experienced member of the broad analytic community, Rawn creates a model of a self-reflective and self-searching psychoanalyst. Writing about her stalemate in the first analysis and contrasting it with the repair effected in the second analysis may influence others in the field to be more open in their published self-assessments. Sharing this process with the reader is something too often missing in the psychoanalytic literature.

Ellen Ruderman, the composer of our last chapter, tells us in her introduction how she draws on her social work heritage to create, together with her analysand, a long and mutually respectful analysis. Here, the understanding of the transference and countertransference, the contrapuntal experience, enable the duo to merge and separate as they digest the history and development of the analysand's personality and character. The analyst not only sees her patient as leading in the dialogue, but also feels that he must be the guide for the theory she can use.

Social work concepts she values are the relationship, the person in the situation, the use of self, and starting where the patient is. These harmonize effectively for her with the more contemporary relational and intersubjective theories. This harmony is evident throughout her clinical examples.

Ruderman also suggests how this mutual effort around the ending of the analysis led to her own growth and repair personally and professionally. She describes changes in her ideas about termination and the newer understandings at which she arrives. Citing Casement (1991), who has a background in social work, Ruderman points to the way in which countertransference can provide both analyst and analysand with new opportunities to resolve old conflicts.

Echoing Mary Richmond (1920), who strongly believed that case work treatment should enrich the social worker as well as the client, Ruderman elucidates some of her own personal changes during this analysis.

What is most striking about this presentation, however, is the hint at the beginning and the fruition at the end that the treatment will end where the patient is: that is, it will not have a definitive end. The analyst sees this termination as the organic outgrowth of her analysand's dynamics and the losses he has suffered. The patient is offered open access to Ruderman, while she keeps in mind the need for independent integration of the analysis. For this analyst, termination is a complex and generative experience, which must follow, as has the entire analysis, the needs and development of the analysand.

Through the voices of these contributors, we have sought to celebrate Jean Sanville's life and her contributions to both social work and psychoanalysis. In doing so, our contributors have pointed to a new relationship between analysis and social work, a relationship that Jean Sanville has done much to foster. We have become accustomed to thinking of what analysis has brought to social work. These case studies proffer evidence that social work brings much to analysis.

A recognition of these contributions comes at a particularly fortuitous time. Analysis is in crisis, both as a set of theoretical constructs and as a therapeutic endeavor. Freud bashing has become a popular pastime. Critics of analytic thinking abound. Increasingly patients are turning to alternative forms of treatment that are cheaper and promise quick results. There is a paucity of those requesting analytic treatment and a similar paucity of potential candidate applicants at institutes. This is particularly true for physicians, who are finding medication more lucrative in a managed care environment that restricts therapy sessions and insists that shorter term treatment modalities are more effective. To increase profits, HMOs devalue and in many cases do not accept analytically educated practitioners on their referral rosters.

Analysts and analytically oriented therapists, through their own organizations and through participation in coalitions of professionals and consumers across the country, actively try to educate the public to the problems caused by managed care. Significant efforts are being made to gain regulation of that industry and eventually to replace it with a more patient-oriented health care system.

Analytic organizations are also beginning attempts at educating the public to the nature of analysis and its benefits. They are identifying the problems within the profession that have contributed to its decline and are seeking to remedy them. The present crisis is being viewed as an opportunity to strengthen and enrich psychoanalysis.

This process leads to the blossoming of theories in the Americas and in Europe to address the needs of an increasingly diverse population of analysands. These theories allow analysts to be more responsive to this varied group of patients, as they draw on them to understand how the particular background of the patient may be affecting the interchange of the analytic couple.

There is growing agreement that analysis must also reckon with the vast changes that are occurring in patterns of work, family life, mobility, and child care. Its leadership, together with its membership, must make analysis more relevant to the grave societal problems we face today, such as poverty, racism, sexism, and the escalation of violence among our young people. Such an endeavor calls for greater flexibility in the analytic frame. Thus analysts, their institutes, and their associations must become more heterogeneous, more flexible, more open to new ideas, more involved in community, and more proactive politically. We believe that social workers have much to contribute to such changes.

Having begun in a profession expressly related to the poor, social workers are familiar with the impact that race, ethnicity, culture, and class have on development and personality as well as on transference, countertransference, and resistance (Tang and Gardner, 1999). There is, however, much more to learn. Maria de Lourdes Mattei (1999) and Rosemarie Perez Foster (1999) are among those faculty in schools of social work who are currently seeking to bring such factors as poverty, ethnicity and race into therapy in more creative and healing ways. That social workers tend to come from diverse racial, socioeconomic, and cultural backgrounds means that those who become analysts will help to expand the heterogeneity that psychoanalysis is seeking today. They can add strength to sensitizing the analytic community to these issues.

While social workers represent a diverse group, the majority are female, as are most of our writers. Among social work applicants to analytic training programs, women predominate. This has both advantages and disadvantages. As analysts, social workers will add to the already increasing number and proportion of women in the field at a time when the number and percentage of men in the field is declining. Regrettably, information from other fields suggests that, when men abandon any occupational category, the field diminishes in status and in pay. Social workers carry an additional burden since their profession has historically been poorly remunerated and regarded as less prestigious than others. Being a mainly female endeavor and being associated with those in society who have the lowest status account for much of this reputation.

But being women and associating with others from all disciplines, social workers are influencing the evolution of both theory and technique in ways that many believe can be valuable to psychoanalysis. The significant growth in analytic understanding of female development in the last 10 or 15 years can be attributed, in part, to this gender shift. Swayed by feminist theories and the questions that feminists have raised about traditional analytic theory, female analysts, along with their male colleagues, have significantly added to our knowledge of female psychology. The greater appreciation of pre-oedipal development and the role of the mother, a focus on object relations theories, an increased appreciation of the importance of the relationship in the therapeutic outcome, all are among those features of contemporary analysis that seem to be particularly congenial to women. There are some, like Ilene Philipson (1993), who are convinced that the paradigm shifts currently being witnessed are related to the simultaneous shift in the gender of practitioners. Whether they are feminists or not, Philipson proposes that the mothering models, especially of Winnicott, speak to the way in which women view the world. This is certainly true within social work.

In our case studies, we have seen how the social work backgrounds of our writers have prepared them for treating more severely troubled patients. Those who were once viewed as unanalyzeable were, as noted in our Overture, referred to social work therapists for guidance and counseling. These therapists developed a sensitivity to play in concert with their usually unplayful clients by adapting to their unique needs and language. When Balint, Fairbairn, Mahler, Spitz, Winnicott, and others began to call attention to the preoedipal baby and her relationship with mother, social workers found guidance for their treatment of these more troubled persons. These analysts also offered conceptual understanding for analysis to begin to encompass those who suffer from the more serious disorders.

Becoming more relevant to community and society is an area very familiar to social workers. Advocacy, social action, community organization, the establishment of programs to promote mental health, the development of needed agencies, working with ancillary agencies and services have been an integral part of social work practice since the time Jane Adams founded Hull House. Now, when analysts are seeking to extend their contributions in these areas, the training and experience that social workers have had can be of considerable value. One excellent example of the kinds of programs that can be developed is the Child Development Community Policing Program, established by the Yale University Child Study Center and the New Haven Department of Police Service. This program is under the direction of Steven Marans (1995), an analyst who has a master's degree in social work from Dr. Sanville's alma mater, Smith College, and a doctorate in psychology. In this program police and analysts work closely together to address the psychological burdens on children and families imposed by their chronic exposure to violence.

Social work analysts are also contributing fresh theoretical perspectives to analysis. Because social workers have drawn from other disciplines those theories which seem best to fit their clients' needs, some professionals from other disciplines have regarded social work as atheoretical. Today, however, many of the current analytic schools of thought include perspectives brought from social work, particularly attention to external context and reality.

Today social work analysts have become leaders of some of the analytic institutes and associations to which they belong. They are presidents, deans, faculty, curriculum chairs, and developers of outreach programs. From their historic adaptability, they are contributing to a freer, more flexible atmosphere in the institutions with which they are affiliated.

As the last discipline to be welcomed into the analytic community, social work looks forward now to joining with all the other disciplines that are being included under the new analytic umbrella. Each brings its own unique contributions. We believe that all disciplines will be influenced by and have influence on the others. Some of us feel that in time we will discover unity in our present divergence. Together we may raise our voices to shape a stronger, more effective psychoanalytic community that will serve and be viewed as a valuable resource for the next century.

References

Applegate, J. S. & Bonovitz, J. M. (1995), *The Facilitating Partnership.* Northvale, NJ: Aronson.

Casement, P. (1991), *Learning from the Patient.* New York: Guilford Press.

de Lourdes Mattei, M. (1999), Editorial comments: Openings in theory and in practice. *Smith Col. Studies in Soc. Work.* 69 (Special issue: Perspectives on intersubjectivity).

Fonagy, P. & Target, M. (1996), Predictors of outcome in child psychoanalysis: A retrospective study of 763 cases at the Anna Freud Centre. *J. Amer. Psychoanal. Assn.,* 44:27–73.

Friedman, L. (1983), Discussion of Piaget and psychoanalysis: Some reflections on insight. *Contemp. Psychoanal.,* 19:339–348.

Helfer, R. E. & Kempe, R. S. (1987), *The Battered Child.* Chicago: Oxford University Press.

Loewald, E. (1982), The baby in mother's therapy. *The Psychoanalytic Study of the Child,* 37:391–404. New Haven, CT: Yale University Press.

Marans, S. (1995), Psychoanalysis on the beat: Children, policies, and urban trauma. *The Psychoanalytic Study of the Child.* 51:522–544. New Haven, CT: Yale University Press.

Perez Foster, R. M. (1999), An intersubjective approach to cross-cultural clinical social work. *Smith Col. Studies in Soc. Work,* 69:269.

Philipson, I. J. (1993), *On the Shoulders of Women.* New York: Guilford Press.

Richmond, M. (1920), *What Is Social Case Work?* New York: Russell Sage Foundation.

Saari, C. (1986), *Clinical Social Work Treatment.* New York: Gardner Press.

Sanville, J. (1991), *The Playground of Psychoanalytic Therapy.* Hillsdale, NJ: The Analytic Press.

——— (1996), *Ferenczi and Psychoanalytic Technique.* A discussion of Andre Haynal's paper, "Occasion: The Birth of the Federation of IPA Societies." Los Angeles, January 13.

Shengold, L. (1989), *Soul Murder*. New York: Fawcett Columbine.

Stern, D. (1985), *The Interpersonal World of the Infant: A View from Psychoanalysis and Developmental Psychology*, New York: Basic Books.

Taft, J. (1937), The relation of function to process in social casework. *J. Soc. Proc.*, 1:1–18.

Tang, N. M. & Gardner, J. (1999), Race, culture, and psychotherapy: Transference to minority therapists. *Psychoanal. Quart.*, 68:1–20.

Winnicott, D. W. (1968), Interpretation in psychoanalysis. In: *The Facilitating Environment: Clinical Applications of Winnicott's Theory*, ed. M. G. Fromm & B. L. Smith. Madison, CT: International Universities Press, 1989, pp. 620–635.

Zalusky, S. (1998), Telephone analysis. *J. Amer. Psychoanal. Assn.*, 46:1221–1242.

Index

DATE DUE

Cat. No. 23-221

BRODART